Jordan Henderson

THE AUTOBIOGRAPHY

Jordan Henderson

with Oliver Holt and Dominic King

THE AUTOBIOGRAPHY

MICHAEL JOSEPH

PENGUIN MICHAEL JOSEPH

UK | USA | Canada | Ireland | Australia
India | New Zealand | South Africa

Penguin Michael Joseph is part of the Penguin Random House group of companies
whose addresses can be found at global.penguinrandomhouse.com

First published 2022

001

Copyright © Jordan Henderson, 2022

The moral right of the author has been asserted

Picture permissions can be found on page 317

Set in 13.5/16 pt Garamond MT Std
Typeset by Couper Street Type Co.
Printed in Great Britain by Clays Ltd, Elcograf S.p.A.

The authorized representative in the EEA is Penguin Random House Ireland,
Morrison Chambers, 32 Nassau Street, Dublin D02 YH68

A CIP catalogue record for this book is available from the British Library

HARDBACK ISBN: 978–0–241–62384–8
OM PAPERBACK ISBN: 978–0–241–62386–2

www.greenpenguin.co.uk

Penguin Random House is committed to a
sustainable future for our business, our readers
and our planet. This book is made from Forest
Stewardship Council® certified paper.

To my family and friends,
my managers and team-mates.

Contents

1. With or Without Me

There was a breakfast bar in our house, and when my dad and his wife, Donna, came down to see us that day – 18 December 2013 – we perched on the stools that were arranged around it and listened to what he had to say. I had been getting more and more worried about their visit ever since he'd told me he wanted to come down from Sunderland to have a chat. I knew it wasn't going to be good.

My dad, Brian, is a retired policeman. Chats aren't normally his thing. To be honest, they wouldn't be my thing either. He isn't the kind of man who shows vulnerability too easily and he has passed it on to me. Where I'm from in the north-east, you just get on with it if things are hard and I don't ever remember it being any different.

I think I am emotionally intelligent. But I am emotionally intelligent for other people, not for myself. That is part of my story. I want to help other people, but I'm not good at accepting help. I want to try to fix other people's troubles, but I always put a shield up around myself.

My problems are my problems, and your problems are my problems. That's my attitude. Maybe that's why I go through some of this turmoil in my career. Sometimes I agonize over small things others would see as insignificant. Maybe that's why I sometimes feel my whole career has been about trying to prove people wrong.

I'm a strange mix like that. I'm not without self-confidence. I'm a good footballer. Perhaps people recognize me as a grafter, and I'm proud that people know I have got everything out of my talent, but there is more to my game than just running about. Much more, in fact. You don't play for Liverpool and England on the back of the ground you cover in a match.

But, saying that, there's another part of me that thinks I don't deserve the accolades or praise that have come my way. When I've been in a position to lift trophies with Liverpool, I've found myself thinking that Jürgen Klopp should be doing it or I should share the stage with James Milner.

It's about the collective here. Nobody has won us a trophy on their own, so why should it be me getting the trophy on my own? I tried to get the gaffer to lift the Champions League trophy in Madrid after we had beaten Tottenham in June 2019. He had shown us the way on this journey, we all followed him – but he was having none of it. I asked Millie if he wanted to join me on the stage. He reacted like Klopp.

I wanted to call this book *With or Without Me* because that's how I feel about the trophies Liverpool have won over the last few years: they'd have won them with or without me. I'm not Luis Suárez or Steven Gerrard or Virgil van Dijk or Mo Salah. The success is not down to me. I play my part, definitely, but I'm not the ultimate reason we win. It's always been my mindset, and that hasn't changed over my professional career.

If I wasn't captain, if I wasn't at Liverpool, they could still have won the trophies they have done, as far as I'm concerned. I may be judged as a good captain, but good times were always going to come under Klopp. He came here in October 2015 with a vision, and the players who were here bought into it. Those who stayed have improved under him; those who signed for him took their performances to new levels.

Yes, I've worn the armband for him, but he could have appointed Millie as captain and I could have left and Liverpool would still have been successful because of the ferocious ambition and belief he has instilled in the team. Maybe I do myself a disservice a little bit, but that's just how I feel.

When I was appointed Liverpool captain in July 2015, after Stevie had moved to LA Galaxy, I knew I could never replicate what he had done. Stevie was a Liverpool lad and the intense connection he had with the club was unique. I knew I was following in the footsteps of legends like Emlyn Hughes, Phil Thompson and Graeme Souness, but I didn't want to compare myself to them. I had to do the job my own way.

How was I going to do it? For starters, I was sure I could help all the lads in the dressing room. I could be there for them, be somebody they could rely on, someone they could come to if anything was bothering them. I dedicate myself to my team-mates – that's how it's always been.

That's what I brought in as a captain. I felt I could bring the best out of everyone on and off the pitch. I could relate to everyone. I wasn't the team superstar. I wanted to be able to make them perform to their best level and I wanted them to know that I was one of them.

I wasn't on a pedestal. I wasn't someone who couldn't be approached.

I've always wanted to help the other players become a proper team so we can be successful together. I want to help them become better. I knew when I took the captaincy I could never replace Stevie, in terms of everything he brought. That wasn't what I wanted to do. But I knew I had to be my own man and I knew I could bring one quality to the table: I felt I could put everyone else before me. Stevie did this, by the way, while juggling his role as the team's talisman.

That's another part of the contradiction. I'm not comfortable being acclaimed as a leader, but I've always wanted to lead and I've always had leadership qualities. I was captain of the England Under-21s and I captained the youth teams at Sunderland. People have always seen those leadership qualities within me.

I've always tried to do everything properly. I love football. I've lived the right way, so I lead by example in that regard. On the pitch, I have always wanted to be a leader, but I didn't want this special thing around being a captain. I wanted to bring people together to form something that can't be broken. My team-mates can look at me and they know 'Yes, we trust him; we'll die for him because he'll die for us.' I want there to be that kind of bond. That's how I have always wanted to lead.

I asked for a low-key announcement when I took over as Liverpool captain. I said there were to be no videos. I wanted to keep it to a paragraph of quotes and a couple of pictures. We're living in an age when clubs go to town on moments like this on their social media channels, with fancy reveals, but that isn't me in the slightest. I didn't want any of that and I hated the idea of it. It was going to be hard enough for people to swallow the fact that Stevie had gone without us making a fuss about me taking over from him.

I knew how it looked from the outside: we were going from Steven Gerrard, arguably the greatest captain of all time in a Liverpool shirt, one of the best players ever, to Jordan Henderson. 'What on earth is going on here?' people were going to be saying. 'Is this a wind-up?' That's how I thought the outside world would view it. Deep inside me, I felt I had the qualities that meant I could lead within the dressing room, but I knew how it would look. At first, I felt a bit uncomfortable and awkward that I was standing there with the captain's armband.

I'd been signed by Liverpool in June 2011 and there were times in the first couple of years, in particular, when I was in a really dark place. I wasn't playing well. Or not well enough, anyway. I wasn't justifying the fee Liverpool had paid Sunderland for me. And so I was coming home after training and shutting myself away in our house in Formby, a few miles north of Liverpool, not talking to my partner, Rebecca – not talking to anyone, for that matter.

I wasn't much company in those times, certainly not to Bec. She and I had known each other since we were eleven years old and she'd moved down from Sunderland with me. We were barely out of our teens. She didn't know anyone, and now she had another stranger sulking

5

around the house. I sometimes wonder how she stuck it out with me.

I asked her about that spell in our lives recently and what she made of my moods. She said she thought I was just morose. To be fair, she called it right. When I was down, I didn't talk to anyone in the team about it. I'd close off, as I thought I'd be a burden. Everyone's got stuff to deal with, haven't they? Everybody's got their own problems, so they don't want me moaning about being injured or fretting about my form. There was no chance of me sharing my feelings with anyone. Not back then, anyway.

I can laugh about some of that now. There was a match, early in Klopp's reign, when we threw away a three-goal lead to Sevilla during a Champions League group game in November 2017 and I blamed myself for it. I was in despair that I'd allowed it to happen when I was playing in a position at the base of midfield, a position where I was supposed to stop that exact thing from happening.

I took all the responsibility for it on my own shoulders, even though it was the culmination of a period when our results had been a bit uneven. In those situations, you think about everything. Well, I do anyway. Was I good enough to play as a No. 6 in this system? Why were we conceding so many goals and looking so vulnerable? What could we do to fulfil our potential? I wanted answers, I wanted to help and I needed to talk to someone. So the next day I texted Adam Lallana, who is one of my best mates, and told him I was going to pick him up and give him a lift in to training. Adam's a smart guy. He's open and he's comfortable in his own skin. He knew something was up, so after we had sat in silence in the car for a bit, he just said, 'Everything okay?' and then it all came spilling out.

So, back to that week before Christmas in 2013 when I found myself sitting in the kitchen with my dad, Rebecca and Donna in Formby, waiting to hear what he had to say. Liverpool were jostling with Arsenal, Manchester City and Chelsea in the Premier League, and for the first time in a while it felt like we were going to be properly involved in a race for a title. I'd come to Liverpool with a dream that we would be champions one day and I wanted to help us win our first title since 1990. The previous Sunday, we had gone to Tottenham and won 5–0. I'd scored and had one of my best games for the club.

But it turned out my dad, who was in his late fifties then, had been keeping his news secret from me for as long as he could. He had been told in November that he was ill and needed surgery, but he hadn't wanted to do anything that might affect me in the biggest season of my life so far. Football came first. Football was all I'd ever wanted, the thing I'd never, ever compromised on.

Sometimes, when I was in the youth teams at Sunderland, my dad would come along to the Academy of Light when I stayed behind after training and help me practise my crossing. He'd feed me passes over and over again so I could bend the balls in from the flanks. He'd make me practise with my weaker left foot. He did whatever he could to try to help me make it.

7

I knew that some of the other lads would snigger a bit about how hard I worked. 'Look at Hendo, still out there, the busy bastard' – that kind of thing. That never bothered me. Putting in the extra hours was normal for me. It wasn't like it was a chore. I loved it. And my dad knew football was everything to me and that I was only just finding my feet at Liverpool after a difficult start, and he didn't want to do anything to interrupt my momentum. But now, he couldn't wait any longer.

So he went into detail. He'd had a cyst removed from his neck and the surgeons had discovered a tumour. Then he had some more tests and they revealed another tumour, on his tongue, and that he had throat cancer. Bec started crying, but my dad was very positive.

He said he was going to have to have surgery and post-operative cancer treatment and he kept trying to reassure me that everything was going to be fine. That's what dads do, don't they? We were all a bit quiet after that. It's hard to know what to say. I was determined to keep it together and not show my dad I was upset. So we watched some television and went to bed early. That was how we did things. That was how we coped. But, really, it was one of those days that shakes your world to its foundations.

I went into training the next day as normal. That's how I have always dealt with things. I suspect many people could relate to that approach. We get this news that turns everything upside down but we get on with a parallel life where we pretend that everything is the same. And so I went into Melwood and I didn't tell anyone what I knew,

I didn't tell anyone about the thoughts I was having and I didn't tell anyone that I didn't really know how to act.

Our first child, Elexa, had been born five months earlier, on 5 July, and so I had all these thoughts rushing around in my head that I couldn't blot out about her maybe growing up without having the chance to get to know her grandad. Again, I kept all that to myself. I closed up. I didn't discuss it with anyone else.

I didn't want to tell anyone at the club because I didn't want it to affect anything. I didn't want anyone to treat me differently or make allowances. There might be days when I was a bit emotional, and I didn't want people thinking they didn't know what to say when it's one of those situations when you can't say anything to make someone feel better. I didn't want any awkwardness.

The week before his operation, which was scheduled for 14 January 2014, Dad came down to stay. 'I've never seen you train at Melwood,' he said. 'Do you think I could come in one day and watch?' Normally, I'd have said, 'No, you can't just come to training.' But I knew what he was getting at and I knew I couldn't say no.

The implication of his question was that he didn't know what was going to happen. In case he didn't come through the operation and the treatment, he wanted to do stuff he hadn't done, bucket-list stuff. That was tough for me. Like I said, I didn't want anyone to know he had cancer, but I couldn't say no so I didn't know how to get around it.

I didn't want the manager, Brendan Rodgers, knowing, and I didn't want the lads to know. But then I saw an opportunity. We played Oldham in the FA Cup third round on 5 January at Anfield and won 2–0. There was a recovery session scheduled in the day after, a kind of light training session for players who had been involved in the game, so I called him and told him I'd take him with me into training that day.

I signed him in at the reception at Melwood and took him up the stairs to the canteen as quickly as I could, desperately hoping we didn't bump into the manager or any of the lads. There was a balcony outside the canteen that had a panoramic view of the training pitches and I thought I might be able to sneak him out on to that to watch the session. He remembers being in good company – Luis Suárez's daughter, Delfina, was there, too, and she wanted help with her colouring books.

Part of me didn't blame him for wanting to come. We've moved to a fantastic new training facility in Kirkby now, but I loved Melwood. You could feel the history all around you. You could imagine Bill Shankly sitting outside the old clubhouse that once stood on the far side of the training ground, near the old entrance on Crown Road, back in the sixties. What a place it was – I couldn't believe it at first when I got there and saw fans standing on purple wheelie bins to watch us train over the walls.

You could feel the traditions of the club at Melwood almost as much as you could at Anfield. You could imagine Sir Kenny Dalglish, the manager who had signed me, the greatest man in the club's history, training there in the seventies and eighties when Liverpool were the kings of England and all of Europe.

Souness played at Melwood, and Tommy Smith, and Alan Hansen and Ray Kennedy and Steve Heighway and Kevin Keegan and Roger Hunt. And modern-day legends like Stevie and Jamie Carragher and Robbie Fowler. Bob Paisley strode around there, and Joe Fagan and Ronnie Moran. And now my team-mates and I were following in the footsteps of those giants.

But my dad had earned this trip too. He was a pretty good golfer at one point and he had got his handicap down to seven, but when I got taken on by Sunderland when I was six years old, not long to turn seven, he started ferrying me round to training and to matches so he didn't play as much golf. Before he knew it, his handicap had shot back up to seventeen.

He used to take me to all Sunderland's home games too. We went with a mate of mine called Michael McKeown and his dad. Michael was a brilliant young footballer, and he and I thought we would make the journey together into being professional footballers. Every other Saturday, we'd watch our heroes playing at the Stadium of Light and dream that, one day, it would be us.

And in May 2003, three weeks before my thirteenth birthday, my dad had taken me to Old Trafford to see the Champions League final between AC Milan and Juventus. He had managed to get a couple of tickets from his business partner, Steve Knox – whose uncle was none other than Archie Knox, one of the great figures within football. It was a surprise trip, and one I'll never forget. Beforehand, we were in a hotel where the corporate guests were being entertained, and I saw Archie, along with Walter

Smith, Neil Lennon and Les Ferdinand. Frankie Dettori, the famous jockey, was there too.

The football, though, was the only thing that mattered to me, and it lit a fire. That occasion was like nothing I'd ever witnessed. It wasn't that it was a great match – Milan won on penalties after a 0–0 draw – but I never forgot the excitement and intensity of the atmosphere around it, and hearing the Champions League anthem being played for the first time. Gianluigi Buffon, Alessandro Del Piero, Lilian Thuram and Edgar Davids were in the Juventus side. The Milan team was incredible, with legends like Paolo Maldini, Gennaro Gattuso, Andriy Shevchenko and Andrea Pirlo. Nine years later, I'd play against Pirlo for England against Italy in our Euro 2012 quarter-final in Kyiv. He was still untouchable then.

But back to that match: when the music started, I turned to my dad and said, '*I* want to play in one of these games one day.' He smiled and nodded, in the way that all dads do. If he thought there wasn't much chance of that happening, he didn't say so. He always believed in me and maybe he had some sense that, sixteen years later, we'd be standing together again in a football stadium at the biggest club game in the world.

So that day in January, I took him up to the canteen at Melwood and introduced him to Carol and Caroline, the two women in the canteen who had worked there for years and years. They're the heart and soul of the training ground. They're always welcoming, always kind and cheerful, and pick people up with their outlook. I asked them to do me a favour and look after my dad, to keep him out of the way and allow him up on the balcony. And then I went out to train.

It turned out that my dad had been keeping another secret from me. He wanted to watch the training, but he also wanted to use it as an opportunity to speak to Brendan and tell him about what was happening the following week because he knew I wasn't going to tell him myself. So while I was outside, he went to see Brendan in his office and told him.

During Brendan's first summer at Liverpool, in 2012, the club tried to sell me – with the manager's full agreement – to Fulham in a swap deal with Clint Dempsey, but I'd worked and worked to convince him I was worth my place at the club. We had reached a point where our relationship was strong. He had made me Stevie's vice-captain and I had come not only to trust him implicitly but also to have the utmost respect for him as a coach.

When I came back in from training that day Brendan came over to me, and when I looked at him I knew straight away that my dad had told him he had cancer. I started sobbing. I broke down in the treatment room and Brendan consoled me. He just said that if I needed any time off to go back and see my dad, I could just go. I didn't even have to ask. 'We're all here for you,' he said.

Despite all my reluctance to talk about it, that was probably the best thing that could have happened to me. Otherwise, I'd have bottled it up, and that wouldn't have done anyone any good. Not long after that, my dad started his treatment. The arc of that treatment will be familiar to so many families whose loved ones have endured it.

My dad was in surgery for fifteen hours to remove lymph nodes in both sides of his neck and the tumour from his tongue; it left a hole in his tongue the size of a 50p piece. He had a three-month course of radiotherapy and a series of chemotherapy treatments too. I found out later he lost four stone in weight during the chemo. I say I found out later, because I didn't see him during his treatment.

He did text me to let me know the treatment had started, but when I told him I had a day off and that I was planning to drive up to see him, he said he didn't want me to make the journey. 'You're not coming up and you're not seeing me like this,' he said. 'Not a chance.'

I knew then that things must be pretty bad.

He couldn't really speak because of all the pain in his tongue and throat so we texted a lot and I spoke to Donna as often as I could. My dad and Donna got together after he split up with my mam when I was six. I wanted to know whether, if he wasn't going to allow me to see him, there was anything I could do to help.

My dad texted me back. 'The only thing you can do,' he said, 'is when you're playing, just get Man of the Match every game – that'll help me get through this period. When I'm in a hospital bed, I can watch the game and I can see you playing, and that is the thing that will help me and spur me on to get better.'

You can imagine what kind of effect that had on me. I broke down again. I get emotional thinking about it now. I could look back at it and think, 'That's a lot of pressure,' but actually it changed my focus. I wasn't thinking about what happened if we lost or how it would affect our position in the title race or how close to Manchester City we were.

The only thing I was thinking about was going out and performing and making my dad proud. I knew that the better I played and the harder I worked and the further I ran, he would see it, and I convinced myself that by doing that I would save his life. I convinced myself in those weeks and months that football really was life and death. I convinced myself that I held my dad's life in my hands.

It gave me the illusion of control. I'm sure that was part of the equation. Those next few months, I felt I was unstoppable. I felt like I *had* to be unstoppable. It helped that I was a player in a brilliant team with genius players like Stevie, Luis Suárez, Daniel Sturridge, Raheem Sterling and Philippe Coutinho. We were in fourth place at the start of the New Year, but then we mounted a title charge.

We went on a winning run that started with a 5–1 demolition of Arsenal at Anfield on 8 February. We beat Fulham at Craven Cottage in the next match, then Swansea, then Southampton, Manchester United at Old Trafford, then Cardiff City, then Sunderland, then Spurs, then West Ham, then Manchester City, then Norwich. I felt I was playing as well as I'd ever played.

I didn't get Man of the Match in every game, but I felt like I was keeping my promise to my dad, that I was doing him proud. It was like I had changed from a boy into a man when Elexa was born and now I was growing up even more, taking on this responsibility and not buckling under it. Instead, I was thriving on it. I had never been that consistent before.

I never actually saw my dad's hospital bed, but I imagined it every time we played. I imagined him lying in it and staring at a television, watching Liverpool playing and Liverpool winning and watching his son playing well and running his heart out and giving everything he could. And I knew he would know that I was thinking of him with every run and tackle I made and every shot I had.

As we got closer and closer to the title, as my dad began to recover, as my world stopped shaking, it started to seem as if Liverpool winning the league that season was meant to be. I told myself that the fairy tale was going to come true and I began to wonder if this would bring the vindication I craved.

I think I wanted respect. Deep down, I always felt I'd never quite been given that. I felt it had always been withheld. And when the title slipped away from us in the last few games of that season, I thought about that idea of respect again and I realized I was going to have to fight even harder to earn it.

2. Into the Light

Sometimes, I hear and see some of the things people say and write about Roy Keane – often when they disagree with something provocative or explosive he may have said on television – and I can tell they don't understand quite what a brilliant footballer he was. When Manchester United dominated English football through the 1990s and 2000s, Keane was their captain, the driving force behind so many unforgettable triumphs.

Maybe people have got used to Roy as a controversial analyst now. Maybe they never knew him as a footballer, in the same way younger fans only know Gary Lineker as the presenter of *Match of the Day* and aren't even aware he is one of England's greatest ever goalscorers, a finisher as deadly as any of the modern greats.

If viewers think Roy takes no prisoners when he offers his opinions, then they should also know that was the way he played. He was one of my favourite players when I was a football-mad kid growing up in Sunderland in the 1990s because he was a brilliant midfielder and he never, ever backed down from a confrontation.

I loved his no-nonsense approach. I'll never forget the footage of him squaring up to Patrick Vieira in February 2005 when he felt the Arsenal captain was trying to intimidate some of his team-mates. 'He wants to pick on

Gary Neville? Tell him to pick on one of us!' Keane shouts, making it clear he is United's leader. That's what captaincy and leadership are all about. I loved that moment before a Champions League quarter-final against Inter Milan in March 1999 when he marched straight past Diego Simeone and Ronaldo rather than wait for them to finish tying their laces and shake their hands.

Roy arrived at Sunderland, where I had been rising up through the age-group teams at the Academy of Light since the age of six, in the August of 2006. Immediately, his presence sent a jolt of electricity through the club. Sunderland had been relegated to the Championship at the end of the previous season, and even though it was Roy's first job in management he soon revived the club and set it on course for a return to the top flight.

He got the team playing good football again and restored a sense of discipline and pride in the players. He did not suffer fools. There was one famous incident in March 2007 when a few of the lads were late for the team bus to Barnsley one afternoon. So Roy told the driver to leave without them. I was sixteen when Roy got the Sunderland job and was as obsessed with football as I had ever been. It was all that had ever mattered to me for as long as I could remember, really. It was everything. I had never thought about doing another job, never dreamed of being an astronaut or a fireman, or a policeman, like my dad. No other career appealed. All I wanted to be was a footballer and nothing was going to stop me.

I grew up in an area of Sunderland called East Herrington and I played for a local kids' team called Fulwell

Juniors who were based in a different part of Wearside, seven miles from my home, across the river. They were worth playing for, though, because they entered more tournaments than other teams, had a great reputation and a great record. It meant more driving for my dad, mind.

I saw recently that the guy who was the manager of our team has a copy of the *Shields Gazette* dated 13 July 1999 and there's an article in it that lists our achievements. We went 60 games unbeaten to win the league and cup, scoring 150 goals along the way.

The article says: 'Michael McKeown and Jordan Henderson shared the league's Player of the Season award, and Shaun Turnbull was voted top manager,' and it goes on to say that Fulwell added the Wansbeck Tournament, the Whitburn Tournament, the Umbro Tournament (my dad still has that trophy at home) and the Darlington Crest Tournament to our titles before travelling to Ireland, where we beat a junior side from the famous Home Farm club.

So Fulwell were a good side and we were watched regularly by Sunderland, even at that age. I was actually spotted by Sunderland when I was six, by a scout called Anthony Smith, and I stayed on the pathway with them all the way through to turning professional. There were plenty of times when I didn't think I'd make it, but I was incredibly single-minded. Nothing was going to get in my way.

I loved Sunderland and I loved going to the Stadium of Light. 'He was never any trouble,' my dad said when he was asked about my childhood for a recent television documentary. 'The only thing he ever wanted to do was play football, to be honest. The first time I ever took

Jordan to the Stadium of Light he was seven or eight. Jordan absolutely loved it, of course. Screaming the whole game, wasn't he?'

I don't know where that determination to be a footballer came from. I do know that I buried myself in football. Maybe a psychologist would say it was something to do with my mam and dad's divorce. Their separation was not a good one, it was quite acrimonious. I saw stuff I wish I hadn't seen in terms of the arguments they had. Even though I was only six, there are moments I can remember vividly. When you're a young lad, and especially if you're an only child, which I was at that point, and your mam and dad break up, it's like the end of the world. It was a horrible time, but I was thankful for the role my nana, Sheila, had in my life back then. I would stay with her a lot and she always looked after me, always providing the comfort and support that I needed. After the split, my dad moved out to Washington, five miles away. I stayed with my mam, Liz, who is a fitness instructor in Summerhill, and saw my dad every other weekend.

A year or so later, my mam met a guy called Peter Conway; eventually he came and lived with us. Peter is a good man and he treated me like his own son. He used to take me to watch Newcastle matches but I only went with him to watch the opposition! Peter and my mam had a baby, my sister, Jodi, and he would take me to training whenever my dad couldn't do it. Things worked out.

I haven't thought too much about the effects the divorce had on me. Maybe that's because everything worked out OK and I felt, in the end, that I had the best of both worlds in terms of the time I spent with each of my parents. But their split has made me very conscious of the impact that seeing parents row can have on children.

I saw arguments, and I never wanted that for my kids. If Bec and I have a disagreement, for whatever reason, we never do it in front of Elexa, Alba and Myles. Bec's mam and dad have been together since they were kids so it's not a big deal for her, but all the time we were going out, right up until we had children, I always told her that I never wanted to get married. Never, ever. I met her in our first year at secondary school in Farringdon. But then, when you have kids, things change. It's easier, for practical reasons. And having kids deepens your relationship. I softened as I got a bit older.

We've got three kids – Elexa, Alba and Myles – and I was at all their births. That was massively important to me. The night before Alba's birth, I was away with the team before an FA Cup quarter-final replay away at Blackburn but rushed to the hospital when I got the call to say Bec was in labour. Alba arrived in the early hours of 8 April, 2015, and I went back to the team hotel and got a bit of sleep before playing in the game at Ewood Park, where Philippe Coutinho's goal sent us to Wembley. What a twenty-four hours that was.

I was a bit of an introvert as a kid, a bit shy, and I just felt happiest with a ball at my feet. My parents' divorce didn't affect my relationship with either of them, really. In fact, as I said, it might even have made it better. I lived with my mam and I've always been fiercely protective of her, and I loved my weekends with my dad. I'd get treats because we didn't see each other day to day and so the times we did spend together became like special occasions. I knew that my mam worked tirelessly and I get a lot of my discipline and work ethic from her.

She has always been into eating the right things and not giving me junk food or taking the easy option with my meals. I always had to be back at a certain time in the evening. If we were down at the park at the end of the road playing football, my friends might have to be back at 9 p.m. but I'd have to be back by eight. I was always the first one who had to leave, so I'd leave it to two minutes to eight then sprint home.

I was lucky with my friends too. My best mate, Ryan Royal, is basically like my brother. We were at nursery together. We've known each other since we were three and were so close that our parents split us up because they thought we were messing around too much and getting each other into trouble. We used to go round to each other's houses to watch the Champions League together. I'm lucky that I've had him as a friend because he's always looked out for me when we've been out and about and he's always made sure I haven't got dragged into any trouble when we've been on a night out. He runs a paint business with his dad and he's been very successful. He's a workaholic and he loves what he does, so we're both lucky that way. I count myself blessed that I've got him by my side.

It's easy when you're younger to be taken down the wrong path by your friends. The path to becoming a professional footballer is so competitive and so unforgiving that sometimes it can take just one wrong turn and you can never get back on it. It's fragile like that. I've seen so many brilliant young players, players blessed with sublime talent, fade out of the game because they didn't have the right people around them. Your prospects can change in the blink of an eye.

One of my other mates at school was Michael McKeown, the lad mentioned in the *Shields Gazette*. Michael lived not too far away, our parents were close, we went to the same school, we went to watch all Sunderland's home games together and he was a brilliant footballer. It was always between the two of us for Player of the Season and we both played in the Sunderland age-group teams together our whole childhoods.

Michael was an amazing player, with a left foot like a magic wand. He was a brilliant passer. He had great vision. We were close friends, but there was always a bit of unspoken rivalry between us too. Well, there was for me anyway. He was more eye-catching than me and, when we were at secondary school, I'd hear our friends saying that Michael was the one out of all of us who was going to make it to the big time.

I used to take it personally, even though I thought he was very, very good. I thought we'd *both* make it. I read a piece in *The Athletic* recently that quoted one of my big influences in the youth coaching set-up at Sunderland, Elliott Dickman, talking about me and Michael and our contrasting styles.

'McKeown would not beat himself up if he tried an outrageous through ball and it did not come off,' the article said, 'but, according to Dickman, there was a sense of shame with Henderson, who always seemed furious with himself whenever he got it wrong. His attitude was, "I've got to win the ball back." Coaches identified Henderson's natural enthusiasm above all his other attributes. Dickman: "He was never standing still; perpetual motion. Good at running forward but even better at running backwards.'"

Michael and I always imagined that we would do it together, that we were on a journey together. But I suppose, at some level, there's a competitive instinct there too. It wasn't that I wanted Michael to fail, but I didn't want him to succeed at my expense. Of course I wanted him to succeed, but I wanted it for myself more.

There was never a moment when I felt pushed into being a footballer. There was never a moment when I resented the sacrifices I had to make. I didn't see them as sacrifices. How can it be a sacrifice to play more football? It was just something I enjoyed. Playing more football, staying late at training, thinking about football 24/7 – that was just normal to me. I come across stuff sometimes about pushy parents and football's 'mad dads', fathers living their lives through their kids and living out their own thwarted ambitions through them, but I never considered my parents pushy. My dad played at a decent level for the police, but I never felt like he wanted me to succeed for his own ends. He wanted me to succeed because he knew how much I loved football.

In the late 1990s and early 2000s, youth team sessions for Sunderland were held at a primary school near a colliery community in Usworth, close to Washington, where my dad lived. We played at the sports grounds of the

Nissan car factory, where there were three pitches and a Portakabin.

Michael and I rose higher and higher up through the age groups at Sunderland until we were sixteen, and then we both faced the decision about whether the club was going to offer us apprenticeships. That's the moment of truth for any kid that has dreams of being a footballer. Often, it's the moment that makes you or breaks you and changes your life.

It was touch and go for me. I knew that. I'd had a massive growth spurt and my body didn't really look properly joined up. I was all arms and legs. I knew the club had worries about whether I was physically strong enough to make it. I knew they liked my attitude and my technical ability, but I was scared that might not be enough.

Michael had always been a midfielder. That was where he excelled. But over the course of the last year at the Academy they had moved him to left back and I'm not sure he enjoyed it as much there. I think he lost a little bit of love for the game at that point. That was the sense I had, anyway. It took away some of his qualities as a midfielder, his passing range and his vision. He went in before me to find out whether he had got an apprenticeship. That night, his dad rang my dad and said the club had let him go.

I went in the next day, not sure which way it was going to go. As I'd thought, the Academy manager, Ged McNamee, said he was worried about me physically but that he and the coaches were willing to take a chance on me because they saw something in me in terms of my mentality. I knew I had an advocate in Elliott Dickman. Maybe that swung it for me.

'We played him in the centre of midfield,' Ged McNamee said in the article in *The Athletic*, about their dilemma over whether to offer me an apprenticeship, 'but other players were bigger than him. We then played him as a withdrawn striker and he didn't have a massive effect on the game. We sat and talked about him a lot. In the end, he was the last player from that age group that we decided to sign as a scholar. It was a decent group of seven or eight. Jack Colback, Martyn Waghorn, Jordan Cook, Michael Kay and Conor Hourihane all signed just after Christmas, but with Jordan, we waited for as long as possible before offering him a deal.'

Michael and I were never quite as close after that. Maybe that was inevitable. There's something unspoken when a decision sends you in opposite directions like that. I was still going to training at the Academy of Light every day, and Michael wasn't. He started having trials at a couple of other clubs and I know that he's had a decent career, but we gradually slipped out of touch.

In 2015, he played in the FA Vase Final at Wembley for North Shields and won the trophy after they beat Glossop North End. He's still regarded as a fine player in the north-east and I know he's back playing in midfield, where he always belonged. He was a phenomenal talent. We just got on different paths and went from being really close to being pushed apart. It's a bit sad, but that happens in football.

I was given a two-year apprenticeship, which wasn't the highest level. It didn't make me a chosen one. Some of the group got longer contracts, with the promise of going professional. Jack Colback was one of them. But I got a standard two years. No guarantees. I was still being asked to prove myself. It has always been a struggle for me to get to the next stage. It's as if it's been bred into me – the struggle, the fight, the constant battle to persuade people that I'm good enough, that I won't let them down. It never leaves me.

When you're young, you're doing it without knowing. I had the desire to prove I was good enough, to become an apprentice, to become a pro, to become a first team player, to get my debut, to become a regular. I don't know if I'd call it a constant battle with doubt because, most of the time, I've believed in myself. I've been happy to back my own ability.

But I suppose my career's been a constant battle with other people's doubts. Touch and go at Sunderland, Sir Alex Ferguson saying I had a dodgy gait, fans saying I was a waste after my first season at Anfield, Brendan agreeing to sell me to Fulham, and so on. Football was the only thing I wanted to do, so it was even more vital to me than it should have been that I was valued on the football pitch.

I wasn't the most confident player. My dad was always on at me to shoot when I had a chance, but I'd often look to pass. Deep inside, though, I did believe in myself. I would have backed myself against anyone, one on one. I wanted to prove I was better than the other player and I wouldn't be shy of having a direct competition to establish that.

I felt my desire to succeed was different to everybody else's. When I was at Sunderland, and fifteen, I was out on the pitches practising my free kicks, practising my crossing, practising my left foot, and now and then my dad would come down and serve me the ball. Now and again, I would get a bit of stick. I got called a 'busy bollocks' – that kind of thing. A teacher's pet. That didn't bother me.

I knew there was a question mark against me physically, so from the point I was taken on as an apprentice I was in the gym every day with the sports science people. When Roy took over he brought his old Manchester United team-mate Michael Clegg in as head of performance and Scott Ainsley as his head of sports science. Scott was a massive help with my running and we used to do sessions at Silksworth Running Track to get us into condition.

I could run all day when I was young. I'd do loads of core work, press-ups, all the upper-body work. After the first six months of my apprenticeship I was a different beast altogether. I had energy and aggression to burn. That was a big part of my game, getting around the pitch and getting in your face. I loved that. I loved the challenge of it. I loved the direct confrontation.

Maybe Roy liked that in me because it was he who gave me my debut at Sunderland. I first came to his attention when we had a pre-season reserve team game at Gateshead at the beginning of the 2008–9 season when I had just turned eighteen. Our side was a mix of youth team players and reserves and the odd first team player who might be coming back from injury or just needing game time in general.

We lost the game 2–0. Roy wasn't there because the game had clashed with a first team training session. But when we got back, he called a team meeting at the training ground. We were sitting in a lounge area and we were all spread out, waiting for him to come in. He took one look at us and started cursing. 'This fucking sums you lot up,' he said. 'Sitting in your separate groups, lounging around.'

I started to feel nervous. I was dripping with sweat. He went through every player, and no one was spared. He got to me and he said, 'And you? Do you think you're good enough to be in the first team?' I said, 'Yeah, I do.' I didn't know what was coming next. I thought there might be an explosion. But there wasn't. 'I'm glad you've said that,' he said, 'because apparently you were the only one that fucking ran today and you're the youngest one.'

I've never been so relieved in my life. The next day I got the call to say I was in the first team squad for a pre-season friendly against Ajax at the Stadium of Light. And, in terms of me becoming a senior player, a professional footballer, that was the beginning of my journey. I came on against Ajax and then, on the first day of November, I travelled with the first team squad to London for the Premier League game against Chelsea at Stamford Bridge. Roy put me on the bench and I sat in the dug-out for the first forty-five minutes. Chelsea were brilliant that day and a goal from their centre half Alex and two more from Nicolas Anelka put them 3–0 up at half-time.

Roy wasn't pleased. In fact, he was sent to the stands in the second half. But before that, he turned to me in the dressing room at half-time and told me I was coming on in place of Steed Malbranque for my debut. It was quite a baptism. Chelsea had Joe Cole, Deco, Frank

Lampard and Florent Malouda in midfield, and because I was playing on the right of midfield I was up against Ashley Cole, who was probably the best left-back in the world at that time.

For Roy to give me my debut in those circumstances gave me a massive confidence boost. I just loved getting out there and playing against a top, top team. It was everything I had dreamed of. We'd conceded two more goals within eight minutes of me coming on, but after that we did at least stop the bleeding. I basically ran around for forty-five minutes, but for someone like Roy, a man who had achieved so much in the game, a player I'd idolized, to trust me to play in that game meant the world. He was the first person who saw something in me that nobody else had.

Was I scared of him? A little, perhaps, but I think that part of Roy's management style is overblown. You always need to have respect for the manager's authority at a club, and if you don't, there's something wrong. Roy could dish out fairly fearsome bollockings to people, but there was nothing particularly unusual about that in a football club.

I wasn't afraid to challenge myself with him, though. He'd give you the eyes and you'd start sweating a bit if you felt you were going to get the benefit of some of his more forthright observations about your play, but the most important thing for me was that I was aware I was being managed by one of the best players ever to play in the Premier League, or in Europe, and I could tap into his experience.

Not many players are lucky enough to be able to say that. Now and again, I'd ask him what I needed to do to get in the first team, and I wasn't afraid to go and knock on his door. I wanted to learn from the best. I wanted to understand what he wanted from me and get any advice I could about what it took to succeed in the Premier League as a midfielder.

I made my first start in a League Cup match against Blackburn Rovers, but then Roy resigned as Sunderland boss before Christmas and our first team coach, Ricky Sbragia, was put in temporary charge. He told me he thought I ought to go out on loan so that I could get some regular playing time at first team level. I could see the logic of that and I was keen to keep progressing. I was sent to Coventry City in the Championship for the rest of the season.

I loved my time there. Chris Coleman was the manager, and he was great to work for. It was my first time living away from home – I lived in a hotel to begin with and then moved into a flat in Leamington Spa – and he and the players made it easy for me to settle in. We had a good side, too. Clinton Morrison, Leon Best and Freddy Eastwood were up front and we had Danny Fox and Scott Dann. There was a really good balance to the team and I came in and played on the right.

I ticked off a few career landmarks while I was there. I scored my first competitive goal, in a 2–1 away win over Norwich City at Carrow Road, and we went on a decent run in the FA Cup. We got to the quarter-finals, but then we came up against Chelsea again and lost 2–0. I broke my metatarsal not long after that and was sent back to Sunderland.

That summer of 2009, Steve Bruce was appointed the new manager of Sunderland. I looked on with a mixture of sadness and astonishment at the criticism he got when he was the manager of Newcastle over the last few years, because that wasn't the manager I knew and I can guarantee you that the players loved working for him. I certainly owe him a huge debt. He was incredibly important in my career.

Steve and his assistant, Eric Black, had been brought in from Wigan Athletic, and I think Eric had seen me play a few times while I was at Coventry. He liked what he saw, apparently. It also helped that I'd recovered from the metatarsal injury and was absolutely flying in pre-season training. I played in a friendly against Benfica at the Amsterdam Arena and afterwards I heard Steve talking to Grant Leadbitter, who was saying what a good game I'd had. I felt ten feet tall.

The previous season, I'd been cleaning Grant's boots, so I guess I must have done a good job! Each apprentice was allocated two players each, and I cleaned the boots of Grant and Carlos Edwards. I loved that whole culture. It was a hard school, but I think I was around too late for the proper old-school stuff that used to go on in football changing rooms and this just taught young players a bit of responsibility and respect.

Kevin Ball, who was a legend at the club, was a big influence on me at that time and he was in charge at the Academy. At the end of the day, you would have a few lads allocated to the jobs, making the dressing room immaculate – toilets cleaned, floor cleaned, everything taken to the laundry room. The sinks where the boots were washed had to be left sparkling too.

Once it was done, you'd go upstairs and tell Bally and then you could leave. Sometimes, balls would have been left out and someone would get a call on the bus home and they'd have to go back to the training ground.

The boot-cleaning culture has died out now – I think it's viewed as too demeaning for young players. That's a shame as it was a way to interact with the first team players. Carlos and Grant were great with me and even gave me a few hundred quid as a Christmas bonus.

Steve was a massive influence in my career. He was old school in terms of doing pre-season running, and I liked that. He wanted me to go out and enjoy playing. I played more games for the club that season than any player apart from Darren Bent and my reputation began to grow. We had a brilliant dressing room, with players like Anton Ferdinand and Lee Cattermole, who were endlessly encouraging to me. It was a close group.

Steve also knew how to get me going, what buttons to push to motivate and get the best out of me. I wasn't intimidated by reputations. In fact, I was inspired by playing against the best players. And now and again, when Steve asked me to do a man-marking job on a star player like Cesc Fàbregas or Ryan Giggs, I absolutely thrived on it.

I was always taught by my dad that when I was on the pitch against big players I should remember they're the same as me. It's eleven versus eleven; there is no hierarchy. You can have respect for them, but when you're on the pitch everyone is equal. I always took that with me when

I went into games. Maybe that could come across to senior players as being disrespectful, but I wasn't frightened of standing up to them or making them angry.

Maybe that was the instinct behind my behaviour in that meme of me squaring up to Diego Costa in Liverpool's League Cup semi-final against Chelsea in January 2015 and him backing away as if he knows he's been confronted by a madman. That still makes me laugh when I see it now.

I actually like Costa as a player. He was the type that loved the hustle and bustle of the Premier League. He liked to have a fight now and again, but I didn't mind that. You'd watch Chelsea and see him winding people up. He liked to play on the edge, and I liked that, too. But when it's against you, it's different. During that particular game, he had done one or two things to a few of the younger lads in the Liverpool team that I didn't particularly like. He was saying stuff, mouthing off, to one or two of the more inexperienced players and I'd had my card marked about it.

There was always an edge in matches between Liverpool and Chelsea in those days – that was during José Mourinho's second spell in charge at Stamford Bridge – and I'd tangled with Cesc in the build-up to that confrontation with Costa. I'm not sure that it was quite as funny in reality as it looked. My recollection is that he might have had to move backwards anyway because we were about to take a free kick. But why spoil a good meme? And I do know this: he was always nice to me when we saw each other after that game . . .

Up until I met Steve Peters, a psychologist who has worked with a lot of sports teams and individual sportsmen and women, I always felt I needed the anger. I felt it was part of me and part of my game. Steve didn't agree. He didn't think I needed it. He thought I could channel that energy in a better way. I didn't think I was too emotional. I hadn't been sent off. I knew where the line was. But he thought I was wasting emotion.

He used the example of a lion before it is about to attack its prey. He pointed out the lion would go very still. There would be calmness, dead eyes and then it would explode into action. I was a shouter and emotional and I was using a lot of energy. It was all or nothing when I was on the pitch. As I've got older and since Steve gave me that perspective, I've tailored that energy more.

I had quite a few shoving matches when I was younger. In my early days at Liverpool we were playing against Manchester United and tensions were high, as they always were. Giggs said something to me and I said something back to him, and I think he took that as a sign of disrespect from a younger player. He was caught on camera, staring at me. 'Watch your fucking mouth,' he said.

I asked myself after the game what the hell I'd been doing, speaking to a player like Ryan Giggs like that, but that was the way I was back then. That was the way I'd been brought up to deal with opponents: to treat them all the same. A few years later I sought him out at a game at the Etihad, where we had both gone to watch Manchester City play Barcelona, and apologized to him. But when I was younger, that was me. I played with my heart on my sleeve.

I didn't care how good opponents were or how big their reputations were – the bigger, the better. I loved playing against Fàbregas, in particular, because that was always lively. We played Arsenal at the Stadium of Light and, before we went out, Steve Bruce said to me: 'Fàbregas, don't let him out of your sight. You stay with him.' It was a bit old school, that kind of man-marking job, but I loved it. Those instructions were music to my ears.

I wanted to prove a point against big players like Fàbregas and I could soon tell Cesc didn't like it. It must have been pretty frustrating. I was young and hungry and wanting to make an impression. Every time he had the ball I was there. I was literally following him around. I wasn't even thinking about what to do when we had the ball, I was focused on him. As soon as they had the ball, my only thought was 'Where is he?'

He was a fiery character anyway, so it wasn't long before he snapped. 'Are you going to fucking follow me into the changing room at half-time?' he said. I was a big fan of his. I thought he was an unbelievable player but, obviously, I knew at that point I had him. When it's difficult to get on the ball, it's so easy to get frustrated and start wandering around trying to make something happen and then lose your man.

As I've got older, I've learned that you've got to sacrifice yourself. If somebody is on you, take them for a ride and leave space for other people. And there were also times when the plan didn't work. There was another afternoon when we played Chelsea at Stamford Bridge and Steve asked me and David Meyler, who was one of my best mates at the club, to do a job on Lampard and Michael Ballack. Meyler and I were the two best runners at the club. He was on Lampard and Ballack was mine.

Steve told us that with our legs and our youth and our attitude, we'd run all over Lampard and Ballack. It didn't quite pan out that way. They were 4–0 up after thirty-four minutes and the BBC report of the match mentions that the first goal came courtesy of a 'sublime' through ball from Ballack. I guess whoever was supposed to be man-marking him that day had bitten off more than he could chew. We lost the game 7–2 in the end.

I was voted the Young Player of the Year for Sunderland in that 2009–10 season, and again in 2010–11. We finished thirteenth in that first season and made the top ten in the second. We had a really good side by then, with Danny Welbeck and Asamoah Gyan up front and Nedum Onuoha and Anton Ferdinand at the heart of our defence. We had good times, and I kept improving to the point where I became aware that other clubs were watching me.

But I owe so much to Sunderland. Everything I was as a player when I moved to Liverpool in the summer of 2011, I owe to the club and its coaches. And everything I was as a person, I owe to my mam and my dad and my friends and the city where I grew up. For a kid who lived for football, to pull on that red-and-white striped shirt of his home-town club and run out in it at the Stadium of Light was the best feeling I could have imagined.

3. An Audience with the King

Towards the end of my last season at Sunderland, then, I was aware that other clubs were looking at me. Danny Welbeck had spent the year with us on loan from Manchester United and one day he revealed that people at Old Trafford had been asking him questions about me. I even found out after one match that a high-profile scout had come up from the north-west to see for himself.

I couldn't believe it. A year earlier, I had been on loan at Coventry; now I was being told that Sir Alex Ferguson, one of the all-time great managers, had given up his time to come over and assess me. To put it mildly, it was unbelievably flattering, but it went no further . . . maybe Welbz hadn't been so generous with his reports after all!

I had also been made aware that Liverpool wanted me. At some point, with Sunderland's permission, my dad drove me down to Southport and we met up with Kenny Dalglish at his house. It was so surreal. I was wide-eyed, only twenty years old, yet here I was at Kenny's place, talking football with one of the greatest players of his generation.

Kenny told me he had gone to Ewood Park in October 2010 to watch me play for Sunderland against Blackburn; it was a Monday night, we'd drawn 0–0, but he had been impressed. He said he was at the start of rebuilding Liverpool and he wanted me to be part of that process. I knew they had signed Luis Suárez and Andy Carroll in the January transfer window and they were at the beginning of an ambitious new project.

There was something else. If I moved to Anfield, I'd have the chance to play with Steven Gerrard. What an opportunity that would be – Steven was someone I'd always looked up to and I'd regarded him as a role model as I was making my way through the ranks at Sunderland. By the time I left Kenny's house that day my mind was already made up. Actually, I tell a lie. I'd made my decision before I'd even walked through his front door.

I met with Damien Comolli too. He'd been appointed as the club's first Director of Football Strategy by the new American owners, New England Sports Ventures (they would later change their name to Fenway Sports Group, shortened to FSG) and he wanted to explain how he saw my role. I felt he and Kenny were aligned in why they wanted to sign me. Kenny was a judge with the eye. Damien was a smart man, who could see how important statistical insight was becoming in the modern game. He opened up a laptop and showed me a page that was full of facts and figures and said this was the reason they were signing me.

I saw one chart that had my name next to David Silva, Samir Nasri, Cesc Fàbregas and a few more leading Premier League midfielders. There were charts about creating chances, assists, final third passes and what the new Liverpool regime was looking for in a midfielder. Damien pointed at my stats and said, 'That's you age twenty, playing for Sunderland: these other guys are playing for City and Arsenal.'

I had heard stuff about *Moneyball* by then and how the study of statistics had revolutionized player recruitment, in Major League Baseball in particular, and I knew Liverpool's new owners also owned the Boston Red Sox, so it all tallied. I could tell Damien was a big fan of mine from what he was saying and he showed a lot of belief in me as a player and a person when things started to get rough and other people fell away. I'll always be grateful to him.

Sunderland and Liverpool agreed a fee of £16 million and so, on 9 June 2011, I broke off from preparations for the European Under-21 Championships in Denmark to begin a new adventure. After making seventy-nine appearances for my home-town club and winning one England cap, in a friendly against France at Wembley the previous November, I agreed a five-year contract and became Liverpool's first summer signing. It was a new club record fee for a player of my age and the hope was that I'd be part of a brave new era.

This was a big moment in time for Liverpool – you could feel it everywhere. Things had changed since Kenny resigned in February 1991 and we were no longer the club to beat. Manchester United had overtaken our record of most league title wins and it didn't take me long to realize how much it hurt fans to be stuck on eighteen champion-ships while United were heading towards their twentieth. When you put Chelsea into the mix too, with everything they were doing with Roman Abramovich's backing, plus the emergence of Manchester City with the wealth from Abu Dhabi, the route back to the top wasn't going to be easy. Liverpool are in fantastic shape now, but twelve months before I signed they were headed to the brink of bankruptcy and administration under Tom Hicks and George Gillett.

One of the things that attracted me to Liverpool, however, was down to those hard times. When things were bad, the fans marched in the streets to protest about what was happening. I loved that because you could see that their club meant everything to them. When you get the back of supporters who are that passionate, you'll run through brick walls for them because you want to give them the success they crave. Thankfully, the new American consortium, led by John W. Henry, Tom Werner and Mike Gordon, seemed altogether different from Hicks and Gillett and they had a track record of success in American sport.

When I got to Liverpool, it was a bit of a culture shock. I found myself at a club that was hungry to make up for lost time and was prepared to spend big on new players to try to catch up fast.

Liverpool had been bought by FSG in October 2010. Roy Hodgson left as manager in January 2011 and Kenny had replaced him, first as caretaker manager, and then, in early May, after some excellent results, as permanent boss for his second spell in charge at the club.

I've been asked on plenty of occasions what Kenny means to Liverpool. The best way I can say it is that he is more than a hero. I've watched the footage of him scoring the goal that beat Club Brugge to win the European Cup in 1978. I know about his feats as manager the first time around, when he won the League and FA Cup double in 1986, won two more titles in 1988 and 1990, plus another FA Cup in 1989.

Football is only one small part of his story, though. Kenny took on an unbelievable role after the tragedy of Hillsborough on 15 April 1989 when ninety-seven of our fans died. He became a leader in a different way, attending so many of the funerals and providing incredible support to the bereaved families and countless others who had been affected.

So for Kenny to be reappointed as manager by FSG was a powerful move. It was also romantic. At that point, it was twenty-one years since Liverpool last won the league title. Arriving on Merseyside, I could feel the desperation of the supporters to end that cycle. Imagine what it would have been like if Kenny had been the man to end the wait?

It was clear that everyone at the club meant business and how serious their ambitions were. Luis Suárez and Andy Carroll were already there by the time I joined, and before the end of that transfer window Charlie Adam, Stewart Downing, José Enrique, Sebastián Coates, Jordon Ibe, Craig Bellamy, João Carlos Teixeira and Alexander Doni would arrive too.

I'm not sure my signing particularly caught the imagination of the Liverpool fans. At a time when they were looking for new heroes, was I anybody's idea of a saviour? Probably not. If anything, people thought Liverpool had paid over the odds for a raw kid. I expect the new owners were impatient to see a return on their investment too.

That just made me even more desperate to succeed. We had finished sixth the previous season and seventh the season before that, and the reality was that we were a long way off clubs like United and Chelsea. We'd been in a mess until Kenny took over, and a situation like that doesn't change overnight. It's a cliché, I know, but I probably tried too hard for a lot of that season. I was so determined not to fail that I forgot how to play my normal game.

It didn't help that Stevie missed more than a hundred days before Christmas with a variety of injuries. Part of the narrative around me joining was that I'd be acting as a foil for the club captain in the centre of midfield and that we would establish what I hoped would be a dynamic new partnership. But Stevie was injured and I wasn't playing in the centre anyway. Nothing seemed to be quite happening in the way I had wanted it to.

Kenny played me on the right of midfield, which wasn't what I'd been expecting, and in our opening game, my Liverpool debut, against Sunderland at Anfield, I was preferred to Dirk Kuyt in that position on the flank. Lucas Leiva and Charlie Adam played in the middle and Stewart Downing was on the left. So three of the midfield four were making their first appearance for the club. I was booked after an hour and then replaced by Kuyt. We drew the game 1–1 after Luis Suárez missed an early penalty. It wasn't exactly a dream start.

But we beat Arsenal 2–0 at the Emirates Stadium in our next game and I scored my first goal for the club, the opener in a 3–1 win over Bolton Wanderers that took us, briefly, to the top of the league. What a feeling it was to score at Anfield – with my left foot, too! It's a good job Martin Kelly, Dirk and Lucas caught me as I raced away celebrating. That was a high point, though, in terms of the Premier League campaign, and we struggled to achieve any consistency as the season wore on. We stayed on the outer fringes of the race for the Champions League spots.

Our season was torn apart and our reputation damaged by the furore that followed an altercation between Luis Suárez and Manchester United defender Patrice Evra at Anfield during our 1–1 draw on 15 October. Luis was accused of racially abusing Patrice. The details are well known and documented, as are the positions taken during it. I don't intend to use these pages to judge any individual's conduct during this period other than my own.

You know when players finish their career and are asked if they have any regrets or if they could go back and change anything? Usually, the answer is no. But this is different. In my case, there is so much I wish I could change about what happened during that episode – chiefly, how we dealt with the situation as a whole.

As a club, we got it wrong – badly wrong. I will always regret it. Within that situation is my own conduct, which in retrospect is more about what I didn't do rather than what I did. I should have thought about Patrice and, the truth is, I didn't. I could come out with excuses and say I was young and inexperienced. I could hide behind others. But when it comes down to it, I have to confront my own failings. I'd been brought up the right way and knew the difference between right and wrong.

The main cause of my regret is that when the controversy was at its highest and the scrutiny on Luis as an individual and us as a club was at its peak, we only looked inside, when we also needed to look outside. Focusing on ourselves was the wrong approach and that quickly became apparent as the saga rumbled on. The rest of football seemed to be looking at us and wondering how we were getting it so wrong. But we did get it wrong and, in my opinion, it was a collective failing.

On 20 December the FA found Luis guilty after a six-day hearing and gave him an eight-match ban and a £40,000 fine. The night after that, we played a Premier League game against Wigan Athletic at the DW Stadium and, in the pre-match warm-up, we wore T-shirts with an image of Luis printed on them to show our support. We were heavily criticized for that, and rightly so. The problem was, we had become so defensive that our judgement had become impaired.

Years later, I spoke to my old Sunderland team-mate Anton Ferdinand about the episode for his BBC documentary, *Football, Racism and Me*. He asked me about the decision to wear the T-shirts and I said that we all learn from experience. Our entire focus was on Luis and how to protect him in that moment. But we should also have thought about Patrice and what he was going through.

People could look at me and put me under the microscope and ask, 'What did you do in that instance?' and I wouldn't be able to argue with them. Not thinking about Patrice and the effect on him was a huge error. I was thinking about Luis because he was my team-mate, my friend and because I know he is not racist. I admired the player and the man. I still do.

You've got Liverpool versus Manchester United, you're in the midst of a maelstrom of emotions and accusations, and so you protect Luis, but you don't think about Patrice. How did he feel? I'm a great believer that responsibility starts and finishes with yourself, and I certainly wish I'd thought more about Patrice – a lot more.

The club has apologized to Patrice since and Jamie Carragher apologized to him on behalf of the club, too, while Patrice was appearing on *Monday Night Football*. It was only right. Sitting here now, I'm still thinking about my own actions through it all. It's why I told Anton that if people want to point me out, I'll take responsibility. People will say, 'That's a bit late,' but it's better late than never, particularly on an issue of such significance.

Talking to Anton was a valuable experience for me and I'm grateful to him for reaching out when he was making his documentary. We shared a dressing room, but in that moment he helped educate me. When he interviewed me, I listened as much as I spoke. What I can say with certainty now is that I have been part of the club as it has matured, faced up to its own failings and worked incredibly hard to ensure they are never repeated. We owe this to ourselves, to everyone else in football and to society as a whole.

Across March and April 2012, we lost six times in seven games. There was a 1–0 defeat at the Stadium of Light (my first return home ended with me being substituted after eighty minutes) and the sequence, which culminated in a 2–0 loss at St James's Park, was Liverpool's worst, we were told, since 1953. The pressure was starting to build on Kenny by then, despite the fact that we had won the Carling Cup at the end of February and had reached the FA Cup Final, where we would meet Chelsea.

I had played on the right again in the Carling Cup final, where we squeezed past Cardiff on penalties after a 2–2 draw at the end of extra time. The midfield that day, from right to left, was me, Stevie, Charlie Adam and Stewart Downing, with Luis playing off Andy Carroll in attack. I played the first hour before I was replaced by Craig Bellamy. Against the backdrop of our poor league form, winning the Carling Cup gave everyone a real boost.

Big days at Wembley are one of the reasons you join Liverpool, but I was struggling. Not physically, but mentally. I was in a dark place. I felt that I wasn't justifying my transfer fee and that I wasn't achieving the standards I had set at Sunderland. When Kenny came under pressure, I felt like I was letting him down as well. I owed him a great debt of loyalty for what he had done for me and I wasn't repaying it.

This was my big move and I felt like I was blowing it. I was twenty-one years old, living away from home, trying to adapt to a new city, a new club, new expectations and under a harsh spotlight, and I wasn't really coping. Damien Comolli lost his job two days before the FA Cup semi-final against Everton on 12 April at Wembley and I felt partly responsible for that, too. One of the biggest sticks that was used to beat him was the size of the transfer fee they had paid for me. It made me angry.

Kenny was massive for me that first season. He pulled me into his office several times to talk. He is a great student of people, but he didn't need to be particularly perceptive to see that I was a bit lost. He kept telling me to calm down, do what you're good at, relax, enjoy playing, but I wanted so much to impress him and to repay the faith he had shown in me that I found it hard to play my own game.

I started the FA Cup Final against Chelsea alongside Jay Spearing as the two holding midfielders in front of a back four, but we went 2–0 down just after half-time. Andy Carroll got one back midway through the second half and he thought he had equalized eight minutes from the end when Petr Čech palmed his header on to the underside of the crossbar and it bounced down and was hacked to safety.

It was in a time just before the introduction of goal-line technology, and the referee, Phil Dowd, ruled that the ball hadn't crossed the line. It was a matter of millimetres. We pressed for an equalizer, but we couldn't find one. The season ended on a low point – then it got worse.

The day after the final match, a 1–0 defeat to Swansea City, Kenny had to go to Boston for face-to-face talks with John W. Henry and Tom Werner about the season. We had finished eighth in the league, thirty-seven points behind champions Manchester City. That wasn't good enough. We all knew it. But I assumed winning the Carling Cup and getting to the FA Cup Final would be seen as reasons for encouragement. I was wrong. On 16 May it was announced that Kenny had lost his job.

I was numb when I heard the news. It also showed me how much I had to learn about football. I was still a naïve kid, and that was a reality check for me. It taught me how ruthless the game can be. Kenny is a great man, a genuinely great man, but the owners wanted to go in another direction.

Kenny dealt with it with typical class. He said he had been disappointed with our results in the league but that he wouldn't have swapped the Carling Cup win for anything because he knew how much it meant to the supporters. And he praised FSG too. He said his departure had been handled in 'an honourable, respectful and dignified way'.

There was some talk initially about Rafa Benítez returning. John W. Henry was pictured having coffee with Roberto Martínez, the Wigan manager, in Miami. Other names linked to the post included Jürgen Klopp, who had just won the double in Germany with Borussia Dortmund, while Louis van Gaal let it be known that he would be interested in the job. But on 1 June the club announced that Brendan Rodgers, who had been manager of Swansea City and had been widely praised as an innovative coach whose teams played attractive, attacking football, was the new Liverpool boss.

I knew Brendan only by reputation. I knew about the work he had done at Chelsea as a youth team coach and reserve team manager under José Mourinho. He was highly rated and respected by players who had played for him, and for having got Swansea, in particular, punching above their weight in the Premier League and playing some really clever football.

He made a brilliant first impression, putting on some great training sessions. There was real clarity about the way he wanted to play. There were some gimmicks, too, like the episode that was filmed in the documentary *Being Liverpool* where he is seen holding three envelopes and saying that he had written the names of three players who would let him down that season.

I think that was an old Ferguson trick – and he never did reveal whose names were written down, or even if he had ever written any down in the first place. The older players might have been a bit sceptical about something like that but, as a young player, I was impressed. I suppose it was just a ruse to try to make sure everyone was pulling their weight.

We were in the third qualifying round of the Europa League so we started the season early. Brendan's first competitive game as Liverpool boss was a 1–0 win away at Gomel in Belarus, and even though I hadn't had much of a pre-season because I had been involved in Euro 2012, I started that game in the centre of midfield. After we had beaten Gomel in the home leg too, I played in the centre again when we beat Hearts at Tynecastle in the first leg of the play-off round. I hadn't played a minute in either of the opening two Premier League games against West Brom and Manchester City, sitting on the bench throughout.

The second leg was scheduled for 30 August, a Thursday night, at Anfield. The day of the game, we were staying at the Hope Street Hotel in the city centre, which was our usual pre-match routine. There was a knock on my door and I was told the manager wanted to see me in his room. I went up there, exchanged a few pleasantries and listened to what he had to say.

I knew by then that a lot of the fans were openly wondering what I could bring to the team. It would be fair to say that some of them had been underwhelmed by my contribution in my first season at the club and, as the manager began to speak, I realized he wasn't exactly a big admirer either.

He said the club was trying to buy Clint Dempsey from Fulham and he had provided a list of Liverpool players they were willing to trade for him. Fulham had come back and said they didn't want anybody on the list but they would be prepared to swap him for me.

There was a bit of an uncomfortable pause. Then Brendan continued. He said he wasn't sure I was going to be starting and playing as much as I would like but that he wasn't going to force me out of the door. He said it was up to me, but he also repeated the fact that he wanted Dempsey, and Fulham wanted me. He said if I decided to stay, there were things he needed me to work on if I was to have any chance of playing regularly.

I was sitting there and trying to take it in, but I knew what the bottom line was: they were prepared to let me go. It was a hammer blow, the kind of news that leaves you hollow. I had only been there one season and I was being told I was surplus to requirements already. I went back to my room, closed the door behind me and cried. Then I phoned my dad, listened to what he had to say, and once I got it out of my system, I knew what I was going to do.

I spoke to my agent, Neil Fewings, and told him what had been said. I told him about Fulham and I told him it wasn't for me. I didn't want to go. I had only been at Liverpool for a year. Leave now? You must be joking. I still had a lot more to give. I hadn't got anywhere near the level I wanted to be at and I had worked so hard to get there. I wanted to stay and fight. I knew I wasn't going to play much, but I was prepared to get my head down and try to force my way back into the team.

I didn't have any more direct conversations with Brendan about it. I'm sure my agent would have spoken to Ian Ayre, the chief executive, and told him I didn't want to go. And I stuck it out. I wouldn't even call it a sliding doors moment, to be honest. I never think about what would have happened if I'd said yes to the idea of going to Fulham because it was never an option for me. I wanted to stay.

I did speak to Brendan about the changes he wanted me to make in my game. I wanted to do whatever it took to convince him I had a future with the club. I asked him about how he wanted me to play and he opened up his laptop and started showing me diagrams about positional sense and where I should be in certain situations, both with and without the ball.

From that moment on, I started working closely with one of his analysts, Chris Davies, who is now his assistant manager at Leicester. To be fair to Brendan, it was probably the first time anybody had tried to teach me that much detail about tactics. I had been much more off the cuff until that point. I hadn't had that kind of instruction before and I buried myself in learning everything I could.

We would analyse my performances in games and what I could do better and how I could improve. You don't want to be like robots and have absolutely set positions for every outcome. It was more where Brendan wanted players during the build-up of a move. I had a tendency to go looking for the ball and leave my position, and he wanted me to correct that.

I was very energetic and I wanted to be everywhere so I was leaving holes and gaps in my wake as I was charging around. I worked on that for a good few months. I didn't play much in the Premier League, but I played a lot of Europa League games. I kept my head down and kept learning and kept waiting for an opportunity.

I started sixteen games in the Premier League but, generally, Joe Allen and Lucas started ahead of me alongside Stevie in midfield. In my first season at the club, I was getting constant criticism about why I was still in the team and it started to affect me as a person and as a player. At least now I was out of the firing line a bit. People were pleased I wasn't playing as much and so there was less reason to have a pop at me. No one was saying I was a waste of money – because I wasn't in the team. I used that respite to do as much extra work as I could behind the scenes.

It was around then that I started to have sessions with Steve Peters, the psychiatrist who has worked with British Cycling and Ronnie O'Sullivan, among others. Brendan brought him in at Liverpool and said it wasn't going to be compulsory for any of us to talk to him but that he thought it might help us cope with the pressures of the modern game and that we were free to go to him if we wanted to.

Still, I can't try to suggest that my second season was anything but a struggle. My family life was non-existent. Rebecca would say that was the worst period of my career in terms of my behaviour at home. I would be out training until late, doing gym work, staying behind, and it would affect my mood when I came home. I'd watch TV, have a bit of food and go to bed without saying much.

It was just me and Bec at that time. It wasn't easy for her. She had left her home in the north-east and now she was here with me, but I wasn't really present. It was a big thing for me to leave home, but what about her? She'd left behind everything she knew, but her patience was unbelievable; Bec is incredible and I wish I could have shown her back then what her love and support meant to me. It wasn't normal, the way I was behaving and how my mind was working. Something was wrong. I had started thinking I needed to see someone just around the time that Brendan mentioned Steve Peters.

The thing was, football was everything to me and now people were saying I wasn't good enough. The fans were saying I wasn't good enough to be at Liverpool. Brendan, or the owners, were saying I wasn't good enough to be at Liverpool. The media were saying I wasn't good enough to be at Liverpool. Everybody, in my head, was against me, and that killed me because I felt I was good enough. I had so much to give, and nobody could see it.

You start questioning how good you are because everyone seems to be against you. You wonder whether other players think you're good enough to be there. I hit rock bottom at that point. Then my mood changed into an aggressive, angry kind of defiance. At the beginning, I was a bit sullen, a bit within myself, and it got to a point where it was making me angry.

I was getting angrier and angrier in training. I didn't mind anger at that time. I wanted to fight anyone and everyone because things weren't going the way I wanted them to go. I felt like I was a punch bag for a lot of people. I'd lose my head in training and fight with players, and that was OK because it told me I had the fire to prove people wrong.

I have always been prepared to fight my own corner and Luis Suárez was aware of that within three months of me arriving at Liverpool. Luis never hid his feelings in training. He'd throw his arms up in frustration if you didn't pass him the ball or if you lost the ball and, one day, I'd had enough. Luis was being particularly dismissive towards me and I was ready to kill him. Something happened and his arms went up, and it was about the third time he'd done it. I lost my head and ran up to him.

'Who the fuck do you think you are?' I said as the red mist descended. Everybody jumped in to separate us and it was a big drama for ten or fifteen seconds. After our confrontation in training, my relationship with Luis improved. Before the next game – Stoke City away in the Carling Cup in October 2011 – Lucas told me Luis had bet him that I would set him up with a goal. And that was how it happened. The ball dropped on the half volley and I crossed it in and he scored with a header. After the game he said he had told Lucas I would set him up. After that, he was brilliant with me and I felt our relationship from that point on was great.

It's important to say a word about Lucas, too. As time went on, I became closer and closer to Lucas. He knew better than anyone what was required at Liverpool to win people over, and his attitude and professionalism were faultless. Lucas was such an important person around the place because he was multilingual and could bring different players together. He is a brilliant character, with a lovely family, and his influence can still be felt in our dressing room. He went viral shouting, 'UNLUCKEE!' once when I was with him filming for the club website, and the lads, particularly Roberto Firmino, still say it now.

There were plenty of other things, however, that weren't so great. And so one day I thought about Steve Peters sitting up in his consulting room at the training ground and said to myself, 'What have I got to lose? The world's against me, so if it can help me even one per cent, then I'm not losing anything. It can't be any worse than this.' I went up and told him how I was feeling and the thoughts I'd been having. I started feeling a bit better and he put my feelings into the perspective of real life.

Steve was the first person I opened up to because I felt he wasn't judging me. He wasn't bothered about whether I was good enough. He wasn't there to coach me. I felt very comfortable, from the first session we had, that I could open up with him. I knew he wouldn't relay what we were talking about to anyone.

Steve always used to say, 'On a bad day, don't forget that you're incredible as a footballer. On a good day, you're phenomenal. You're in a different atmosphere. Remember that. The amount of work and sacrifice you've had to do to get to this place makes you one in a million.'

That helped put things in perspective. I stopped worrying about 'They don't want me to stay, the fans don't like me, the owners regret buying me.' I started to banish those thoughts and concentrate on the things I could affect. Talking to Steve helped me open up. I started to channel the anger in a way that benefited me. I became stronger mentally. I wasn't bothered about anything else.

I was physically fit. I was focused on getting back into the team, trying to prove Brendan wrong, the fans wrong, everybody wrong. It was just about how good I could be and being ready for the opportunity when it came. All the work I'd done behind the scenes had helped me and I was ready to grab a second chance.

There isn't one moment I can point to when I knew I had turned a corner and that everything was going to be all right, but I do remember scoring the only goal away against Udinese in December 2012 to put us through to the Europa League knockout stages. After that, I started doing things naturally. I got a couple of breaks and found myself playing more in the first team. When you play more, you gain a lot more confidence. My chest was out, I was doing things I hadn't done before and I was learning all the time from people like Carra, Stevie and Luis.

Luis was an incredible player to play alongside. He would talk to me about how to find him, he explained his movements and what he was thinking several moves ahead, how he reacted when the ball was in certain positions. The forging of that relationship, on and off the pitch, was a massive thing for me. As soon as I got the ball, I always looked for him.

If Luis is lining up next to you in the tunnel, you look around at him and think, 'We're not losing today.' He was on a different level in those three seasons we were together. I would look for him, give him the ball, he'd take five people on and put it in the top corner and I'd have an assist. He made me look unbelievable, and all I was doing was what he'd asked – 'Give me the ball.'

We had signed Philippe Coutinho and Daniel Sturridge in the January window and we only lost once in the last twelve league games of the season. Even though we finished seventh, we felt we were on the rise at last. And I felt I was on the rise too. I was a starter again. I scored in a 2–1 win at Aston Villa and there were a couple in a 6–0 win at Newcastle, which was nice. More than anything, I felt the beginnings of an attitude towards me from others that I had been craving for two years: it was called acceptance.

4. Make Us Dream

It doesn't seem enough to say that the birth of our first child was the best day of my life because nothing can ever capture the elation you feel when you become a parent. When Elexa was born in July 2013 she lit up our world and helped us see things in a different way. Over the past three or four years, I'd learned a lot. I'd learned about growing up, leaving childhood behind, taking on more responsibility, and I'd found out that you can't please everybody. Most of all, though, I'd learned about adversity and it had made me stronger. Elexa's arrival came at the best possible time: I felt ready.

It changes your whole perspective, having a child. Until then, I'd been doing everything for myself, but now there was something else. Football was everything I had ever loved, and sometimes that might have been too much because I had no release. It was football, football, football, and maybe it was unhealthy at times.

Then we had Elexa and, all of a sudden, the world flips and this little dot who has been in your life for five minutes is the most important thing in the world. That helped me, because it took my mind away from football and away from overthinking because, believe me, I am just about the world's worst overthinker.

Now I had this tiny baby in my arms when I got back home from training and she was all I cared about. And that changed things for me. I felt ready, personally and professionally. I felt it was my time to go and show people what I was all about. I wasn't a kid any more, a point emphasized to me by my international situation. I was too old to play for England's Under-21s and I hated the idea that breaks in the season meant I would remain at Melwood while my team-mates went elsewhere with their countries. This was going to be a big season, but I was going to attack it with everything I had. We went on a pre-season tour to Indonesia, Australia and Thailand for our preparations and while I was over there I gave an interview to the *Daily Mail*. The point I wanted to make was clear: I was a father now, and there were no excuses. This was my time and it was about becoming a man.

I was optimistic about the new season, especially because of the way we had finished the previous one. But it wasn't all rosy. Luis Suárez had been banned for ten games towards the end of the previous season for biting Branislav Ivanović during a 2–2 draw with Chelsea at Anfield in April.

The situation around Luis was complicated, though. Arsenal were desperate to sign him and, while we were in Melbourne at the end of July, they offered £40,000,001, because anything over £40 million meant that Liverpool would have to tell Luis that another club was interested in him. It was unsettling for Luis and, in early August, he gave two newspaper interviews, making it clear he wanted to leave. He believed Liverpool had to sell him if an offer in

excess of £40 million came through, and I'm sure the fact
that Arsenal were playing in the Champions League was
attractive to him. But Brendan said repeatedly he wasn't
for sale – so, too, did John W. Henry – and to the relief of
everyone at the club, Luis stayed at Anfield.

In some ways, our absence from Europe helped us that
season. It was a blow to the club's pride not to be involved
in any way, but fewer games and less travel kept us fresh
and hungry. Brendan's training sessions were excellent too,
and I went into every game feeling in top condition and
absolutely raring to go.

Perhaps it helped that people didn't expect too much of
us either. We might have ended the previous campaign well
but we had still finished in seventh place, to go with eighth
place the season before and sixth place the season before
that. People were used to us not being involved in the title
race. They didn't see any reason to rank us among the
favourites with Manchester City, Chelsea and Manchester
United this time; in fact, we started as 33/1 shots.

I had played well enough at the end of the previous
season to make some of the Liverpool fans revise their
opinion of me and thought I should be in the starting line-
up at the beginning of the new season. And that's what
happened. We won each of our first three games 1–0,
thanks to goals from Daniel Sturridge – Stoke at home,
Aston Villa and then Manchester United at Anfield in their
first season without Sir Alex Ferguson. I started all of them.

Sir Alex's autobiography was published early that
autumn and, to my surprise, I got a mention. He addressed
the fact that United had thought about buying me when I

was at Sunderland. 'We looked at Jordan Henderson a lot,' Sir Alex wrote, 'and Steve Bruce was unfailingly enthusiastic about him. Against that, we noticed that Henderson runs from his knees, with a straight back, while the modern footballer runs from his hips. We thought his gait might cause him problems later in his career.'

I've been asked a lot whether I was hurt by it or if I felt Sir Alex was criticizing me, but I didn't see it that way at all. Actually, it solved a bit of a mystery for me because I had wondered why United didn't come in for me after they had watched me play. And the book suggested it was more of a medical concern than one about my quality or about me as a player. I wasn't offended. I was just flattered that one of the greatest managers of all time had been thinking about signing me at all. Sir Alex said some nice things about me recently, about missing out on a good player and a good person, which was very nice of him. It goes without saying he is someone I have an immense amount of respect for.

With Luis still unavailable, Brendan played a 4–2–3–1 system, with Stevie and Lucas sitting in front of the back four and me, Philippe Coutinho and Iago Aspas in a bank of three behind Daniel Sturridge. Raheem Sterling started those games on the bench, but he came more and more to the fore as the season went on and his brilliance became impossible to ignore. We fell to our first loss midway through September, 1–0 at home to Southampton, but that game signalled the end of Luis' suspension. He started a Capital One Cup defeat to Manchester United the following Wednesday and that set him up perfectly for a weekend trip to Sunderland on Sunday, 29 September. He and Studge linked brilliantly in that game and Daniel laid on two goals for him in a 3–1. Luis lifted up his shirt at one point to reveal a message on his T-shirt. I held my breath for a minute, as I didn't want him to get into any more trouble, but I needn't have worried. It was a picture of his family and a message that translated as 'I love them.'

We went top of the table when we beat Crystal Palace 3–1 at Anfield in our next game and, even though we had blips at Arsenal and Hull City, we went on a spectacular run at the beginning of December when we put five past Norwich, four past West Ham, five past Spurs at White Hart Lane and three past Cardiff City. Luis scored ten goals in those four games. He was unstoppable – the things he was doing on the pitch were frightening. If you get a chance, go back and watch the four goals he scored against Norwich. Everything he was doing in training was coming off in a match situation – it was like he was on a crusade. Everybody was talking about him again, but this time it was for all the right reasons. The best way I can explain it is that you knew if you put the ball into a certain area for him, he was going to put it away. Stevie told me Luis was the best striker he had played with, and that kind of compliment told you everything about his quality.

We had what seemed like a bit of a setback when we lost narrowly to both Manchester City and Chelsea 2–1 in quick succession between Christmas and New Year, but then we went on another run and started to build momentum. It began to feel as though something special was happening and everything began to come together. Suddenly, we felt like we were title contenders.

Brendan managed it all brilliantly and, sometime in January 2014, unbeknown to the players, he began to ask someone close to one of us to write a letter about that person's journey for Brendan to read out to the team in the build-up to our matches. They were often very emotional and very motivational, which was the point.

We played Fulham on 12 February and when Brendan gave the team talk at the hotel before we left for the game at Craven Cottage he told me it was my turn to have a letter read out. 'This one's from Jordan's dad, Brian,' he told the rest of the lads. Things were very raw for me at that point because Dad was only in the first stages of his course of radiotherapy, having undergone surgery for throat cancer twenty-nine days earlier. When Brendan started reading the letter out, I was gone emotionally. I was trying to block my ears because I didn't want to hear what Dad had said. I just wanted to think about the game. It was very emotional. My dad had written about how proud he was of me and how proud he was of the team, and I was a wreck by the end of it.

On the bus from the hotel to the stadium I was still in pieces, and I'm not sure it helped my performance. I wasn't very good in that game at all, but we came from behind twice to win 3–2 with an added time penalty from Stevie. And if I felt a bit drained by my dad's letter, I felt inspired by listening to the letters that other people's loved ones had written to them. Brendan had got a lot of stick for his stunt with the envelopes the previous season, but I think he should have got more credit for the letters. It was great man-management. It brought everyone together even more. Everything going on in your personal life was out there and it made us closer. It was a team playing on emotion.

Emotion made us dangerous. There was so much whirling around my head, not least what Dad had said about going out to get Man of the Match in every game to help his recovery. Not long after we played Fulham, we took on Swansea at Anfield and I scored twice in a 4–3 win, the second one clinching the three points. I was told afterwards that I'd run seven and a half miles in the game, which was half a mile more than anyone else involved. I felt unstoppable, but so did plenty of the others. Luis, by now, had made himself the favourite to win the PFA Player of the Year award; alongside him, 'Studge' was having the season of his life. It shouldn't be forgotten how magical he was during that campaign and the way it was all gelling together was something that had got the Anfield crowd going. It was the first time I had properly heard them bringing the noise to matches – and who could blame them? We beat Arsenal, who were top of the table at the time, 5–1 one Saturday afternoon and the energy in the stadium made you want to run through brick walls. Teams simply couldn't live with us.

Sometimes, I think people forget just how exciting and open the title race was that season. Arsenal were top on New Year's Day, City were second, Chelsea were third and we were fourth. Arsenal fell away, but there's also a tendency to think the fight for the title became a two-horse race between us and City, whereas the reality was that

Chelsea were right in it too. We hit the top of the table at the end of March – our target had changed after we had gone to Old Trafford and run all over Manchester United. We won 3–0, effectively putting them out of the race for the top four that day, and I was doing all I could to take it all in. Qualifying for the Champions League was in our grasp, but something even more incredible was in touching distance. The fans had started singing about our football being 'poetry in motion', and that summed it up perfectly because, in so many positions, outstanding players were doing world-class things. To play your part in it is all you ever want.

When we put four past Spurs – I scored the last goal that day – we were on top and looked like we would stay there. At the end of that game we walked to the Kop to show our appreciation, as always, but I heard a noise from them different to anything I had ever heard before: it was a scream that made the hairs on the back of your neck stand up, a roar that suggested they felt the twenty-four-year wait to be champions might soon be over. Chelsea were second, but City were in a false position in third because they had two games in hand. Chelsea were dangerous, but we felt City were our biggest threat. When we played City at Anfield on 13 April, two days before the twenty-fifth anniversary of Hillsborough, we knew a victory would be enough to put the destiny of the title in our own hands. If we beat City and won the last four games of the season, we would be champions.

The game against City was incredibly highly charged, partly because the stakes were so high and partly because of Hillsborough. In our minds, this game was everything. This was what would decide the title. We knew that we had to throw everything we had at it, and the fans knew it, too. I still have some video footage of it somewhere. The crowds that greeted us on our way into the stadium had been building during the season, but before the City game they were bigger than ever. As soon as our team bus pulled on to the Anfield Road and got to the King Harry pub, the fans were lining the pavements on both sides of the street.

The closer we edged to the stadium, the deeper the crowds got. Soon, they were ten deep; there were people standing on brick walls and clinging to lampposts and flares being waved and supporters chanting and cheering and roaring us on. It was like we were being carried to the ground on a wave of emotion and, in these situations, you're terrified of letting people down. I'd never seen anything like this. It's become more commonplace since some of our recent successes but, back then, the fervour that we were unleashing felt like something wonderful and unfamiliar. You could see the longing in those scenes, the longing to be crowned the best team in the country again, the desire to let us know how badly they wanted this and how much they believed in us and the emotions that we were unleashing in them after so many years of watching the success of others.

My memories of the day are crystal clear, from the frenzy outside to the silence inside before kick-off when we paid our respects to those who had lost their lives at Hillsborough. I wasn't born when Hillsborough happened, but I've spoken to enough people and immersed myself in enough information to know the impact it had on the club and the city. That particular day in 2014, on such a significant anniversary, was as emotional as I have ever known. We carried the emotion into the game. We had made a habit of making fast starts, and we did it again against City. There were only six minutes gone when Luis, who had already been booked for a late challenge on Martín Demichelis, played Raheem in on goal, but when Vincent Kompany and Joe Hart both raced to the edge of the area to block his path, it seemed like they had controlled the danger.

Raheem just squared them up, feinted to go one way and then went the other. He sold both of them, did a sidestep to his right and then slotted the ball into the empty net. It was a stunning piece of trickery and it took Anfield to fever pitch. We were absolutely flying, overwhelming City with our pace and our pressing. Twenty minutes later, we went further ahead. Hart pulled off a brilliant one-handed save to keep out a header from Stevie, but when Stevie swung the resulting corner over to the near post, Martin Škrtel rose above everybody to guide it into the Kop end net. Absolute bedlam. For a second, I thought the ball might come to me, as I was on the back post – next thing I know, Luis and I are sprinting as fast as we can, screaming as loud as we can, to join the celebrations. These are the moments you wish you could bottle. Two–nil at half-time could easily have been 4–0.

Then City came back at us. It's strange to look back at their first goal now and see James Milner playing a clever

1–2 with Fernandinho and putting in a superb cross for David Silva to equalize twelve minutes after half-time. It was only a little over a year later that he was pulling on a Liverpool shirt. His signing must rate as one of the best free transfers in English football history.

But he was on the wrong side then and, five minutes after he had set up City's first goal, they had a second when Silva's shot deflected off Glen Johnson and deceived Simon Mignolet in our goal. All that dominance in the first half suddenly counted for nothing. City were level, and now people thought they were the most likely winners. But we had developed a huge amount of resilience and spirit in that season and scored a lot of late goals, and we always believed we had another goal in us. There were twelve minutes left when Kompany made a rare error and sliced an attempted clearance to the edge of their box. Philippe Coutinho was on it in a flash and smashed a shot past Harty's left hand. Anfield went wild again. This time, we were determined not to let the lead slip again. We all knew how much it meant. We knew how much every tackle meant, and every clearance and every pass. We were so close to getting the win we needed and we could not let it fall out of our grasp again.

We were deep into injury time when it happened. We cleared a City corner and Victor Moses burst forward with it as if we were going in search of a fourth goal to put the game out of reach. He was tackled by Kompany, but the ball fell to me as I ran forward. I cushioned the ball on my thigh as I ran and then took another touch, but the second touch was a heavy one and it ran away from me.

It ran towards Samir Nasri, who was standing on the halfway line. I thought I could get to it first and I was desperate not to concede possession to City again. I didn't want them to be able to mount one last attack. I launched my left foot at the ball. I got the ball, but maybe I went over the top of it a bit and maybe I also got part of Nasri's foot. Nasri rode the challenge, I think, but Mark Clattenburg, the referee, brought the red card out straight away and I was a bit in disbelief. It wasn't a great challenge, I have to accept that. It was just that it happened so quickly and it had never happened before. It was the first straight red of my career. When I think back, it feels like watching a car crash, when everything is in slow motion, a scene from my nightmares. I see Nasri hitting the floor and then Kompany, who was right there, gesturing at Clattenburg to give me a card. I see David Silva pointing me to the changing room, then I see Clattenburg hold up the red card. Then, finally, I see Silva beckoning Joe Hart and telling him to take the free kick for the last attack I so wanted to avoid.

. I lingered for a few seconds and then I accepted my fate. I knew there could only be a few seconds left, but I was thinking, 'We'd better win, we'd better hold on to this or I'll have let everybody down.' I was in the dressing room, praying to God we got through the game without conceding another equalizer, and then I heard the final whistle go and the cheers, and someone came running in and said we had won. It was our tenth league win in succession.

Part of me was devastated by the way things had ended for me, but part of me was filled with this incredible elation that we had won the game. We had one hand on the trophy.

That was what it seemed like. This was the biggest hurdle, in our minds, and we had just overcome it. The emotion was overwhelming, and that was just for me in the quiet of the dressing room. Out on the pitch, everything was even more heightened. As I sat inside, coming to terms with my conflicted feelings, I saw footage of Stevie and the players at the final whistle. Stevie was struggling to keep it together, and he got the players in a huddle around him and urged them on and reminded them that it was not over. 'This does not fucking slip! This is gone!' he yelled above the din. 'Next week, we go to Norwich, we do this, exactly the same! Come on!'

There was so much elation and relief about what we had done while I was at the stadium that it was only really on the drive home that I started thinking about the reality of my suspension. It started to sink in. We had four games left – Norwich, Chelsea at home, Crystal Palace away and Newcastle at home – and I could only play the last one. I knew that was going to be tough to take, but I tried to give myself a pep talk. There was still time for me to contribute if it went to the final day, and I was going to help however I could. I tried to think what else I could do. The media side of things was going to go crazy now, so I took our communications manager, Matt McCann, to one side and told him that if there were any community appearances or interviews to do, I'd do them to save the other lads. Strange though it may sound, nobody was interested in speaking with the lad who couldn't play!

I travelled with the squad to Carrow Road on Easter Sunday. No one was going to keep me away, even if I was suspended. We got a boost the day before when Chelsea lost at home to Sunderland, and then Raheem put us ahead early on with a blistering shot from outside the area. Raz was playing some of the best football of his career. I know that's a high bar, and I know that he has gone on to do great things since that season, but it was exciting to watch his talent flowering. He set up our second goal for Luis after eleven minutes and even though Norwich pulled one back Raz got our third and that was enough. The table showed we were five points clear of Chelsea at the top and nine points clear of City. We had three games left to play, but City still had those two games in hand and now we had to play Mourinho's Chelsea at Anfield. We were seven points from the title at that stage. Two wins and a draw in those last three games would have taken us over the line.

Still, I couldn't help but feel nervous about Chelsea. They had pretty much blown their chance of the title themselves, but I thought that might actually help them. And this was exactly the kind of situation that Mourinho thrives in. In many, many ways, this match was made for him. It played right into his hands. He has many attributes, and among them is being a spoiler. Right from the first whistle, he set out to frustrate us and play on the nerves of the crowd and the players. From that first whistle, there was something about the match that made me uneasy. The crowd was nervous and fretful and Mourinho was in his element. He knew Liverpool fans hated him, but he loved having the opportunity to wind them up and wanted to avenge the events of 2005, when Luis García's 'ghost goal' took Liverpool into the final of that year's Champions League. That was probably Mourinho's best chance of winning the competition with Chelsea, and we ruined it for him. He never forgot that.

They were time-wasting from the first minute. I knew they were going to do that. They were going to do that all day and kill the tempo. I was sitting in the directors' box at Anfield, watching it all unfold. It was like torture, and it got worse in added time at the end of the first half when Mamadou Sakho played a short ball inside to Stevie, Stevie lost his footing and Demba Ba ran through and slid his shot past Simon Mignolet. If my red card against City was bad, the reaction to this around the stadium was even more intense, going by the gasps.

The whole thing was scrambling my head. It was like Mourinho had caught us in a trap. Chelsea were a good side with great players and they were also experienced at playing this kind of game, massing their defence, 'parking the bus', wasting time, complaining relentlessly to the referee, playing on the frustration of the opposition and then pouncing on any error and punishing it ruthlessly. What was happening was right out of the Mourinho playbook. My heart was in my mouth. I knew Stevie was experienced enough to get going again and crack on. He could overcome it. There was still plenty of time left. I didn't think it would be the defining moment of the game. It was very positive at half-time. We were pushing, pushing, pushing, but they defended for their lives, we became more and more desperate and we just could not find a way through.

A draw would not have been the end of the world. In fact, a draw would still have left the title in our hands. We searched and searched for the equalizer, but Mark Schwarzer in their goal made some good saves and Branislav Ivanović and Tomáš Kalas in their defence soaked up everything that was thrown at them. We were still attacking deep into injury time when Chelsea broke away and Fernando Torres, once a great hero at Anfield, ran clear and slipped a square pass to Willian, who tapped it into the empty net. Game over. I went down afterwards to try to lift the lads, but it was impossible. This was as bad and emotional a situation in a dressing room as I had experienced up to this point. It was horrendous.

The PFA awards were being held in London that night. We were all supposed to be flying down, but, in the end, Luis was the only one who went. He had won Player of the Year, so he had to go. No one else could face it. Even though there were two games left, it was City's to lose now, and we knew it. This was City pre-Pep, obviously, but they were still a formidable side. They won 2–0 at Palace later in the day so they were three points behind us with a game in hand. And, crucially, their goal difference was now +58 and ours was +50.

We still had a chance, but we were odds against now. City played at Everton the following week and Everton had had a good season and were still right in the hunt for a place in the top four. It was the most difficult of City's remaining fixtures, but they played at Goodison Park on Saturday teatime and won 3–2, putting the pressure on us ahead of our Monday-night game at Selhurst Park. We knew we had to go for it against Palace. Our goal difference was now nine worse than City's, but Joe Allen put us ahead with a header midway through the first half. We couldn't add to the total before half-time, but when Daniel Sturridge and Luis scored two goals in two minutes early in the second half to put us 3–0 up with thirty-five minutes to play, suddenly we glimpsed a bit of hope.

Our goal difference was now only six worse than City's. If we could get another three goals, say, with the home game against Newcastle still to come, then who knew? But that was a dangerous way of thinking. Even though we threw everything we could at them in the next twenty minutes, we couldn't break them down again. Instead, they got one back. Damien Delaney scored after seventy-nine minutes and, when that went in, our world caved in. It went from bad to worse. Palace were decent and Dwight Gayle grabbed a second almost immediately, then a third two minutes from the end.

It was practically impossible to watch, seeing your dream die, and even eight years on it's still difficult to talk about now. We had given everything – literally everything – and with a bit of good fortune and some better performances, we would have done it. If we'd won it, we would have deserved it too, because the football was as good as anything I had ever played in.

Nobody would have deserved to have been champions more than Stevie or Luis, who pulled his shirt over his head to hide his face and his emotions as he walked off the pitch. He had been through so much turmoil and I wonder if maybe he felt that winning the title would somehow have justified it all and given it some meaning in his mind. And now that had been taken away. He kept the shirt over his head as he walked towards the tunnel, which is at the far end of the ground at Selhurst Park. A television camera tried to get up close to him and Stevie ushered it away and he and Kolo Touré helped Luis off the pitch as if they were guiding a man who could not see. The vision that we had had for our season had been blurred out of existence.

The draw took us back to the top of the table, but we were only a point ahead of City and they had that game in hand. 'Never has going top of the Premier League with one game to play been greeted by such an outpouring of grief, despair and disappointment,' Phil McNulty wrote on the BBC website in his match report from south London, and he was right.

There has been a tendency to report the Palace game as the match where we lost the title, but that has always struck me as inaccurate. The Chelsea game was the critical moment. By the time we got to Palace, we knew we needed something extraordinary to happen to win the title and we tried to make that happen at Selhurst Park by racking up a cricket score. By doing that, by throwing caution to the wind, we left ourselves vulnerable to the kind of comeback that Palace mounted, but by that point, we had nothing to lose. City's closing results vindicate the approach we took at Palace. It was all or nothing.

City had two home games left. They won their first one, their game in hand, by hammering Aston Villa 4–0. That meant that their goal difference was thirteen better than ours going into the final Sunday. We were at home to

Newcastle. They were at home to West Ham. That made goal difference an irrelevance. Our only hope was that West Ham could somehow pull off a stunning shock by winning at the Etihad.

My suspension was finally spent so I was back for the Newcastle game. It was like I had returned to a different world. My last taste of action had been during the euphoria and joy of the win over Manchester City, but now the euphoria had disappeared and all that was left was defiance and a tiny sliver of hope. We went behind to Newcastle, but Daniel Agger and Daniel Sturridge hit back for us and we won the game 2–1. We had scored more than a hundred goals in a season for only the second time in the club's history. It was scant consolation. City cruised to victory against West Ham, never providing us with even a glimmer of hope.

It was a devastating outcome for us when we had got so close, and it was particularly hard for Stevie because he probably knew he would never get that close again. Some people, predictably, took great glee in his slip and in the fact that he never won the title for Liverpool, and I know he has said that the memory of that game against Chelsea still haunts him. There is an easy response to those who got some enjoyment from that moment, though. Stevie doesn't need me to talk for him, but he was one of the best players in the Premier League for more than a decade and he won the Champions League with his home-town team and had an FA Cup Final named after him. He's a Liverpool hero, a one-club man in England, a player whose legend will never fade. Not many players can claim that kind of legacy.

Nobody should be blamed for the fact we didn't win the title. It was an unbelievable adventure and we played some amazing football, to the shock of all those who didn't think we would get into such a position. If people want to look for someone to blame, I deserve my share for the red card, but I have never thought that, if I had played, then things would have been different.

What I did regret was that I wasn't there with my team-mates when they were going through that adversity against Chelsea and Crystal Palace. I should have been going through it with them. It might not have made any difference whatsoever to the outcome, but I would at least have been part of the struggle.

There was a famous banner at Anfield that season that said 'Make Us Dream'. It caught the mood somehow. It said something about the wonderful improbability of what was happening. We had come out of nowhere that season and it had given us the belief that we could be contenders again. At some level, perhaps, the club had stopped dreaming in the last few years of its upheavals, but the way we had played, the goals we had scored, the ambition we had shown and the joy we took in the game during that season under Brendan, a season that ran on emotion and passion, paved the way for what was to come.

5. Walking on Broken Glass

For all the joy Luis Suárez brought me on the pitch, for all the respect I had for him as a player with such frightening ability, I'll never forget the misery he brought me in the summer of 2014. He was the reason England were knocked out of the World Cup in the group stages, when he inspired Uruguay in Brazil with both goals in a 2–1 win. The feeling of that defeat was horrendous but, to make it worse, when I shook hands with him afterwards, something in the pit of my stomach told me our days as team-mates were numbered.

What you saw that night in São Paulo was Luis in a nutshell. He had a knee problem that he'd been managing in the build-up to the World Cup. He had keyhole surgery just after the end of the season, but nothing was going to stop him facing England and he played on one leg against us. I never doubted for a minute he would be firing on all cylinders, even with that problem, because I'd seen some of the things he had done at Liverpool. If the medical department told Luis he had an issue, he wouldn't listen. He'd ask for anti-inflammatory tablets or extra strapping to be applied, and that would be him. I'm not naïve enough to think that Luis is a player who is loved universally, I can only tell you about my own experiences with him. He was one of the best in the world at that time, one of the best I ever played with, and when I heard Barcelona had made him their transfer priority in the summer of 2014 I had a horrible feeling about what was coming. The best Liverpool could do in the situation was to get as much money for him as they could in return, and that's what they did.

Luis joined Barcelona for £75 million on 11 July, just before I was due back in pre-season training. It's an exaggeration to say that's all you need to know about how the following season went, but it's not far off. How things might have turned out if Alexis Sánchez had been signed as his replacement, we can only guess, but the fact remained that Luis was one of those special talents who is irreplaceable. We had other brilliant players, but he brought everything together. He scored goals out of nothing and he made goals out of nothing. In that 2014–15 season, he went to even better levels. I knew he would have no problem fitting in alongside Lionel Messi and Neymar and I knew he was going to win a load of trophies: twelve months after leaving us, he had won the Treble and scored in the Champions League final, as Barcelona beat Juventus 3–1. Let me say it again: what a player.

In the squad we have now at Liverpool, we'd still miss a player like Luis. Any team would. But we have been building for a lot longer than we had been under Brendan and I'd like to think we would adapt in the same way we will have to adapt without Sadio Mané. The side that came so close to winning the title in 2013–14 came out of nowhere and its foundations were still fragile. Losing Luis was like one of the main bricks coming out of a Jenga tower.

We tried to replace him. Alexis Sánchez would have been brilliant; Brendan also did his best to sign Radamel Falcao. The club were committed to investing, though, and we spent over £100 million in that window. We bought Rickie Lambert, Adam Lallana, Mario Balotelli, Emre Can, Lazar Marković, Dejan Lovren, Divock Origi and Alberto Moreno. Some of those players turned out to be brilliant signings. Adam was part of England's World Cup squad, and I'll never forget his excitement when he knew that his move from Southampton was going to go through. He would become an integral part of everything we achieved under Jürgen Klopp, and there was a time when I thought he was one of the best players in Europe as a number 8. As for Divock, what can I say? Aside from all those goals against Everton (I'm smiling as I write that), without his input against Barcelona and Tottenham in the spring of 2019, we wouldn't have won the Champions League – it's that simple. A great lad, a brilliant striker and a club legend. It's not a bad way to be described, is it? Dejan was another good lad, a big character in the dressing room who always did his best for us. He was outstanding in the 2018 Champions League final, among other big performances.

But with so many new signings, it was inevitable that 2014–15 was going to have an element of transition about it. It wasn't the kind of progression we had hoped for when we ran Manchester City so close at the top of the league the previous season, but things change fast in football. By the time Christmas came around, we had been knocked out of the Champions League and there were suggestions that Brendan was facing the sack.

I wasn't a wide-eyed kid any more. I'd seen what had happened to Kenny Dalglish three years earlier and, if it could happen to him, it could happen to anyone. Brendan had credit in the bank after the impact he had made at the club, but when we only won four of our first twelve Premier League games, he came under pressure. Daniel Agger had also left the club in the summer and I had been appointed vice-captain in his place, which was a huge honour. At the same time, though, I was having some issues with my contract, which was unsettling me. My contract was running down and the owners weren't exactly rushing to sort out a new one.

It was a loaded subject for me. I was still smarting a bit from the difficult start I had had at the club, when I felt like the owners, the manager, the fans and some of the players thought the club had paid too much money for me. That stung, and it left a few scars that were still healing. I'd been rejuvenated by playing a full part in such a charged season the year before and by the acceptance from the crowd that came with it. I thought the club would be keen to extend my contract and that I had proven myself. When the negotiations started, I had hoped that my performances would be reflected in the club's stance – all my numbers were improving and I was taking more responsibility. Instead, Ian Ayre, the chief executive at the time, made my agent, Neil Fewings, a low offer. I thought that might be an initial ploy, but then the lines of communication went dead.

By the time we got to March 2015, we were having a difficult time in the league and we knew we were not going to finish in the top four after we had lost at home to Manchester United. Brendan was under pressure, Stevie had made the decision to leave and there was a general feeling of uncertainty. The disappointment continued as we lost the semi-finals of both domestic cups, to Chelsea and Aston Villa. We were still nowhere near close to agreement on my contract and I wondered whether the club might be preparing to sell me. It got to the stage where I thought I might be leaving in the summer. I didn't feel wanted at the club. I didn't feel wanted at all. They weren't even putting up a pretence of it being a priority for them to do the contract.

Then Mike Gordon, the FSG president and someone I respect immensely, rang and said he wanted to apologize for how everything had been handled and that he wanted to get the situation sorted out immediately. He was great on the phone, but I still had a few reservations because I wasn't sure why the other people handling it had taken so long. Brendan and I lived close to each other in Formby at that time and I went round to his house one day to talk through some of his plans for the future. I got the impression from him, at least, that I was very much part of his thinking. Brendan went through the offer they had made to me and, not long after that, the club came back with a much better one.

Neil had said that if I wanted to move I would have two or three big clubs on the table, and I knew if their interest was followed through I would have the opportunity to play Champions League football. I was still young, I was in the England set-up and both those things were going to play well with potential suitors. But the truth was I didn't want to move. You don't leave Liverpool easily. There's no other club like it, and my mind kept going back to how I felt when I first arrived from Sunderland. I was going to be a success here, I was determined to be part of good times and I just wanted people to recognize how much I was giving for them. So I decided to accept the club's offer and let all the reservations go. The idea that at some point in the course of my contract I would become the club captain and the responsibility that would mean and the honour of leading the club was a big thing for me. They wouldn't make me captain if they didn't want me, would they?

It helped, too, that I had had that bit of dialogue with Mike. It's not like I'm on the phone to him regularly, by the way, and I know that there are some managers who wouldn't want part of the ownership group talking to one of the players. But Brendan wasn't like that and Jürgen isn't like that. In fact, the relationship between Jürgen and Mike is very strong and Jürgen encourages the dialogue, particularly if it's something I can relay to the rest of the players.

I don't agree with every decision the owners have made, but whenever they have made mistakes, they have been quick to correct them and say sorry. To concentrate on the bad things would be stupid, and it has to be said they have got plenty right. What they have done for the club has been incredible. Anfield, thanks to the rebuild they have overseen, is almost unrecognizable now, compared to how it was a decade ago. They have invested in the squad, they've never been afraid to break the transfer record if it meant we could get an outstanding player; they've built a new training ground, with every kind of facility and gadget a professional footballer could want and need. Above all, they were the owners who recruited Jürgen Klopp and changed the course of our history. The business side of football gets lost in emotion sometimes, but as far as my relationship with them goes, ultimately, they're running a business and our relationship is a business relationship. At one point, maybe they did think they had spent too much money on me, but I hope they believe now it was a good deal. If I needed to prove anyone wrong, so be it. It hasn't ended up working out too badly for us all, has it?

That season, though, we were a shadow of the team that had taken the title race to the last weekend back in May. We were never in the hunt for the title this time and we finished third in our Champions League group, behind Real Madrid and Basel. When we lost 3–0 at home to Real in October, it marked the first time we had ever been three down at half-time at Anfield in Europe, but in some respects the 1–0 defeat in Madrid a couple of weeks later was even worse. I was one of several players 'rested' for a game in the Bernabéu that we needed to win, but the team that was picked suggested the priority was a Premier League game against Chelsea the following weekend. Brendan got a lot of criticism for the approach he took that night, and I have to be honest and say it was a shock that I was on the bench with Stevie, Raheem and several others. It was a shock for all of us.

Speaking of shocks, though, the biggest one of all was coming in January. On New Year's Day, Stevie announced he would be leaving when his contract expired and that he was going to join LA Galaxy. Stevie was heading towards the end of his career – we all knew that – but it was almost impossible for me to imagine the club without him. Its identity had become wrapped up in his in the years that he graced the league. He had been our driving force and our figurehead for so long, and there had been talk in the media that he would be offered a new contract and that he would accept it.

People found it hard to envisage him ever leaving. I certainly did. That's why I can't forget where I was when he told me the news: in the gym at Melwood, on the morning of 2 January 2015. We'd heard the news the night before, but when he came in the following morning – he'd scored two penalties the previous day in a 2–2 draw with Leicester at Anfield – it was like the building was in a period of mourning. I'd looked up to him since the day I arrived at Liverpool. He'd always been good to me, and I think it's because he knew how much football mattered to me and how much I was trying to make it work. He'd helped me settle in, and it was a privilege to play alongside him. There's not much I can say about him as a player that hasn't already been said, but he wasn't just like that in big matches. He was like that in training every single day. What a man and what a leader.

Once more, the fates didn't play fair with him when they made his last game in a Liverpool shirt a 6–1 defeat at Stoke on the last day of the season. Stoke scored three goals in eight minutes in one first-half spell. It was the first time we had conceded six goals or more in a top-flight game for more than fifty years. Stevie scored our only goal, midway through the second half. He deserved a lot better. The fans, certainly, deserved a lot better. We had arranged a going-away present for Stevie – a few days together in Dubai – and we had to go to Manchester airport after the game in Stoke. We had some pretty tough discussions about whether we should go, and it was only because it was his gift that we got on the plane. Thinking back to that flight, I remember how quiet we all were. We'd embarrassed ourselves with that performance; we deserved every bit of criticism that came our way. There are days I will never forget for as long as I live, and that, unfortunately, is one of them.

The result inevitably led to suggestions that Brendan was on borrowed time. His problems were piling up. It emerged before the game that Raheem had refused to sign a new contract and so he was dropped to the bench. The idea that this was to have been a transitional season had implied that there would be something good at the end of it, but we seemed further away from success now than we had been in August. We finished the season in sixth place.

Raheem joined Manchester City in the summer, which was another blow, and after Steve had officially left for LA Galaxy I was confirmed as the new Liverpool skipper. I know I wasn't the popular choice, but there was nobody prouder. I've spoken about how I didn't want a big song and dance being made around the announcement, but don't ever confuse that with not wanting the job. Captaining Liverpool? It's one of the greatest honours in football. I'd captained the side a few times in games Stevie had missed the previous season, and when it was announced he was leaving Brendan called me into his office at the training ground and said that the leadership qualities I had shown over the last couple of years meant I was the perfect choice as captain for him and the team.

I was over the moon. I felt a huge responsibility, but I was over the moon because I felt I had something that I could bring, I felt I could lead by example and that I was the right person to take on the role. I knew the outside perception would be rather different because the drop-off from Stevie to me was so big. I knew I would be compared to Stevie constantly and that would be difficult, but I felt I was strong enough to do it after everything I had been through. I wasn't afraid to get advice from people who had been around the club for a long time either, and they explained what I knew already: I had to be my own man, I couldn't impersonate or replicate what Stevie did.

I struggled with the expectations a bit and I realized I would be the one in the firing line when things weren't going well, but I had to take that on the chin because I knew that would be the case. I'd wanted the job, so it was a bit late to start complaining. When you lose, you suffer a lot more as captain because you take more of the responsibility, but I suffered anyway as a player when we lost a game. Anyway, people said I was good with pain. Stevie was typically generous with me. He took me aside when we were at the Hope Street Hotel before a game and said to me that he couldn't be giving the captaincy to a better person. That made me amazingly pleased, obviously, but he also warned me that it wouldn't be a bed of roses and that there would be ups and downs. The one thing that stood out in what he said to me was that, as a captain, you will always be judged by what you win.

You could be the best captain in the world and not win anything and then everybody from the outside thinks you're useless. As soon as you win a big trophy, you're this great leader. I'm at a stage now where, statistically, I have been involved in a team that has won more than the teams he was involved in. But you put Stevie in our team, with Jürgen as the boss, and he wins everything. It's not down to me.

I have written this before, but it's worth repeating: if I wasn't captain, if I wasn't at Liverpool, Liverpool would still win the trophies they win, as far as I'm concerned. I may be judged as a good captain because we've won what we've won, but I know there are other people at the club who would have led us to those trophies too. When it comes down to it, it's just timing.

I didn't make the most auspicious start to my Liverpool captaincy. I played in the first two games of the season – 1–0 wins over Stoke and Bournemouth – but I was increasingly being troubled by sharp, shooting pains in the sole of my foot – plantar fasciitis. I'd been in a lot of pain with it and I had felt it first during the defeat at Stoke. It's not a widely known condition, but the plantar fascia is a band of tissue that connects your heel bone to the base of your toes. It supports the arch of the foot and absorbs shock when you walk. Tension and stress on the fascia can cause small tears, and with me it had got to the point where every time I put my foot down it felt like a knife was being stabbed through it. It was like walking on broken glass.

I was in pain every day, but none of the treatments were working. I did stuff in the gym, I got treatment, I did everything I'd been asked to do, but as soon as I went outside and had a jog I couldn't put my foot down, it was so painful. They knew I had a tear in the plantar fascia, but even though there was a diagnosis there didn't seem to be a solution. The medical staff, headed by Chris Morgan, consulted people at the Royal Ballet, British Athletics, the Rugby Football Union, as well as at Cricket Australia, because of the prevalence of the problem among dancers, fast bowlers and Australian Rules Football. They also consulted doctors at the Boston Red Sox in the search for a solution, but I was still told there was no immediate cure. Trying to fix it was like trying to grab hold of a wet bar of soap. I was ringing Chris and sending him messages at all hours, having already gone on YouTube to see what we could do and what – if anything – he had found out.

The club thought the issue had arisen from a chronic overload on the heel over several years. I hadn't had a proper summer break for more than a decade and they thought that might be a contributory factor. Obviously, someone in the media came up with the idea that Sir Alex Ferguson had been right all along and that these problems were being caused by my gait. The medical department said that was rubbish. The club found a surgeon in New Jersey in the States who does an operation that obliterates the nerves on the sole of the foot, and the club and I decided it was worth a try because we'd exhausted almost every other option. The surgeon carried out the nerve ablation procedure and said it had been a success. He gave me orthotics to wear in my trainers that would help with the rehabilitation – or so I thought.

I put them in, and they were really hard. When there's no flex, it's supposed to aid rehabilitation by stiffening the sole of the foot. I was walking around the day after the operation and there seemed to have been an improvement. When I got back to England, I kept the orthotics in and I began to think that I might be able to train again. I had been out for around a month by then and so I told the medical staff I felt ready to get back out there because I wanted to see if the surgery had worked.

Morgo said he wasn't sure it was a good idea, but I insisted I was going to train. I kept the orthotics in my boots because I had got used to them and I associated them with feeling better. But ten minutes into training I made a pass, went to turn, felt my foot roll off the orthotic and heard a click. Within seconds, I couldn't put my foot down. I knew I'd broken a bone. So I had to hobble off the pitch, in tears. The club sent me for a scan and I was convinced it was going to be bad. The scan showed I had broken my fifth metatarsal on the right side. I'd been the author of my own downfall in a way, because I wasn't supposed to wear the orthotic in my boot; it was intended for my trainers. Breaking the metatarsal was caused by my foot rolling off the edge of the orthotic. It meant I would be out for ten weeks.

I tried to stay positive and I thought maybe that would give my plantar fascia time to settle down and that everything would be fine by the time I came back, but when I did, the pain was still there. So I still couldn't train.

I felt hopeless. I had tried so many different things and nothing had worked. It was the worst time I had ever had with an injury. The last resort was to inject it with a steroid, play on it and rupture it. The experience of some other players suggested that after the initial swelling caused by the rupture and rest for a week or so the problem would finally go away. I was at my wits' end with it by then, so I agreed to the steroid injections. I had been having regular pain-killing injections in my heel anyway so it didn't make much difference.

As soon as the steroid went in, it felt miles better. I could train without real pain at last. I had another steroid injection and played at Sunderland away on 30 December. After twenty or thirty minutes, I sprinted for a ball and it felt as if I had trodden on something on the ground, a bottle cap or something, and there was a popping noise. I looked back, but there was nothing there. The noise was my plantar fascia snapping. I got injections into my foot at half-time to numb it, but I only lasted fifteen minutes of the second half before I had to come off. I had to play with injections for a long period, but once it had ruptured that day at the Stadium of Light the pain went.

A lot of athletes have suffered from plantar fasciitis, but for many of them the pain is manageable. For me, I just couldn't put my foot on the ground because of the pain. I felt like it was never going to go away. Sometime later, I developed the same problem in my right foot, and this time I went straight for the steroid injections and went through the same process with the rupture. When you've got pain every day, it gets you down. That was a really tough time.

Brendan must have been silently cursing his new skipper. He was coming under more and more pressure, and I was out injured and no one could tell him when I'd be back. It was obvious we were struggling, and I felt helpless. I was desperate to play, but I was still recovering from my metatarsal injury when Brendan's time at Liverpool came to an end.

After winning our first two games, we only won one of the next six and losing a lead at Everton in the sixth of those games would have major consequences. The game was played on a Sunday afternoon at Goodison Park; I'd gone with the squad, as normal, and we took the coach back to Melwood, four miles away. Ian Ayre was there waiting for Brendan, and he followed him into the main building when he got off the bus. None of us in the squad had any idea what was coming – nobody had been consulted. There had been speculation for weeks about his position but, even so, when the news came it was a huge shock to us all. Did I feel the sacking was fair? Probably not. I thought he got a rough deal. Yes, we'd struggled with results the previous season and we hadn't made a great start this time either, but Brendan kept having the ground shift under his feet. He kept having his best players sold out from under him or retiring and it's hard to build any kind of momentum at a club when that happens.

I loved being a part of that 2013–14 season and, if we could have kept that team together, then who knows what would have happened. But Brendan had lost Jamie Carragher to retirement in May 2013, then he lost Luis to

Barcelona the following year, then Stevie twelve months later, and then Raheem. That's a big talent drain. It's a lot of blows to absorb and, in the end, Brendan just lost one player too many.

Our relationship was good by the time Brendan left. I was a little bit angry and out to prove him wrong in the aftermath of the episode with Clint Dempsey and Fulham. But I also needed his help. I needed him to give me opportunities and teach me tactically, and eventually he made me captain of the club. For him to recognize the effort I had put in to be the player he wanted me to be, to acknowledge that I had grown in terms of my tactical awareness and to give me opportunities says a lot about him. Kenny had brought the club back together and Brendan had shown us what was possible at Liverpool, in an era when we were competing with clubs owned by oligarchs and nation states, if we could keep a hungry, talented team together. He deserves more credit than he gets.

6. This is Just the Beginning

My mind was racing; my eyes were trying to take everything in. It was 30 April 2013, a Tuesday night in Madrid, and I was at the Bernabéu, staring out at that beautiful stadium with its steep, elegant tiers and its packed stands. Jamie Carragher was retiring in two weeks and, to give him a big send-off, it had been arranged that we would go to Spain for the night, have a bit of crack and some food and then do the thing that Carra loves to do more than anything else – watch football. Carra had enjoyed an amazing career, he was someone I looked up to so much, and there was nothing he didn't know about the game. He was in his element when we got to Madrid – but he wasn't the only one.

It was the second leg of the Champions League semi-final between Real Madrid and Borussia Dortmund. Back then, it was still the kind of match I could only dream of playing in. We weren't even in the Champions League at that point, let alone getting to the latter stages of the competition. Part of me was still that little lad who had gone to Old Trafford with his dad ten years earlier to watch the final between AC Milan and Juventus, the football obsessive who just wanted to study all the players on the pitch and the gifts they had.

I was there to watch Dortmund, really. It's easy for me to say now. I know what you're thinking: nice words for the boss, if he's reading! But honestly, I was there for them. I'd watched them before on television and I could not believe what I was seeing. The way they played – the press, the counter-press, and all that energy. I wondered, even then, what Jürgen Klopp was like, a man who could get his players playing like Dortmund's players played for him. Everything I had seen from Klopp's Dortmund had me saying two words: yes, please.

Six days earlier, Dortmund had won the first leg of that semi-final 4–1 at the Westfalenstadion and Robert Lewandowski had scored all four of their goals. But Dortmund were about a lot more than Lewandowski and, as I watched that night in the Bernabéu, I loved the fact that they didn't have big names but that they were a unit. They exemplified the power of the team and the strength of the collective will. That sat perfectly with my philosophy of football too.

Madrid had Sergio Ramos and Michael Essien and Luka Modrić and Mesut Özil and Ángel di María and Cristiano Ronaldo. They had Karim Benzema and Kaká on the bench. And Dortmund? Well, they had really good players but they weren't star names. Not then, anyway. They had Sven Bender and İlkay Gündoğan and Marco Reus and Mario Götze and Jakub Błaszczykowski and Lewandowski. And they played like fire. They lost 2–0 that night, but only when Madrid got a couple late on. Dortmund still went through to the final. I still loved the way they played. They were full of energy, they won the ball back quickly, they were brave and committed. I thought that the way they played would suit me down to a tee. I thought I would suit them, too.

Dortmund were punching above their weight as well. That wasn't lost on me. Under Klopp, they had beaten Bayern Munich to the Bundesliga title two years in succession in 2010–11 and 2011–12 and I know their progress under Klopp had caught the eye of Fenway Sports Group even then. To put that achievement in perspective, those are the only times a team other than Bayern has won the German title in the last thirteen years. It was testimony to Klopp's acumen and his powers of motivation.

So I thought about that night and the excitement I'd felt watching Dortmund when, on 8 October 2015, four days after Brendan Rodgers left, it was announced that Klopp was going to be our new manager. He had taken a few months out of the game after he left Dortmund and now FSG had chosen him as Brendan's replacement. It felt like a huge coup that we had got him, a proper statement of intent. He'd had approaches from other clubs, including Manchester United, but thankfully none of the offers captured his imagination. With Liverpool, it was different. He sensed he and the club would be a good fit. He was right.

Part of me felt a bit guilty for feeling so excited about his arrival. Footballers move on when a manager is sacked. And we tend to move on fast. You don't have much choice if you want to stay in a job. So when Brendan left, I thanked him for what he had done for me and then I began to think about who the next manager would be and whether he would want me in the team or whether he would replace me and sell me.

That's it. You wipe the slate clean and start from scratch with the new man. It was harsh that Brendan hadn't got the chance to finish what he had started, and I owed him a lot for what he had done for me, but I had to pour all my efforts into the future. I did my absolute utmost for him while he was at the club and I'm content in my own mind that that was enough.

I was excited about Jürgen arriving but, equally, I was a little anxious, too. I was injured so I was concerned about not being able to have the chance to impress him immediately. I knew him by reputation and I knew he was a populist and a man whose dynamism rubbed off on everybody around him, but I didn't know what he was really like. What would he think of a player like me? I just wanted to get on the pitch because he told everyone in his first few days that you needed a good period of training with him to understand his methods. I wanted to be a sponge, I wanted to soak up everything he did. My broken metatarsal, however, meant that others got a head start on me. What if the lads played really well and I couldn't get back into the team? No one could tell me when I'd be fit again, and managers hate that kind of uncertainty. So that was difficult. Still, the first meeting I had with him was memorable. I was in the gym at Melwood, doing a leg press, doing my rehab, and he came in and gave me a high-five and a hug and introduced himself. Straight away, he put me at ease, as he told me he couldn't wait until I was fit. First impressions are important and, instantly, I had got a good feeling from him.

This injury, however, could not have been worse timed. I wondered whether he would want me as captain but, most of all, I was worried about persuading him that I was worth a place in the team. He spread energy around the place as soon as he arrived and there was a sense this could be the beginning of something special. I wanted to make sure I was part of it. The main thing is that you want to be playing football, and playing for Liverpool. That's the number one. Everything else looks after itself when you are fit. It was a bit of an adjustment for me because I'd never really had a period in my career where I had been out for a prolonged spell on the sidelines, but I wasn't going to be out of sight, out of mind. Jürgen's first game was against Spurs at White Hart Lane, and I asked him if I could travel. He seemed a bit surprised.

'Haven't you got any rehab to be doing?' he asked.

I told him I'd do my rehab before I travelled. I felt a responsibility to be there and I wanted to be around the team. I was new to the captaincy and yet I'd been an absentee most of the season. Even if I couldn't play, I wanted to listen to what the new manager was saying in his team talk. I wanted to hear what he wanted so that, when I was fit, I had an idea of what he was all about. I didn't want him to forget about me.

The impact he made in that first game was madness. I watched it from the directors' box, and the intensity levels were through the roof. The numbers after that game, the running stats, were new records for us. Collectively, we ran seventy-two miles, and there was this amazing picture of Adam Lallana almost falling into the gaffer's arms when he was substituted because he had put so much effort in.

We were the first team to run more than Tottenham that season. We competed like maniacs, and after the game Jürgen was out on the pitch, hugging the players and congratulating them for their efforts. We had drawn 0–0. Usually I'd never be too happy with a point, but there were so many positives to take from the performances we came away with a definite bounce.

Jürgen was totally different to anything I had seen before. After the Spurs game, I kept asking him if I could travel to games. I think he must have got sick of me asking, but I just wanted to be involved. I wanted to hear and see. I would stay behind after my rehab to watch sessions. He changed training times to the afternoon, which wasn't how things were normally done and wasn't particularly popular. Footballers are very stuck in their ways, and he shook things up. We were coming in at 2.30 p.m. rather than going home at 2.30 p.m. In the winter, when the clocks had gone back, we were training with the floodlights on and, at first, the lads were struggling to get used to it. They asked me to speak to Jürgen so, as captain, I felt it was something I needed to broach and I headed to his office.

'Gaffer, a few of the lads are struggling with late training times – do you think we could maybe train in the mornings?' I asked.

There is a face he pulls when he either doesn't like what he's hearing or doesn't understand what's being said, and this would be the first time I saw it.

'And what players don't like it?' he replied.

There was no way I was going to stitch anyone up by naming names, so I was thinking on my feet.

'There's a good few – that's why I've come to ask you.' He paused.

'Well,' he said, 'you tell the players who have the issue to come and speak to me directly.'

There was another pause. I think you can guess what happened next . . . nobody said a thing and afternoon training was here to stay – and I also thought that I wouldn't be going into his office any time soon! So I would stand on the balcony at Melwood, and some of the sessions were brilliant. Even the shooting drills were different. There was never a rest period, never a chance to catch your breath.

Normally, after you've taken your shot, you'd be admiring your work or thinking about what you could have done better, but with Jürgen's drills there was no time to stop. Whether you scored or missed, you were getting another ball straight away so you didn't have time to think where the previous one had gone. You're not just thinking about shooting. You're reacting to what happens next. In a game, the keeper might save your shot and you have to react to different things and different possibilities. It was a bit like the keeper drill, where the keeper saves then has to get back up and save again. We got a lot of muscle injuries in the treatment room in that first season. We were working at an intensity that was new to us. It was hard work, but it made you feel brilliant, like you couldn't wait for the next one. It felt like a jolt of electricity had been shot through the club.

I'd be lying to you if I said I felt totally comfortable. I didn't. I could see how impressed Jürgen was with Adam Lallana, and Roberto Firmino was a different player under Jürgen. Brendan had signed Bobby, but I just remember when Jürgen came in there was a big thing about Bobby. The gaffer said in one meeting, 'People don't realize how good this guy is.' He had known him from playing for Hoffenheim in the Bundesliga. I really hadn't seen anything that I thought warranted that reaction but, suddenly, a switch had been flicked. Boom! Different player, different level. Now I got it. The first few months of Klopp being here, Bobby was everything. He could defend, he could link play, he started scoring goals. The manager knew it was there from day one, to be fair.

Bobby does stuff that nobody else can do, the positions he takes up. I've got a very good relationship with Bobby. People think he doesn't speak English, but he's fine, believe me! We talk, and he's a good laugh. He's always smiling; he walks in and lights up a room. You don't see him in anything other than a good mood. He's funny, he gets involved in the banter. What a player he has been.

A lot of people were talking about the connection Jürgen had made with Emre Can and how Emre was responding well to being played in midfield again rather than chopping and changing positions. Maybe he felt that I was secure in my self-belief, but I was worried I was being left behind. Maybe he didn't think I would be worried about that, but I was. I got very down on myself. I was stuck on the sidelines. I was powerless. When I'm like that, I'll make sure I'm working incredibly hard in the gym so that when I do get back I'm in top condition. When I got home, though, I'd be watching telly in bed and then out to training, moping around, not talking to anyone.

Perhaps because I was feeling jumpy about my situation, something else spooked me. A couple of months after Jürgen arrived, when I had barely figured in any of his teams because of my foot issues, some of the newspapers ran stories linking me with a move to Spurs. Jürgen was asked about the speculation in a press conference and was very dismissive. He said he didn't comment on speculation, but any player who didn't want to be at the club didn't need to be at the club. Some of the papers loved that. It was interpreted in various ways, among them that Jürgen was telling me I could leave and that no one's place was safe. I didn't really interpret it that way, but it still played on my insecurities.

I came back on 29 November, in a 1–0 home win over Swansea. I hadn't really recovered from the foot injury and wasn't really up to speed for the first couple of months. Saying that, I scored a goal in a 2–2 draw with West Brom, a game that was memorable because Jürgen lined the team up in front of the Kop at the final whistle because we had scored a last-minute equalizer. Plenty of critics had a go at him, but he was being clever, creating a bond between the fans and the team, as he knew it needed repairing. I ruptured my plantar fascia in the game at Sunderland just before New Year and then got back in the team after that. At the end of February 2016, I played in the Capital One Cup Final, which we lost on penalties to Manchester City.

Then we played Dortmund in the Westfalenstadion in the first leg of the quarter-final of the Europa League, a match which the media dubbed El Kloppico. I tore the lateral collateral ligament in my knee in the first half and left the stadium on crutches. I was told I'd be out for six to eight weeks, which was the typical amount of time to rehab that particular injury.

That meant more pain and frustration. The second leg of that quarter-final turned into one of those great European classics at Anfield – the first our particular generation of players had seen – when we came back from 3–1 down to win 4–3 with a last-gasp injury-time goal from Dejan. It was a brilliant night and I raced down from the directors' box on my crutches to join in the celebrations. I know this sounds selfish: I was delighted we had won, but I was gutted I hadn't played in it. When I look at other players doing well, that's great. I want the team to do well, always. However, you want the team to be doing well with you in it. You don't want to believe they don't need you any more. I felt in that first season under Jürgen that they were doing just fine without me. I've told you I overthink things, and my mind was going into overdrive now.

I knew, if I was fit, I should have a part to play, but you never quite know whether you're going to be given the opportunity again. I wasn't fit, and even on the rare occasions I was in the side, I wasn't fully fit. I didn't blame Jürgen. I knew it was difficult for him to see what I was all about. We made it through to the Europa League Final, where we would play Sevilla in Basel. The match was set for 18 May and I was desperate to recover from my LCL injury in time to play some part in it. I came back earlier than expected, and the night before the game I ran around like a madman in the final practice in the stadium to try to prove I was fit. I was one of the players chosen to do the pre-match press conference, and I kept looking at the trophy, which was perched on a desk next to us. Imagine lifting that for Liverpool! I didn't make the starting eleven; I wasn't expecting to. But I did make the bench and I did allow myself to dream. You wouldn't be human if you didn't – how many players get to be involved in European finals in their career?

We played well in the first half and took the lead with a brilliant goal from Daniel Sturridge, but by midway through the second half we were 3–1 down and I was itching to get on. I thought if I could get on for twenty minutes, then maybe I could help turn things around. It was all or nothing and we had staked so much on this game. If we won it, we would be in the Champions League the following season. But Jürgen brought on Divock and Joe Allen and then, with seven minutes left, my last chance to get off the bench disappeared when he replaced Kolo Touré with Christian Benteke. I wasn't the only one who didn't get on. I wasn't the only one who was disappointed. We were all devastated by the result and dismayed at losing a second final in one season.

We got another taste of how Jürgen's mentality is different that night. When we got back to our hotel after the game, the Novotel Basel City, he stood up at the front of the coach and said that he expected everyone to come to the restaurant area, which had been blocked off for the party we had been planning to have if we'd won. I was sceptical. I didn't want to go to any party. What did we have to celebrate? It wasn't for me, and I wasn't alone in having such thoughts.

I was with Millie and Adam, and we went over to the restaurant and there was music playing. I don't think there was anywhere I wanted to be less than in that restaurant that night, and Millie and Adam felt the same. I wanted to go straight to bed and blot everything out. Then Jürgen came over. 'Are you just going to sit here all night with your faces up your arse?' he said to us.

We are looking at him, thinking, 'Eh? We've just lost a final – what do you want us to do?' But he got out into the middle of what passed for the dance floor and made a speech. He said it was fine to be disappointed. Then he said, 'It was shit before. It still feels shit now, but this is just the beginning. So we are going to celebrate today because we did well to get to this point and from this point we will go further. There will be more finals.'

The last words were said with absolute certainty and conviction. Millie, Ads and I were a hard audience, but this was a different mentality. I was still feeling vulnerable, I had been injured for the majority of the season, I was annoyed I hadn't got on. And yet here the manager was, getting everyone up on the dance floor, giving a speech and leading some communal singing. He loves his music and he started belting it out on the microphone.

We are Liverpool, tra la la la la,
We are Liverpool, tra la la la la la,

We are Liverpool, tra la la la la,
The best football team in the world – yes we are!

We carried on until night became daylight, and everyone
tried to buy into it. I still went up to my room as soon as
we were allowed, and at the time I couldn't quite get my
head round it. But I did know we had got ourselves a
manager who wasn't like anyone I had met before, someone whose spirit was unquenchable and who always knew
the right thing to say. *This is just the beginning* – how right he
was. Looking back on that now, I just think: 'Genius.'

What makes you want to play for him? You know that
if you do what he says, you win. If you do what he wants
you to do as a team, then you win. And that's all you want
as a footballer. You want to be successful. I believed in him
from day one. He has an aura. It's partly his delivery – you
believe everything that he says and you know absolutely
that he cares, one hundred per cent.

At the very beginning, he was a lot more intense. He
would push us to levels that tested us both mentally and
physically. As time has gone on, he has built a relationship
with the players so he trusts us and we trust him. The
relationship has evolved and got stronger. I think, even
as a journalist or a fan, you could sense the gift he has
from his first press conference. You know he has got
something special. He sees things in a unique way, and he
doesn't act the way someone else would. Positivity is part
of it. The way he sees things in football, in life. He likes
to help his players. He's like a father figure to us, and you
have fall-outs with your dad but, ultimately, there is that

love and respect. You always want to make him proud and fight for him.

Put it this way – all of the lads would run through a brick wall for him. If I am ever a manager one day and I have the whole team wanting to run through a brick wall for me, I'll take that. I will have done something right if that happens. That must be an amazing feeling for him. He can have arguments, he can demand, he can leave players out because he has to, and to still have all that squad willing to die for you on that pitch, well, I don't think any other manager has that gift. He has the perfect balance of demand and reassurance. He knows when you need a kick up the backside or an arm round the shoulder. If something's not right in your life, he can sense it. He knows. There have been plenty of times when something's not going right for me and he'll pull me into his office and get to the core of it. He's good at picking up on anything that might be affecting the players.

He sells a dream. You believe what he says. If he said, 'Go and jump off that wall,' I'd do it. If he said, 'Go and jump off there and, if you do that, this is going to happen,' I'd do it, because I'd believe him. I'd trust him. And I believe that he cares for the players deeply, more than the players probably know.

It must be incredibly difficult, with my rational head on, to leave players out and let players go. To care and have a relationship with the players is so difficult, and I don't think there's another manager that has both the football intelligence and the emotional intelligence that he has. What you see on the telly with Jürgen is pretty much what you get. Everybody loves him, even if you're not a Liverpool fan. He's infectious as a character, and that's the way he is with us. It's not all a bed of roses. You'll argue and you'll fight but in the end you always have that respect and you're out to try to please him.

Tactically? Intensity is the key with the style of play he promotes. Intensity and relentlessness. He always said he didn't want to be the coach of the best team in the world, he wanted to be the coach of the team that can beat the best team in the world. That means us being every team's least favourite side to play against. When people see Liverpool, he would want them to say, 'Oh, for fuck's sake, not them.' He wants them to look at us and think to themselves, 'This is going to be like playing against thirteen players; they don't stop, they never stop, regardless of the score. They're in your face, but when they get the ball they can play, they can play through lines, they can score from wide, they can score goals from counter-attack, from build-up.'

The intensity was right there from the beginning. The coaching staff are always trying to improve aspects of the game we can be better at. We are constantly evolving. Without the ball, Jürgen wants us to be the ugliest team in world football to play against. With the ball, he wants us to be the most incisive and the most creative. He wants the full package.

That night after the game in Basel, I didn't sleep a wink. We flew back to England and, on the plane, I was thinking, 'This could be me finished at Liverpool.' My talent for overthinking was in full swing. I know that wasn't a rational reaction. At a basic level, I understood Jürgen's decision not to play me. I had rushed back, I'd had a lot of problems, he didn't really know what he was going to get and it probably made sense not to risk setting me back in my recovery from the LCL. My reaction was an emotional one: I hadn't got on to the pitch and so my tendency to fret and worry was going into overdrive.

Maybe it was just destiny that I wasn't going to get the opportunity I wanted. On the bus from Liverpool airport back to Melwood, where we were going to collect our cars and then drive off until next season, that thought kept going round and round my head; it was starting to torture me. The previous night, lying in bed, I'd thought I couldn't stand the uncertainty of disappearing into the off-season not knowing what was in store for me, whether my career and my life were about to be thrown into turmoil.

As we were walking into the building at the training ground, I asked if I could see the gaffer for ten minutes in his office. When I went in, I was emotional, a bit angry. Football was everything to me. Liverpool was everything. And to me, this was make or break.

All the worries and the frustrations that had built up during the months I'd been struggling with injury and doubt came pouring out. I said I knew he hadn't seen the best of me yet and I realized he couldn't tell me if I was going to play or not but I just wanted to know if I was going to be in his plans for next season.

What happened next could not have been more perfect or simple. Jürgen sorted the situation with three words.

'Yes,' he said. 'You are.'

7. Sixes and Eights

It doesn't matter how long you've been at Liverpool, there's always one challenge facing every player the first day you report back for pre-season training: prove yourself. You can be a kid coming out of the Academy or a big-money signing or someone who has played a few hundred games – the minute you take your foot off the pedal or think you've got it cracked, you'll be in trouble.

You'll know by now that I've never operated in any kind of comfort zone, but I came back in the summer of 2016 ready to rock and roll. It was going to be a massive season for us all, with Jürgen really getting down to work, and while I felt physically good – not to mention reassured after what the gaffer had said to me following the Europa League final – a big part of me was anxious.

Jürgen had a new role in mind for me, playing as a number 6 in a 4–3–3 system. He didn't have any doubts that I could be effective there, but this was a new world for me, screening the defence and harnessing my natural instincts. Now I was going to be at the base of the team, setting the tempo, dictating the play. It's like any new challenge. You ask yourself questions – am I good enough to do this? – and it takes time to settle. You can see, then, why I had anxieties. Not only was I trying to prove myself good enough to be at Liverpool, I was trying to prove myself in a different part of the team. Of course there were times when I had doubts. I'm sure everyone had doubts about me.

I didn't make a great start in the role. We won our opening game away at Arsenal, but it was a goal-fest and I wasn't sure I controlled the area in front of our back four in the way I was supposed to. We lost the next game – against Burnley at Turf Moor– 2–0, and I looked lost and felt lost. I got plenty of criticism, and I deserved it. People were generally mystified about why Jürgen was playing me there.

We had signed Sadio Mané and Gini Wijnaldum that summer and Jürgen's team was starting to take shape. Loris Karius had been brought in from Mainz, too, and would gradually take over from Simon Mignolet in goal. Gini was brought in to play 8, and that was obviously one of the reasons why I was being moved to 6, but a defensive midfielder in a 4–3–3 formation is a very different role to an 8. Did the gaffer not think I could play that role? More questions. I was pleased to be in the team, but I didn't really know how to take it.

He had brought Adam in as an 8 on the other side, switching him from a more attacking role. That was where I'd assumed I'd be playing. It was an interesting development and immediately it paid off; playing Adam there was a stroke of genius and I wondered why he hadn't been playing there his whole career. He was world class in that position. Everything Jürgen wanted from him there, Adam gave him: the energy, the counter-press, the aggression, the ability on the ball to create things, his touch, his positioning. He was a revelation.

So Gini and Adam had those positions nailed down and I thought that Emre Can was a more natural 6 than me and I knew he had a good relationship with the manager. I was questioning myself. Am I a squad player now? The doubts came back. Jürgen told me he was going to try me as a 6 because it played to a lot of my strengths. He must have liked what he saw in pre-season and training because he persevered with me. My energy levels were good. The difficult part for me was the discipline. When I should have been sitting and patrolling, suddenly you would see me sprinting in behind the defence or counter-pressing high up the pitch and leaving space where I should be.

To begin with, it felt like I was playing with handcuffs on. I couldn't do what was natural and I was fighting that urge all the time. There were some games where I was miles off it and where I looked exactly what I was: a novice, learning a new position. There was noise from the outside, questions about why he was playing me at 6 and how I couldn't do the job there.

I thought he would take me out of the team after the game at Turf Moor, but he stuck with me. He coached me on the position and told me what he wanted. There were elements of it that I was good at. When we lost the ball, I could react and win it back quickly. I thought I could influence the game more elsewhere, but the gaffer wanted me to do a new job, and what he wants is what I've got to do because that's the best for the team.

The fact that he stuck with me gave me confidence. He could see something in me that I couldn't necessarily see. I gradually began to be more comfortable, and there was a big moment early on, when I scored in a 2–1 win at Stamford Bridge on a Friday night. I don't mind saying it's one of my favourites, a right-foot curler that flew past Thibaut Courtois into the top corner, and it set us on the way to that win. I had a bit of confidence now and I also had a new understanding of what Jürgen wanted. He improved my game a lot and I started to see the game differently. When you're a 6, you can see everything in front of you. He made me a high-performance player in two different positions. I genuinely owe him so much. I didn't think I had the attributes or the qualities to do what he wanted, but I grew and grew in that position and by midway through the season I was anchoring a team that was solidly in the top four and heading for a finishing position that meant we would achieve the prime objective: qualification for the Champions League.

Unfortunately, I missed a big chunk of the second half of the season with another metatarsal injury. I didn't break it this time, but I kicked the bottom of someone's boot in training, just after we had beaten Tottenham 2–0 at Anfield in February 2017, and their studs impacted on my metatarsal. It caused a build-up of fluid and bruising of the bone, which was getting worse every time I played, and that forced me on to the sidelines. It was horrible sitting through the run-in, but an element of comfort was provided by being back in the top four and the opportunities that would present us with.

The team was evolving fast. We signed Mo from Roma that summer – it was a statement of intent because he was a club record buy – and Andy Robertson from Hull City, while Alex Oxlade-Chamberlain arrived just before the window closed. I was delighted we had got Ox, someone I'd played with at different levels for England, and I had been on at the scouting department, telling them he'd be perfect for us. It was the first time the famous front three of Mo, Bobby and Sadio would play together. People talk about MSN (Messi, Suárez and Neymar) and BBC (Benzema, Bale and Cristiano Ronaldo) at Real Madrid, but I wouldn't have swapped our front three for either of those trios.

I started 2017–18 in the same position, and there were still times that I struggled. I suppose you could say our defence was in a period of transition, and there were certainly moments when I felt I didn't protect them well enough. One of those occasions, when we played Sevilla away in the group stages of the Champions League in November, caused me a real crisis of confidence about playing a 6. It was a crazy match from start to finish in the Estadio Ramón Sánchez-Pizjuán. Bobby put us 1–0 up after eighty-five seconds, which was the fastest Liverpool goal ever in the Champions League, and by half-time we were three up and cruising towards qualifying for the last sixteen of the competition with a game to spare. This was what it was all about.

We were playing well and the atmosphere was brilliant, but we came out in the second half and everything changed. We got sucked into wave after wave of their attacks; they created chance after chance and I didn't know how to stop it. It ended up with Guido Pizarro grabbing an equalizer for them – getting to a loose ball just before me – in the ninety-third minute, which earned them a dramatic draw and meant we would be sweating on qualifying for the last sixteen until the final group game against Spartak Moscow.

This was one of the most difficult situations I had faced during my time at Liverpool. I knew that blowing a comfortable lead like that should never be happening when I was playing as a 6. I felt like I was lost in that second half; I didn't know where I needed to be. I spoke to the press after the game – when you're captain, you have to front up in those situations – but I didn't really know what I could say in the circumstances to make it better. I took that really, really hard. I didn't sleep at all after that game. After wrestling and wrestling with it in the early hours after we flew back from Spain, I decided to go into training the next day and tell Jürgen of the doubts I had about myself playing as a 6 and that I felt I was letting the team down – as a player but also as their captain.

I needed to talk to someone, but I'm not good at asking for help, as I mentioned earlier, so I went around the houses. I texted Adam and told him I would give him a lift into training. I picked him up from his house, but I knew that if he started asking questions I'd get upset. In my mind, I'd decided I was going to drive in to speak to Jürgen. I was even questioning whether I should be captain. When I'm in that frame of mind, I'll run over every possible situation to see what I can do to help the team – it's always about the team – and I couldn't accept what was happening. Adam could sense there was something wrong. He just said, 'Everything OK?' and that was enough to set me off.

There were a lot of games – not just that against Sevilla – where we surrendered leads and I was thinking that, as captain, I should see us over the line. And it wasn't happening. My view was that whoever leads Liverpool has to stand up in big moments in games. I was taking a lot of responsibility on my shoulders and the manager sensed it was weighing me down. I have learned to grow into the captaincy role because of Jürgen. He felt it. He knew people would always refer to Stevie and compare me to him. He told me I wasn't Steven Gerrard and that I should be happy being who I was. He said I was taking on too much responsibility and that I needed to concentrate more on my own game.

I tried to shrug it off with Adam, but my mind was running in all kinds of different directions. Adam was brilliant. I'd go to him with anything and have absolute trust in him. We'd got friendly when we were coming back from an away game in Europe and we were sitting next to each other on the plane, talking about family and injury and how we'd got to where we were. From then on, Adam was the person I relied on in the team. So eventually, as we made our way down the M6, I told him that I was thinking about going to see Jürgen, and why. He told me not to do it. He said I was taking too much responsibility for something that was not my fault. He knew I was struggling, but he said, 'Please, do me one favour, if you feel like this tomorrow, fine. But today, leave it.'

So I took his advice. I went in, did my recovery, didn't say anything and went home. Adam and I talked again on the drive back and I gradually started to feel a bit better.

Then we played the league leaders, Chelsea, the following weekend and drew 1–1, and I played okay. I'd gone from rock bottom to playing steady. I got my confidence back. That was the first step back in the right direction.

We had strengthened the side with the signings of Mo and Robbo and then, in January, we made what many observers consider to be the most important signing of all in the development of this Liverpool team when we paid Southampton £75 million for Virgil van Dijk. We had been trying to sign Virgil for some time. We'd missed out on him in the summer, but I was a massive fan of his and I'd always hoped we would go back for him in the January window. In fact, when we won the league in 2020, Virgil showed me a text I'd written to him around the time he'd signed, doing everything I possibly could to get him to come to Liverpool. I wrote in that message:

I believe we can achieve something special in the next few seasons. We have one of the best managers in the world and we have great players already in the squad. But the main thing for me is the togetherness of the team and how much we have improved under the manager. I think you would have a huge impact on this team and help us to become very successful.

That's both as a player and a person. I know you would fit in really well with the lads and enjoy it here. Obviously, Liverpool is one of the biggest and best clubs in the world, but the manager and his staff are also the best I have ever worked with and I believe they are capable of taking the team to the next level. I know you

and my dad soaking up the sun on holiday . . .

he has always been there for me.

Aged twenty-three months, w. my mam, on the day Sunderla played Liverpool in the 1992 F Cup Final. Who would have known then how much those clubs would come to mean to me?

As a little boy, I was a Sunderland fanatic and my dad (*left*) organized this day out for me and my late uncle, Chris (*right*), and cousin, Scott, to meet club legend Niall Quinn (*centre*). After this picture was taken, I played head tennis in the gym with Niall and his strike partner Kevin Phillips.

action at a tournament for Fulwell Juniors, aged eight.

. we had a brilliant team and
on so many trophies in 1999.

Roy Keane was one of my childhood heroes. It was one of my proudest days ever when I signed professional terms with Sunderland.

Keeping my eye on the ball in an FA Youth Cup tie against Manchester City in March 2008.

This was a day I will never
forget – making my
Liverpool debut at Anfield
against my first club,
Sunderland, in August 2011.
It was a 1–1 draw, and this is
me battling for possession
with Stéphane Sessègnon.

One of the best afternoons
in the year I call my
breakthrough at Liverpool.
This was me celebrating our
second goal in a 5–0 win at
Tottenham in December
2013. I had spent a lot of
time working on my game
with Brendan Rodgers, and
he helped me improve
massively.

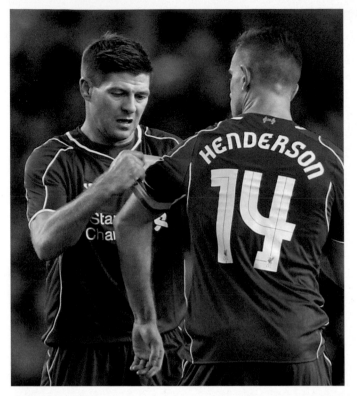

What can I say about Steven Gerrard? He was a role model when I was a kid, a mentor when I joined Liverpool and an inspiration. It was one of the biggest honours of my career to follow him as captain at our great club.

Standing my ground with Diego Costa in a League Cup semi-final in January 2015. I've never had a problem with him since then!

ery kid dreams they will captain
gland one day and this was the
ht I first received the honour, in
World Cup qualifier against Slovenia
Ljubljana in October 2016. Gareth
uthgate had told me the armband
s coming my way when we walked
oss the runway at Luton airport to
ard our flight.

elt like time stood still when Colombia goalkeeper David Ospina saved my penalty in the shoot-out of
gland's last sixteen tie at the 2018 World Cup in Russia. Thankfully it wasn't costly and we got through
route to the semi-finals.

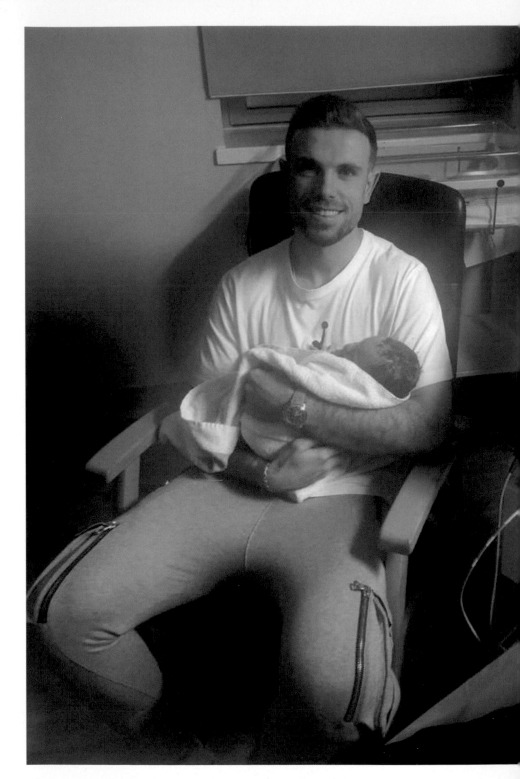

Family means everything to me and this was the night in February 2020 that we welcomed our third ch[ild], Myles. His elder sisters, Elexa and Alba, dote on him and I call him 'my little shadow' because whereve[r] I go, he's always there.

must have had plenty of offers from different clubs
from all over the world but Liverpool is a very special
and unique club. I have been here for more than six
years and I feel like now is the best time to be at Liverpool.
I'm sorry this is a very long message but I want to give
you as much detail as possible.

I was out with a hamstring injury when the deal was
completed and the first time I saw Virg was at Anfield.
He'd arrived in his own clothes, rather than club kit, and
he just looked a million dollars. He was massive, even his
hair was perfect and I thought to myself, 'He's got to be
good.' He just looked the part. It was a big, big signing. If
you want to call it a game-changer, you could. He and
Alisson Becker, who came the following summer, gave us
something we'd been missing. Virg brings everything that
a team needs from a centre half. Leadership, for a start.
He's the best defender in the world, and that brings so
much confidence to the team, from the centre half who is
next to him to the full back who is next to him to the
midfielder in front of him.

He brought a totally different dynamic to the team. He
just had that confidence where he knew that anything that
went in behind him, he would be there. He's quick, so we
know we can play a high line and defend confidently
against pace. We can afford to go one on one if we need
to. He's massive, so he wins everything in the air. He's great
in the dressing room, a great lad, and so positive. He just
ticked every box. I remember playing against him when he
was at Southampton and thinking, 'Yeah, he's good,' but I

didn't realize how good until he came and started training here. He's a one-off. That's the best way to say it.

I'd been told by other people what he was like as a person. The professional culture is very important at Liverpool as well and I knew Virgil would fit like a glove. Liverpool are very good at signing not just the player but the person behind the player. I felt he was exactly what we needed. That is no disrespect to the centre halves we had at the time, but I knew one of them at least wanted to move on. Virgil could play with the ball on the deck and he was so difficult to beat. Players like Suárez, Virgil, Stevie and Mo, you line up next to them in the tunnel and look at them and think, 'We're going to be all right.' We had lost Philippe Coutinho, who was one of the best players in the world at that moment, to Barcelona, but we got a good fee for him and we used the money on Virgil and Alisson.

Virgil made his debut for Liverpool on 5 January in the FA Cup third round and he scored the winning goal with a late header in a 2–1 victory against Everton, becoming the first player since Bill White in 1901 to score on his debut in the Merseyside derby. It was the perfect start. We loved him, the fans loved him and the biggest thing about it all was the fact he had arrived for a world-record fee for a defender but nobody was talking about his price tag. We had a training camp in Dubai soon after the Everton game and that helped him settle in straight away. After that, it was as if he had been at Liverpool his whole career. In a team full of leaders, we had just got one of the best leaders in the game.

The Sevilla game was a low point for me, but things got better after that. Around that time, we were trying to outscore teams, but we were conceding plenty of goals ourselves. We were never really in the hunt for the title that season, but we beat Brighton on the final day to ensure that we finished in fourth place in the Premier League and qualified for the Champions League again the following year. By then, though, our season had come to be dominated by our run to the Champions League final. I'd had a conversation with a friend before Christmas, and we were both of the same mind that a trip to Kyiv in May might not be out of the question – and things took off after we had beaten Porto quite comfortably in the last sixteen.

It set up a clash with Manchester City in the quarter-finals, one that nobody gave us much hope of winning. City would get a hundred points in the Premier League that season and the majority of pundits expected them to deal with us, but we ran all over them in the first half of the first leg, winning 3–0. We had to survive a storm in the return in Manchester but, again, we got through it. Mo equalized just after half-time to make it 1–1, before Bobby clinched the victory. I was suspended that night and had to sit through the torture from the directors' box, but the lads did brilliantly. We were flying now – we couldn't wait for what was to come.

Roma in the semi-final was surreal. We demolished them in the first leg at Anfield and we were 5–0 up after sixty-nine minutes, but we gave them a glimmer of hope by conceding two late goals. We repeated the trick in the second leg. We were level at 2–2 on the night with four minutes to go but conceded two more goals to make it 4–2 to them. It was closer than it should have been, but we were through. It was a dream for me to be in a Champions League final, where Real Madrid would be waiting, but the two matches against Roma were overshadowed for us by serious injuries suffered by one of our fans, Sean Cox, who was attacked by Roma fans before the first leg at Anfield. He was knocked unconscious and suffered brain injuries, which he is still fighting to recover from.

Everyone at the club was shocked and appalled by what had happened, and when we were playing the second leg in the Stadio Olimpico, I noticed that a group of Liverpool fans in the away section had brought a banner that read, 'Sean Cox: You'll Never Walk Alone'. After the final whistle, I took the lads over to it and we took that banner out on to the pitch with us and gathered around it to celebrate with the supporters. Jürgen dedicated the victory to Sean. 'It's hundred per cent a final for Sean Cox,' he told the media.

I read something on the *Anfield Wrap* website later that summer that referenced what the players had done that night. 'The scenes after the semi-final second leg in Rome were unlike anything I've seen in my Liverpool-supporting life,' Josh Sexton wrote. 'It showed a team who are so in tune with what we want as supporters. It isn't forced, it's not a "say something like this . . ." tweet forced upon the players by some PR company. It's a group of lads who that sort of thing comes naturally to. It's a manager who only knows how to be that way. It's not an accident.'

I was glad it had come across like that. It wasn't planned.

It wasn't complicated. It was just the right thing to do, to honour a fan who had given a lot for us and needed our support.

It's strange now to think of the final being played in Kyiv. As always, we didn't see much of the host city when we were there, just the hotel and the stadium and the road in from the airport. But I saw enough of its handsome streets and domed churches to know that it's a beautiful city. I saw enough to feel shocked at seeing pictures on the news of barricades in its streets and tales of barbarism on its outskirts during the Russian invasion.

We had a thirteen-day break between the end of the domestic season and the Champions League final, and preparations, as you would expect, were intense. All my energies were being channelled into that game.

On the Tuesday before we travelled to Kyiv, we were training at Anfield when I received a phone call from Gareth Southgate, England's head coach, who had news for me. Gareth was going into camp ahead of the 2018 World Cup in Russia and he had made a decision on who would be captain.

Gareth had rung to tell me that Harry Kane was his choice for the role. I respected the decision, and it was never going to change the way I was around the squad. I was part of Gareth's leadership group and I made it clear I would support Harry as best I could.

But this wasn't something I could dwell on. My full focus was on Real Madrid, and I needed to move on quickly. The biggest game of my life was coming, and I didn't want distractions.

I couldn't sleep the night before the final. This was something I had dreamed of my whole career, my whole life. I was aware of what it meant to Liverpool too. I was acutely aware of the club's history in this competition, and even if I'd only seen the feats of the Liverpool teams of the seventies and eighties on YouTube clips, the details of the Miracle of Istanbul in 2005 were vivid in my memory and had immortalized people I now considered friends, like Carra and Stevie.

The magnitude of what was ahead of me kept me awake, eyes wide open as I lay in bed. There were too many things going round in my head. It got to midnight, then 1 a.m. I was thinking about the game, the history, the texts that were coming in, my dad saying he didn't want to text on the day of the game so he was texting now and how proud he was of me. I was thinking about how I didn't want to let anybody down. I slept a little bit in the early hours, but I was still wired the next day. I wasn't tired. I was ready. The adrenaline was flowing through me all day. I always had a quiet confidence about that game, partly because no one had expected us to get there in the first place and no one gave us a chance. The talk before the game was about how every Madrid player in the starting line-up had played in a Champions League final before. None of our players had.

Madrid were the Galácticos: Ramos, Kroos, Modrić, Benzema, Ronaldo. Bale couldn't even get into the starting line-up. I had the utmost respect for them, but I thought to myself, 'I'm not sure they know what's coming here.' I knew their side was full of experienced, world-class players who had seen it all, but I still wondered if they might be taken aback by our intensity. We started well and things were even for the first half-hour, but then something happened that changed the mood of the game. Mo and Sergio Ramos were competing for a ball midway inside the Real half and Ramos grabbed hold of Mo's right arm and dragged him down. It was a bit like a judo move and Mo crashed to the ground and landed heavily on his right shoulder. It was obvious straight away he was in trouble. He got treatment, but he couldn't continue and he left the pitch in tears. Adam Lallana, who had barely played since he had been injured at Crystal Palace at the end of March, came on to replace him.

Only Ramos knows if he meant to do that to Mo. I suppose you could call it the challenge of an experienced professional. It was the kind of challenge you're going to get away with in terms of the referee because it's not obvious what you're doing. In that moment, even I wasn't sure what had happened, as it looked innocuous. With the benefit of replays, it is easier to go with a rather different interpretation of the defender's attentions.

It was a bitter blow for us. Mo had become our talisman that season. There were times when he was unstoppable. In fact, he was unstoppable most of the season. He scored thirty-two goals in thirty-six Premier League games and ten more in the Champions League. He scored forty-four altogether and won the PFA Player of the Year Award. Losing him before half-time hit us hard and we didn't deal with it particularly well, but we still went in at half-time level.

We just weren't as good in the second half. Mo's injury had affected the supporters too and then, five minutes after the interval, we went behind to a freak goal. Loris gathered a ball on the edge of his area and there was no danger. I saw Virgil turn towards me to shout an instruction of some sort and then I saw Loris roll the ball out towards Dejan.

Except, as soon as the ball left his hands, Benzema stuck his right leg out and blocked the throw. The ball trickled about ten yards towards the goal and rolled just inside the post. I only half saw it. I turned in time to see it going over the line and I instinctively raised my hand above my head to appeal to the referee for a foul. But there was no foul. Madrid were a goal up.

It emerged in the following days that Loris was probably suffering from concussion after an earlier clash with Ramos. Jürgen said that tests conducted after the match had indicated he had suffered a head injury and that it was possible that the concussion had contributed to his performance that evening. We didn't know that then, of course. To go behind in that way was like a punch in the stomach none of us expected and it was a gift for Madrid. They hadn't even had to work for it. But five minutes later, we were level. Millie swung a corner deep into the box, hanging it up high, and Dejan won it and nodded it across the goal. Sadio reacted quickest and prodded it in from close range. I can still hear the noise now and remember the thought that, just maybe, we were going to do it.

But then Bale came on for Isco just after the hour, and three minutes later the game changed spectacularly.

Marcelo got the ball on the left and cut inside on to his right foot. He crossed it into the box and it flew over my head. I turned in time to see Bale in mid-air, connecting with the ball with an amazing bicycle kick with his left foot. Loris had no chance. The greatest Champions League final goal of all time? It's got to be up there. Zinedine Zidane's volley for Madrid against Bayer Leverkusen at Hampden Park in 2002 would probably top most polls, but this ran it close. Zidane, of course, was standing on the sideline that night in Kyiv as Real's manager. We tried to get going again but, seven minutes from the end, Bale tried a shot from long range. Loris tried to catch it and it slipped through his hands and bounced into the net. That was it. Game over. And that's Madrid. They didn't play particularly well, but with the quality they've got, they can hurt you at any moment. It was the third year in succession they had lifted the trophy.

We all consoled each other at the end. I went over to Loris and had a few words with him. A lot of the other lads did the same. It's a cliché, but we win together and we lose together. There were some observations after the match that he had been left to walk alone when we were trudging around the pitch to thank the fans, but that was a misinterpretation of what was happening. Loris had gone over to the fans himself and held up his hands to gesture that he was sorry for the way things had turned out. We were all alone with our thoughts a bit in the minutes after the medal presentation. There was no question of his being abandoned or anything like that. I think he wanted a bit of time by himself. We all did.

It had been my dream to play in a Champions League final, but to be so close to lifting it and getting over the line and falling at the last hurdle was hard to take. When I walked over to the touchline after the final whistle and the trophy was still sitting there on its plinth, I couldn't bear to look at it. Even now, I can remember the Madrid players lifting it and celebrating as if this was just another trophy, an everyday occurrence. We had to deal with a lot of different setbacks that evening. It just wasn't our night – maybe, in the grand scheme of things, it was an ordeal we had to go through to accelerate our development, even if we had to contend with criticism that we didn't know how to win the biggest matches. This, after all, was our third defeat in a final under Jürgen.

I went back into the changing room, and Mo had got back from the hospital. He was distraught. He had had a dream season, but it had ended like this. It wasn't just losing the final that was making him so distraught. Egypt had qualified for the World Cup later that summer and he knew that he would be struggling to be fit in time. You know deep down you can't say anything to make it better. You do your best to console team-mates in situations like that, but sometimes the best thing is just to leave people to their thoughts.

I left Loris alone for a bit on the night, but on the plane home in the early hours, I went over and sat next to him. How was he? He wasn't great, obviously. What made it worse was I knew what was coming in terms of the media coverage, and especially the reaction on social media. I told him to go away, have a break, stay off social media and ignore the idiots who wanted to abuse him. These things happen, and we had lost as a team. It wasn't his fault. We don't make scapegoats here. We never have done and we never will.

But the truth is, football can be cruel and it can be ruthless. It can hinge on moments in big games. That's why there is so much pressure on players to perform when you get to the highest level. Goalkeepers are particularly exposed. And even if that defeat was not Loris's fault, even if one defeat didn't change the fact that he was an exceptional goalkeeper, the reality is that he never played for Liverpool again. We signed Alisson later that summer and Loris went out on loan to Beşiktaş.

I tried to put things in perspective on the flight back to England. I knew we were still building, and I kept that in my mind when we arrived back at Melwood to see our families – many of whom were still in tears. I knew there was another transfer window coming and that we would add to the team. Alisson was on his way. Fabinho would be bought from Monaco, Naby Keïta was going to finally arrive from RB Leipzig after a deal that had been done twelve months earlier. There was a feeling that the final pieces were being slotted into the jigsaw.

The reason I tried to find some positivity came from a conversation that had happened just before I left the stadium in Kyiv. I walked over to the bus, and the manager was there, having a smoke. He gave me a hug.

'Don't worry,' he said. 'We'll be back next year.' And because it was Jürgen, I believed him.

8. England, What a Feeling

The Royal Garden Hotel in Kensington will forever be linked to England's football team, as that's where the heroes of 1966 stayed after they won the World Cup. Personally, I'll always link it to the England team because that's where I was staying when I received my first senior call.

It was Saturday night, 13 November 2010. I was in my room, waiting to go down for something to eat, when my phone started buzzing with a message from Michelle Farrar, the FA's Director of Team Operations, to tell me I had been included in the squad to play France. The World Cup had been disappointing, and I was told Fabio Capello wanted to assess some young players as he began the build-up to Euro 2012.

Talk about a change in fortunes. Two weeks earlier, I had played in the Tyne and Wear Derby and Sunderland had lost 5–1. I'd barely left my house in that fortnight, and I'm not saying that for effect. Losing 5–1 at St James's Park? I'd never known frustration like it. I was so embarrassed I was literally going from home to the training ground and back again. I felt I just couldn't show my face. Now I was being told I had to report to the Grove Hotel on a certain day to meet Capello and his staff.

Initially, part of me thought it was all a wind-up and I was in disbelief when I put the phone down. Before I told anyone, I went down to double-check with people from the club. I needn't have worried. Steve Bruce was waiting downstairs for me with a big smile on his face and some words that I will never forget.

'I never got an England cap, son, and I so wish I had; you've got the chance at twenty years of age to achieve something magnificent, because it's the pinnacle to represent your country,' he said. 'We're all absolutely over the moon for you.'

Steve was right. Playing for England *is* the pinnacle, something I'd dreamed of doing since watching Michael Owen at the 1998 World Cup in France. What an unbelievable feeling. To top it all off, Sunderland beat Chelsea 3–0 at Stamford Bridge the following day and I headed back to the north-east hardly able to take it all in. Every little boy and girl who kicks a football one day thinks they will run out at Wembley for England, and here, after one Under-19 cap and a handful of Under-21 appearances for Stuart Pearce, I had an opportunity.

I wanted to tell that story in so much detail so you could understand how much it means to me to have been an international footballer and the challenges I had to overcome to establish myself. When you get the chance to represent England, you never want to let it go, and the experiences I had – going back to that night against France – will stay with me for a lifetime.

Andy Carroll and I both made our debuts that evening in an international friendly at Wembley against France, a side that had also disappointed at the World Cup, on Wednesday, 17 November 2010. Ben Foster played in goal;

Phil Jagielka, Rio Ferdinand, Joleon Lescott and Kieran Gibbs were the back four. Midfield was Theo Walcott on the right, me, Steven Gerrard and Gareth Barry in the middle, and James Milner on the left, with Andy up front.

France, to be fair, were the better side. They had Karim Benzema, Samir Nasri and Florent Malouda, and they won 2–1. I got booked for a foul on Yoann Gourcuff, but I enjoyed the game, even if it left me under no illusion that I had so much to learn. I dropped back down to the Under-21s for the next eighteen months before another message from Michelle, out of the blue, provided another unbelievable moment, this time with Roy Hodgson as the manager.

I had played bit-parts in the warm-up games for Euro 2012 against Norway in Oslo and then against Belgium at Wembley. There were a few boos when I came on for Stevie against Belgium, which hurt a little bit. I was only twenty-one. I hadn't had a great season at Liverpool, but I hadn't had time to do anything wrong for England. It's an odd way to treat a young player. I didn't make the squad for the Euros, but I was put in the group of players on standby in case anyone got injured.

I had plans to go on holiday to Cancún in Mexico with my best mate Ryan and some of my old Sunderland team-mates, including David Meyler and Fraizer Campbell. Ryan has always been by my side, and Meyler and Fraiz are diamonds who really helped me feel comfortable in the first environment when I was coming through the ranks, and always looked out for me. We would go out for food and go around to each other's houses most days. We became really close friends, and I'm still close to them to this day.

I was on the train down from Sunderland to London to head over to Heathrow and I was somewhere near York when my phone rang. Michelle told me that Frank Lampard had got a thigh injury in the first training session and I was going to be his replacement.

So I got to London and then jumped in a car up to the Grove. Any regrets about missing two weeks in Cancún? Not a chance! There was, though, some debate about my selection, and it became a talking point in the media. I was aware of things that were being said.

Even though he was in Mexico by then, Meyler felt the need to speak out on my behalf, so he did an interview with talkSPORT. He told fans to get off my back then said I'd prove myself at Liverpool and that I wouldn't let England down in Poland and Ukraine. Meyler finished by saying, 'He'll captain England one day.' Nobody was taking him seriously.

Stevie came to my defence as well. 'I was twenty-one, too, and was nowhere near the finished article when I got into the England team,' he said. 'I can guarantee you that, if the public are criticizing Jordan, they will change their opinion of him very soon. He will prove them wrong. He is good enough to do it and will thrive on what is coming up.'

The negativity in the media was a small lesson in what it had been like in the past for players joining up with England. There are times, I know, when players dreaded joining up with the national team and braced themselves for the media and public criticism they knew was coming their way. I'm not sure why I had to fight that constant battle to prove myself. Perhaps everyone has to; perhaps it's just that you're more aware of it when you are at the centre of it. But nothing was going to stop me. Nothing whatsoever. The same way I was never going to leave Liverpool at the first possible opportunity, there was no way I was going to allow negative opinions stop me from living this dream.

I joined up with the squad knowing I was still trying to improve and learn from different players and managers. I knew I was a long way from where I wanted to be, but I understood that people are impatient. Football fans can be insular and tribal, even when they're following the national team, and I knew I was in their sights. But I was buzzing to go to the Euros. There's not much more you can ask for and, even though I only had a cameo role, I got a taste of the atmosphere.

Most importantly, I played in a tournament. I came on for Scott Parker for the last ten minutes of the group game with France, a 1–1 draw in Donetsk. Then Roy brought me on, for Scott again, in injury time of the goalless draw with Italy in the quarter-finals in Kyiv. What a test that was, coming on against Andrea Pirlo, the guy I had seen at Old Trafford nine years earlier, and Daniele De Rossi.

I had been watching Pirlo while I was on the bench, thinking, 'He's not bad, is he?' The game went to penalties, and the one he scored – a Panenka – was a joke. Italy, unfortunately for us, won the shoot-out 4–2. I was anxious that it might come to me to take one, but if it did I was determined to put the experience to good use, in the hope I would be able to call upon it at a future tournament . . .

To say that I have played in every tournament since for the senior team, in two World Cups and another two European Championships, is a source of unbelievable pride. It's been a roller-coaster, one that has brought every possible emotion – and Brazil in 2014 was a prime example of that. I felt like I had gone there as an established player, not someone whose inclusion in the squad invited criticism. I'd had my best season in the Premier League and I loved the idea of playing a World Cup in Brazil.

Everyone has a soft spot for Brazil, don't they? My dad's generation would talk about the team of Pelé and Jairzinho that won the 1970 World Cup in Mexico; I know other people love the 1982 team, with Zico and Socrates. My favourites were the team of 1998 that reached the final with Ronaldo. I had the kit, and I loved the Nike advert from that World Cup which had the Brazil players running through an airport, with Ronaldo doing tricks on the baggage carousels and Roberto Carlos swerving a shot around a plane. I was transfixed by it all.

So I loved being in Brazil. We stayed in Rio de Janeiro, too, in a hotel near the beach in the suburb of São Conrado, and we trained at a ground in the shadow of the Sugar Loaf Mountain. One day after training, a few of us asked the FA security guy, Tony Conniford, if we could go out and get a coffee. There was me, Studge, Welbz and Chris Smalling. We weren't exactly the high-profile guys, like Wayne Rooney or Stevie. Nobody was going to have a clue who we were, surely? But Tony wasn't happy about the idea.

We pestered him until he gave in and got a car to come round to the back of the hotel, pick us up and drive us the couple of hundred yards to the coffee shop we wanted to go to. It all felt a bit excessive, but I was being naïve. We had our coffee, chilled out for a bit and then we decided we'd have a little stroll on the beach on our way back to the hotel. Everything was relaxed. We took off our shirts and soaked up the sun. All sounds good? Not really. A few people spotted us. Next thing, there are kids asking for photos and suddenly we're surrounded by hundreds of people. Everybody's running, there are paparazzi and camera crews, and Tony's having kittens. Eventually, we get back into the hotel, but it's lively. We laughed about it but, from the rollicking Tony gave us, I don't think he saw the funny side!

Our first game was against Italy, up in Manaus, in the north-west in Amazonas. Everybody said that we were going to melt in the heat, but I liked the fact that it took us out of our comfort zone. It was a World Cup – things should be different. And we played well. At Liverpool, I was playing as more of a box-to-box midfielder, but with England I had a slightly different role, sitting in front of the back four in a two with Stevie. I had a decent shot early on that was pushed away by Salvatore Sirigu, but then Italy scored with a clever corner routine that ended up with Claudio Marchisio lashing a shot past Joe Hart ten minutes before half-time. We equalized two minutes later with a really good goal from Studge, after a great cross by Wayne, but Mario Balotelli won it for them with a header early in the second half. It wasn't a bad performance and Italy are a decent side, but we were under pressure, with games left against Uruguay and Costa Rica. Saying that, we thought we'd get something out of them.

So we went to São Paulo to play Uruguay, still confident we'd progress to the knockout stages. There was a doubt about whether Luis Suárez would play because he had an injury that lots of people expected would keep him out of the tournament altogether. What did I think? I've never been more certain that someone was going to play in a match in all my life. Luis miss playing against England? You must be joking. There were times it felt like I had a team-mate at Liverpool who was superhuman, because the pain he could play through was mind-blowing. Any normal player would have been on the sidelines after having keyhole surgery on their right knee, but Luis wasn't your normal player. Before one match against Norwich at Anfield in December 2013, his foot and his ankle were so swollen he couldn't get his right boot on. The medical department told him he couldn't play. He didn't listen and borrowed a pair of Stevie's boots, which were a size bigger than his. I didn't think there was any chance he'd be able to function, as his ankle looked bent out of shape. He started the match. And he scored – four times in a 5–1 win. He almost had a Goal of the Month competition on his own! I couldn't believe what I was seeing. To produce a performance like that in the pain that he was in and wearing someone else's boots – I couldn't really comprehend it.

So all that was lurking at the back of my mind. Stevie and I told the rest of the squad that Luis would play. Even if his knee was hanging off, he'd be playing. And he played.

He started. He scored. He scored twice, one after peeling away from his marker to bury a header, the other an unstoppable shot lashed past Joe Hart with his supposed bad leg. Wayne's equalizer turned out to be nothing other than a consolation. We were going home after two matches; the final game against Costa Rica was just for the statistics. I was devastated. We had a good side that year and I think we could have challenged at the World Cup. Instead, the adventure of a lifetime was done and dusted within five days.

Euro 2016 in France? The least said about that the better, really. I squeezed into the squad at the last minute, having proved my fitness after recovering from the lateral collateral ligament injury, and I was on the bench for the first couple of group games against Russia and Wales but played in the dead rubber against Slovakia in Saint-Étienne. Then it was Iceland in Nice. Iceland were the smallest nation ever to qualify for the Euros when they made it to the finals, and we were widely expected to win. We didn't win. It turned into a dark moment in our football history.

I was on the bench. I walked out into the stadium and saw the houses on the hillsides of the Côte d'Azur rising behind the stands. I saw the Iceland fans with their arms in the air and heard the Viking Clap for the first time. It was a horrible, horrible day for us. Wayne opened the scoring in the fourth minute with a penalty, but they were 2–1 up after eighteen minutes and we never looked like equalizing. We lost. It was called the most humiliating result in England's football history since our defeat by the

USA in the finals of the 1950 World Cup. People said we had let the country down – and they were right.

During a career in football, some games and memories can merge into one another, but everything about that night remains clear in my mind. I didn't play a minute, but I'll never forget the anger and the way fans were screaming at us as we walked off. That was bad, but worse was to come in the dressing room, when Roy resigned. Roy is a good man, and to see him so upset, telling us all that he knew his time was over, was awful. You could hear a pin drop when he spoke. We had let our country down, and we had let him down. I never wanted to feel that way again.

After Sam Allardyce's short reign, Gareth Southgate came in. Everybody knows he's a top guy, and I saw that straight away. It hadn't necessarily been Gareth's burning ambition to manage the senior team and he had enjoyed three good years with the Under-21s, but he stepped forward at a time when his country needed him. He made massive strides with the team immediately. He wants to empower the players. He sits down with everyone individually, gets into the little details of how we feel when we play for England – what's good, what's bad, what could be better.

One of the first conversations we had is another one of those moments that will stay with me for ever. We were going out to Slovenia, for a World Cup qualifier. It was his second game in charge as caretaker, and we were on the runway at Luton airport, ready to fly out to Ljubljana.

'You're going to be captain tomorrow night,' he said.

What a feeling. Gareth wanted to give us more responsibility and independence, and his ambition was that us being given this responsibility would turn into positive results. One of the things he worked on was finding a way to reconnect the players and the public. There was a sense that the players had become separated from the public, and the way we had lost to Iceland had only led to a deepening of the divide. Gareth had felt the tension in the atmosphere at England games and he wanted to fix it.

It seems like a vague notion, but at its heart it is performance related. Gareth knew that if he got back to a situation where the fans, the media, the staff and the players were all pulling in the same direction, if there was a more positive, less adversarial atmosphere, then it would free up the players to play. I had seen it myself, particularly at Euro 2016. The relationship between the players and the media was very uneasy. There was definitely a divide and everything was very guarded. We were trying to keep the media at arm's length, and they knew it. It was them and us. It wasn't exactly a new thing and, in the past, say at the 1990 World Cup, England teams have used a hostile relationship with the media as a motivation to succeed.

But these are different times, so Gareth tried to reconnect with the public and the media so they were more with us than against us. One of the cornerstones of that plan was a Media Day at St George's Park a couple of weeks before the 2018 World Cup in Russia. Gareth had made a couple of visits to the Super Bowl and had witnessed the Media Day there, when every single player from each of the two rival teams is made available to the media for an hour at the stadium a few days before the game. He asked us before we left for Russia if we would cooperate with something similar, and the players said yes. I thought it was a clever idea. For the journalists, it was a breath of fresh air, and most of the players enjoyed it. We're used to interviews with the media being closely monitored and supervised by press officers at our clubs, but this was more of a free-for-all. There was little or no supervision; it was an exercise in establishing trust, and it worked.

We had some good conversations with journalists. When you're closed off from the media, they have a perception of the players from the outside; they don't really know us as people. They are judging us by how we are on the pitch. It's human nature that, when you talk to people, you tend to warm towards them and build relationships. It's harder for a journalist to slag a player off when they have got to know them a bit, and if the players believe there's a reduced chance they are going to be slaughtered in the media for a misplaced pass or a bad result, then it's going to loosen them up a little. Maybe it doesn't make that big a difference. Maybe it's only going to improve performance by one or two per cent. But even if it's one or two per cent, it's worth it.

Winning a World Cup is all about marginal gains. We were based just outside St Petersburg, at a resort in the village of Repino on the Gulf of Finland, a place where residents of the city come for summer day trips or to stay in their holiday homes. But our first match was against

Tunisia in Volgograd, over a thousand miles to the south-east. I played as a pivot in the 3–1–4–2 formation that Gareth favoured for the tournament, behind a midfield four of Kieran Trippier, Jesse Lingard, Dele Alli and Ashley Young. The selection has been criticized for being too conservative but, unfortunately for the critics, it seemed to get us results.

Not that it was easy against Tunisia – it was anything but. Harry Kane put us ahead early in the first half when he rammed in a rebound after the goalkeeper had pushed out a bullet header from John Stones, but they equalized with a penalty ten minutes before half-time. The holding on Harry at corners was more like a WWE contest than a football match, but the referee waved away all our appeals for penalties. VAR ignored it, too. We had no idea why.

We wasted several gilt-edged chances and it looked like the game was going to end in stalemate, but then, in stoppage time at the end of the match, Harry Maguire flicked on a corner and Harry Kane, unmarked at the far post, powered his header into the back of the net. Our celebrations were as much about relief as triumph. It was the first time I had been on a winning team at a World Cup and I don't mind repeating those three words: what a feeling.

From there, we put six past Panama – the highest score ever recorded by an England team at a World Cup – in our second game, Harry Kane getting a hat-trick. It meant we had qualified for the knockout stages with a game to spare. It was an altogether more positive scenario than the way our opening two World Cup games had played out in Brazil four years earlier. I was rested for the final group game against Belgium in Kaliningrad, which we lost 1–0. Even though it was a dead rubber, and even though neither route to the latter stages of the tournament seemed appreciably easier than the other, Gareth got slated for leaving first-choice players out. People said that we should have gone all out for the win to secure a better route to the final. Then, after the tournament was over, Gareth's detractors said the only reason we had done well was because we had secured an easy route to the semi-final. That's football – and that's England.

We had a few days back in Repino before our second-round match against Colombia in Moscow. The media had their own set-up not far from the team hotel and, in the spirit of the more positive relationship between us, we had a darts match every day between a player and a journalist. I played Rob Dorsett from Sky Sports. It was no contest. He got twenty-three with three darts. Me? I go, twenty, twenty, twenty with each of my three arrows. It was the biggest score any of the England players had got up to that point. Not that I'm competitive or anything.

9. The Obsession

It was late in Moscow. Tuesday, 3 July was about ten minutes from turning into Wednesday, 4 July in the Spartak Stadium. I remember walking towards the penalty spot, juggling the ball with my right foot as I got to the edge of the area, trying to look calm. Actually, I was calm – relatively speaking, anyway. I felt okay because I'd practised my penalties.

We had all practised penalties. How could we not? Penalties and England in a major tournament seem to go hand in hand, and I was thinking back six years, to the night we played Italy in Kyiv in the quarter-finals of Euro 2012. I had been nervous about the possibility of being asked to step forward, but this time was different. I was ready for the situation and I felt confident.

I was the third England penalty taker in the shoot-out with Colombia. Our second-round match at the 2018 World Cup had ended in a 1–1 draw after Yerry Mina scored a last-gasp equalizer at the end of normal time. Colombia had scored their first three kicks; Harry Kane and Marcus Rashford had scored our first two.

When you start that walk forward from the centre circle, you don't think about history. The records of our teams in previous tournaments don't matter, and it would hardly help to start running through what happened in years gone by. So that meant I wasn't even thinking about Gareth Southgate, our manager, who was standing on the touchline in a waistcoat with his arm on the shoulder of his assistant, Steve Holland. Gareth had dealt with questions about missed penalties for twenty-two years, going back to what happened against Germany in the semi-final at Euro 96 when his kick in sudden death was saved by Andreas Köpke. He, more than anyone, did not want us thinking that way and we had been taught to concentrate on positivity.

Our preparations could not have been better. We had spoken to psychologists. We were filmed practising our penalties in training and had studied the film. We had practised over and over and we knew who, statistically, our best takers were. I was one of them, and I was third in line.

So, no, I wasn't thinking about 'Football's Coming Home' or any of the scenes of wild celebration in England that we had been watching from our base near St Petersburg as we'd progressed through the group stage to this point. I knew that everyone who knew me would be sick with nerves when I began to walk forward, but it honestly never entered my head about how awful it would be if I failed with this penalty and it contributed to this journey coming to an end. I wasn't thinking about the consequences of missing or people abusing me and singing, 'You've let your country down' – this was just another hurdle to get over.

I said that, statistically, I was one of our best takers, but something was telling me that Jamie Vardy was supposed to take our third that night. Gareth had brought him on a couple of minutes before the end of normal time, but it seemed like he had picked up an injury during extra time. Anyway, there was some reason his name was absent from the list. I wasn't thinking about that either. No point.

I was feeling good about taking a pen. It had become an obsession for us to win one of these, after so much heartbreak. My dad remembers us losing to West Germany in the semis of the 1990 World Cup when Stuart Pearce and Chris Waddle missed, but I was only a month old then. I had a dim memory of us losing to Argentina on penalties in the last sixteen of the 1998 World Cup, but I remembered David Beckham getting sent off more clearly than the penalties. I remember us losing to Portugal on penalties in 2006, but I remember Cristiano Ronaldo's wink more clearly after Wayne Rooney had been sent off than the penalties. I wasn't thinking about any of that, either. Honestly, I wasn't.

I believed we were going to win this time, but I knew it was in the balance. Radamel Falcao had taken Colombia's first kick and blasted it down the middle, high and confident. Jordan Pickford dived to his right and looked over his shoulder as the ball flew over the place where his feet were. Harry Kane took our first, and that was always going to be the case. I noticed that David Ospina, the Colombia goalkeeper, was standing a little to the right of his goal, as we looked. He was trying to play mind games, but Harry blasted his kick low to Ospina's right. Even though he dived that way, he couldn't stop it. Harry wins that game.

Juan Cuadrado was Colombia's second taker. Jordan was jumping up and down on the line, punching the roof of the net. Cuadrado wasn't fazed and smashed his kick high to the right. Jordan went the right way, but it didn't matter. No chance. It ripped into the net again.

Then it was Marcus. He placed the ball on the spot, took some deliberate steps back and then danced to his left, once, twice, then a third time. Then he ran up and drilled his penalty low to Ospina's right-hand side. Ospina guessed correctly, again, but he didn't get close.

The tension was rising now. I knew it was nearly my turn, but not quite yet. Luis Muriel was Colombia's third man. I thought he looked nervous. Pickford was bouncing on his line again, punching the roof of the net. Muriel ran up, waited for Pickford to commit and slid the ball slowly the other way. Some nerve on that guy.

So I walked forward. I stopped juggling the ball and placed it down on the spot. I was feeling okay. I had adrenaline shooting through me and my mouth had gone a little bit dry, but that happens. That's okay. That's normal. I had a routine, and I was sticking to it. I was keeping my mind clear, using my routine to block out other thoughts and taking comfort in the routine. We had spoken about this process over and over again. I was sticking to my routine.

The last thing I wanted to be doing when I was walking up to the spot was to be thinking, 'I can't fucking miss this.'

I had taken a penalty against Ospina before, which was bizarre, because I hardly ever take penalties. My memory tells me it was three years earlier. It was late in a 4–1 Liverpool defeat to Arsenal at the Emirates. There wasn't anything riding on that kick, as we were being well beaten at the time and the penalty was nothing other than a consolation, but I remember I put the kick to Ospina's right.

So I knew where I was going to put it this time. I was going to put it the other way, to his left. I was going to open my foot up and put it low in the corner. I had practised it. I'd practised it and practised it well. I followed my routine and did not waver, counting my steps back. One, two, three, four. I didn't rush. I stood at the end of my run-up for a couple of seconds. Then I jogged to the spot. Then I ran forward and accelerated towards the point of contact. I hit the ball well. I felt it speed cleanly away from my right foot. I didn't slip or mishit it and it felt good. But it wasn't low. It wasn't low enough. It was a good height for the goalkeeper – that's what they always say when the goalkeeper saves it.

Ospina guessed correctly. I saw his body lurch to his left. Actually, 'lurch' is unkind. His body darted to the left. He was agile and lithe and he got down fast – and his left hand reached for the ball. I saw his left hand hit the ball. I saw the ball loop up into the air, in what seemed like slow motion. I kept watching it. It spun up and it landed on the grass at the side of the goal and bounced over the advertising hoardings before it clipped a photographer who was standing there.

Ospina saved it. I had missed. Same difference. I had missed. That's how it was going to be remembered. Jordan Henderson was the one who missed. 'A missed penalty by Jordan Henderson saw England knocked out of the World Cup tonight,' they would say. I could hear it already. I could hear someone shouting it in my head.

I turned and cursed and kept my eyes down. Inside, I was dying. My world was crashing down. Football is everything to me. England is everything to me, so if I missed a penalty in the World Cup and it meant we got knocked out of the World Cup, how was I going to cope with that? I couldn't think as I walked back towards the red shirts waiting for me on the halfway line. I felt their sympathy and their dread. I walked towards Harry and Marcus. Everyone knew there was nothing they could say to make this better. I tried to remain calm but, inside, all kinds of thoughts were taking over. I'd let everybody down – the manager, my team-mates, my family. For fuck's sake, I had let the whole of England down. A couple of the lads said, 'It's all right; it'll be all right.' All I was thinking was, 'I can't go back to England if we lose this.'

I mean, I was literally thinking that. For a few seconds, I was thinking, I'll never go back to England – that's it. My England career? Over. Life as it exists? Over. I was never going back. How could I go back? I'd let the whole nation down. Then hope gripped me. Mateus Uribe walked up to the spot to take Colombia's fourth penalty. He looked nervous, too, the poor bastard. He bent down to place the ball on the spot and kissed it before he lay it on the turf. In my head, four words began repeating over and over: *please, Jordan – save it.*

Uribe took a couple of deep breaths. He still looked nervous. Next thing, he ran up and smacked the shit out of the ball. Jordan didn't save it, but it crashed against the underside of the crossbar and bounced out. Oh my God! I could breathe again; I could actually breathe again. We were back in it, and the relief was overwhelming. It's temporary, but it's overwhelming.

Kieran Trippier was next up. He's frightening with the dead ball. He's one of our best on free kicks. He ran up and slammed the ball high to the keeper's right. It was our best penalty so far and we had levelled things up. I felt a bit more relieved. Carlos Bacca took the fifth for Colombia. He stood at the top of his run-up, legs planted and spread wide, like Cristiano Ronaldo might. He hit it well, towards the right of Jordan's goal. I was looking at it, thinking, 'Hang on – this is a good height.'

Jordan almost guessed too well. The ball was behind him, but he flung up his left hand instinctively as he fell and somehow he made it a strong enough hand to stop the ball and keep it out. It was the first time an England goalkeeper had saved a penalty in a World Cup shoot-out since David Seaman stopped one from Hernán Crespo twenty years ago in Saint-Étienne.

We ran forward, some of us, from our thin red line, unable to control our excitement. Just a few steps. Then we stopped and regrouped. We put our arms around each other's shoulders again. My mind was working overtime. I asked Harry Kane for assurance – are we through if we score? We checked what the score was and Harry nodded. We got back in our red line, me next to Marcus.

Eric Dier walked up to the spot. Before the tournament began, people had been talking about how maybe he and I were in competition for one spot in midfield. But now we were both on the pitch and I had everything invested in him. Come on, Eric. Please . . . I noticed Ospina was standing a little off centre again, in the same spot he stood in for our first penalty, Harry's penalty. He's daring Eric to put it to the right, just like he dared Harry to do it. Eric takes the dare. He hits it to Ospina's right. Ospina goes for it. He can't reach it. We had won.

I was sipping from a bottle of energy drink. I froze – I didn't move. The bottle stayed at my lips. Everyone else was running. The red line had dissolved. Marcus ripped his arm away from my shoulder and took off. People were running to Jordan, people were running to Eric. People were running to Gareth. I couldn't run. I just fell to my knees. It was relief, just overwhelming relief. We had escaped. I had escaped. Life wasn't over! We were in the quarter-finals of the World Cup, and it was Sweden next, in Samara, on Saturday.

Eventually I got up. I ran to join the other lads, who had gone to the end where most of the England fans had congregated and had all piled on top of each other. It was bedlam, the joy was washing all over us, and you just knew this night had the potential to be spoken about for many years to come. It didn't matter now that I'd missed a penalty. I was the guy who got bailed out by his mates. I wasn't a pariah. The lads had saved me.

'I apologize to back home, to anybody who skipped a heartbeat,' I said to a television camera.

I did a post-match interview with Gabriel Clarke for ITV.

'Your old Sunderland mate, Jordan Pickford, has got you off the hook tonight, hasn't he?' he said.

I was grinning by now.

'Big time,' I say.

You'd think that was the end of me and penalties, wouldn't you? But it wasn't. Now I was obsessed. I was thinking to myself that I couldn't let it happen again. I couldn't miss again. I couldn't. I couldn't face the thought of losing everything again. We got back to Repino. We only did a light session, a recovery session. We were still tired after the game and after the ordeal and the emotional release. The session ended. The other boys went in. I didn't.

I stayed out. I took penalties. I practised penalties. I practised penalty after penalty after penalty. *I can't miss another one. I can't.* So now I'm convincing myself I'm a bad taker. Each one I practised, I thought was too high, too low, too close to the middle or that it was a good height for the keeper. I knew I was overthinking things, but I was obsessed. In the end, Steve Holland came over and yelled at me to get inside.

The next day, I woke up and got out of bed. My groin was tight. For fuck's sake! It felt sore. I had injured myself taking penalties. I trained with the rest of the lads. I could feel it was tight, but I wasn't going to say anything to anyone because I knew how I'd done it and I felt stupid. *It's okay, anyway. It's okay. It's just a scare.* So we played Sweden. It was a World Cup quarter-final, but it was straightforward. It wasn't easy, but it was straightforward. We won 2–0. Two headers from Dele and Harry Maguire. I could feel my groin, tight from taking too many penalties, but it didn't impede me. We were into the semi-final. This, for all of us, was childhood-dream territory.

We were playing Croatia in the Luzhniki Stadium in Moscow. They were good. Modrić, Rakitić, Mandžukić,

Perišić. Good players. Good, technical players. Modrić is the best of them, the only guy to win the Ballon d'Or apart from Messi or Ronaldo for about a hundred years. But I was still thinking about penalties. If the semi-final went to penalties, I needed to be ready. So I practised some more penalties – seriously. The whole team practised this time. Not just me.

I took a few pens. After one of them, I felt my groin twinge again and it gave me a fright. Imagine missing a World Cup semi-final after injuring yourself practising penalties? How would that look? I had some treatment and it felt okay. There was a bit of discomfort, but not much, and thankfully I was fit to play. But I was still obsessed with the idea that if the semi-final went to a penalty shoot-out again, I needed to score . . .

We started well, so well. It was the kind of start you would have if you were writing a story. Tripps scored in the sixth minute with a free kick that he curled and dipped over the top of the Croatia wall. We should have gone 2–0 up, but Harry Kane has a shot cleared off the line. Still, we were leading at half-time. We were forty-five minutes from the World Cup final.

Then we were twenty-two minutes from the World Cup final. But Croatia came into the game more and more and the momentum changed. Modrić had gone up a gear and we couldn't deal with their width. They were switching the play and, when we got the ball, we couldn't get it out wide. Then our world changes. They cross a ball into the box, Tripps goes to head it, but Perišić's foot is high and he gets his high foot to it first; it goes into the net off the underside of his foot. I wonder if it's going to be disallowed for dangerous play. It isn't.

They nearly scored again. Perišić cuts in off the flank and hits the face of the post. It comes out. They got the rebound, but they hit it straight at Pickford. He caught it and we were still in it. Still level. It went to extra time.

John Stones had a header cleared off the line. I started to feel my groin. My penalty taker's groin. It's the seventh minute of extra time and we made a substitution. I looked over at the touchline. My number came up on the electronic board. I walked over; Eric came on for me. We got to half-time of extra time. Still level. Still anybody's. Maybe Croatia had the edge. Pickford makes a save from Mandžukić. Then Perišić nods a ball on, Mandžukić gets it behind and sweeps it into our goal. Eleven minutes left. We couldn't get it back. We didn't quite have enough.

The whistle goes and it's over. In a way, though, it wasn't over. No one thought we'd get that far. Not after 2014. Not after Iceland and the embarrassment in Nice. This felt like a different England now, a new England. Maybe I had been watching too many of the scenes from back home, but it felt as if the fans had fallen in love with us again and the reconnection that Gareth was looking for had been established. Nothing will ever ease the pain of losing a World Cup semi-final, don't get me wrong. But coming back from Moscow, it didn't feel like the end. It felt like the beginning.

10. The Comeback

For all that Jürgen had given me some reason to be optimistic after we had lost to Real Madrid with his comforting message, there was no hiding the fact I returned to pre-season training in 2018 feeling impatient.

With time to think back on what had happened over the summer – losing in Kyiv, then in Moscow – I was asking myself questions once more, but this one had a different twist: how long have I got to wait to win something again?

I could have asked a million people and nobody would have been able to provide an accurate answer.

Whether I liked it or not, I couldn't argue if someone had said I was a 'nearly man' or that we, as a team, were 'nearly men'. I know I'd won the League Cup in 2012 but, suddenly, that felt like a lifetime ago. I used to look at other teams celebrating big moments and it would drive me mad. Why couldn't it be us? The title race in 2013–14; two semi-finals in 2015; the League Cup and Europa League finals in 2016; the Champions League final in 2018; and then a World Cup semi-final. All I wanted was to get over the line.

I didn't think of myself this way, but I know what football is like and I know the way people think: I was a loser. It wasn't just me who was the target of cheap shots, either. Jürgen had lost six finals in succession, three with Borussia Dortmund before he got to us, and his critics loved that. I knew I had to snap the streak and snap it fast, but by late in that 2018–19 season, I could see it all happening again.

The mad thing is, I couldn't understand how it looked like it might happen again. We had played some brilliant football in the Premier League. We'd gone twenty games unbeaten at the start of the season and, in any other year, we'd have been away and clear. But this wasn't any other year. We had taken our consistency and performances to frightening levels, but Manchester City had done the same and, in the final weeks of the campaign, they wouldn't blink, no matter how much pressure we put on them.

And even though we had reached the semi-finals of the Champions League against Barcelona, and even though we had played well, we had come up against the genius of Lionel Messi and lost 3–0 in the first leg. Most people assumed there was no way back. Yes, I've been blessed to have some fantastic times in the last couple of years but, for a brief spell in the spring of 2019, the idea of winning had never felt so far away.

There was another thing. Two days after we had returned from Kyiv, Liverpool signed the Brazil international midfielder Fabinho for £43 million from Monaco. As far as I knew, Fabinho was a 6. He was one of the best holding midfielders in the world. I'd been playing at 6. So I'm thinking, 'Okay, £43 million for a 6 – what's happening? Am I moving to play as an 8? Or what?' I was worried.

Fab took a little time to adapt. The pace of the Premier League is a bit different to the pace of the French League. But it was obvious he was the real deal. I carried on playing at 6 for a while, but then he started our 3–1 victory over Manchester United at Anfield a week before Christmas and he was absolutely outstanding, cleaning things up, keeping it simple, excelling.

I was sitting there on the bench, thinking, 'Wow, now that's a 6.' Then I thought, 'So hang on a second – where am I playing?' I was in and out of the side a little bit. After a few weeks of Fab playing regularly, I could see that he had settled and that he was brilliant. So it was important to turn the situation around – maybe it was time to have an impact in a position that felt more natural to me.

We were seven points clear of City in the league on the morning of 3 January 2019. It was the day we were going to the Etihad Stadium, and I'm adamant that if we had gone ten points clear, even City wouldn't have overhauled us. Early in the game, there was an incident that many looked back on later as the decisive moment in the race for the title. Mo and Bobby played a brilliant one–two in the middle of the pitch, and Mo slipped a ball through for Sadio to run on to. He clipped it past Ederson, as the City goalkeeper ran out to meet him, but the ball came back off the post. John Stones tried to clear it, but he smashed it straight into Ederson, who was scrambling back.

The ball looped up and seemed to have gone in, before Stonesy, a player whose quality I know well from our time with England, recovered to hack it clear. We all looked at referee Anthony Taylor, hoping his watch would vibrate and we would have the goal our play deserved, but technology showed the ball was 11.7 mm from crossing the line in its entirety. City were saved by a sliver, and they went on to win the match 2–1. It was to be our only defeat of the season, but it cut our lead to four points and City chipped away at it and edged past us in the spring. To give it further context, they needed to win fourteen consecutive Premier League games. Their consistency, unfortunately, was just incredible.

I put off my chat with Jürgen for a while and then, some time towards the end of March, I went to see the manager about my frustrations. A month earlier at Old Trafford, I was substituted in a o–o draw and I missed his gesture to shake hands as I was coming off, as I was in a world of my own. Jürgen wasn't happy, but it was a complete misunderstanding. It was said we had a row in the dressing room afterwards, but that would have been a physical impossibility because I had been selected for random drug testing . . .

Still, I was restless. I said I understood how well Fabinho had done and that I could understand how well the team was playing and that I would like to have an opportunity to play as an 8 again. I knew Gini had one of those positions nailed down, but I hoped I could compete for the other. The gaffer was receptive – up to a point. He said he thought I could play in both roles and it didn't really matter to him which one it was from game to game. At the start of the next game, away at Southampton on 5 April, I was on the bench. 'Okay,' I thought. 'Maybe that chat didn't go quite as well as I felt it did.'

So I was on the bench at St Mary's, simmering. When I don't play, I can get a bit angry. I'll try to put a poker face on, but I find it difficult to hide my disappointment. Over time, I have learned to deal with it a lot better. Early on, the manager had given me a rocket a few times. He'd said that I'm the captain of the team and told me I couldn't behave like that and, looking back, he was right. That disappointment, though, is part of who I am.

We were losing 1–0 at Southampton to an early goal from Shane Long and the gaffer brought me on with half an hour to go. Pete Krawietz, one of our assistant managers, the one Jürgen calls 'The Eyes', was going through our set plays with me while I was waiting on the touchline, and he said to me: 'The team needs you now – off you go.'

I came on for Gini, so I was playing as a number 8, and I knew that even though there wasn't long, I needed to make an impression in the position. I got an assist. It was an assist in name only, really. I headed clear on the edge of our box and Mo dribbled half the length of the pitch to score, but it looked good on paper.

And then, four minutes from the end, when we were 2–1 up, I burst into the area and got on to a perfect pass from Bobby. I drilled it into the back of the net with my left foot and then cupped my hands around my ears as I ran over to the fans. Then I turned away and punched the air. From that moment, everything changed. I played in the Champions League the following week in the first leg of the quarter-finals against Porto, and I played as an 8, alongside Fabinho. The manager could see that I was hungry to succeed and he kept playing me in that role for much of the run-in.

We were tucked in right behind City at that point, winning every game, chasing them relentlessly, waiting for them to make just one mistake. We played Chelsea at home after Southampton, and I started alongside Fabinho and got another assist, breaking to the byline to chip a ball to the back post for Sadio to score the first in a 2–0 win. I was a man on a mission, to the point where Jürgen made a joke of it in one of his post-match press conferences.

'Sorry for playing Hendo at 6!' he said, and he got a big laugh, because everyone knew what he was referring to and everyone knew how hungry I was to cement my place in the side.

Then it was Barcelona away in the first leg of the Champions League semi-final. I was excited. I had never played in the Nou Camp. I was playing so well that it didn't occur to me that I wouldn't be in the side, but then the day before the game, we did shape in training and I wasn't in the team. He was going with a midfield three of Millie, Fabinho and Naby. Angry doesn't begin to explain how I was feeling. As usual before a match, we played 'Young v Old' in training, but my head was all over the shop. I ended up scoring a good goal for the winner, but I walked straight in. I needed to get in the shower or get in the gym and clear my head before I said something I shouldn't.

We travelled to Barcelona, and I still couldn't get my head around it. I was waiting in the lift at the hotel, pressing the button to go to my room, and Tim, the security guard, went, 'Hang on, hang on, one more,' and Jürgen walked in. I stood there. No one said anything. We were going up all the floors, stopping at every single one. We didn't say a single word. I understand rotation, but when it's you getting rotated, it feels personal. It isn't personal, but it feels personal. The longer you know a manager and the more respect you develop for him, the more you start to learn about how the manager thinks and the decisions he has to take.

When you're young, you feel that if you're playing well and doing everything right, you should be in the team. It's a simple equation for you at that age. I'm fit, I'm good, I should be playing every game. The manager talks about rotation and you think, 'I don't need to be rotated, I'm fresh, I can play every three days.' But the manager has got twenty-three players to choose from and quality everywhere, and maybe there are certain games where he thinks someone can do a specific job in specific circumstances. There's a difference between being able to play every three days and being a bit physically and mentally tired and being rested for a game and then coming back super-sharp.

I do wonder at times if the gaffer leaves people out to get a reaction. I've never spoken to him about that part of it. Does he know how people are going to react? He left Gini out of the second leg against Barcelona, for instance, and then when Gini came on, he was like a hurricane. Gini says he could never remember being as angry as he was that night. That was a stroke of genius with Gini. I think Jürgen knew he wasn't going to sulk and mess around. I've stopped trying to judge what the manager's doing. I have learned to accept that I'm not going to be happy when I'm left out and get on with it.

You can't just stop being angry. You're angry because you want to play, but you accept it's not going to change anything. Sometimes, players say of a manager that 'the problem was he didn't communicate with me'. But it's not the communication. It's the decision. The manager could sing me a song on a piano to explain it and I still wouldn't like it.

To be fair, I understand he has decisions to make. And, looking at it, he doesn't make bad decisions, so you suck it up. Channel it in the right way and make sure you're ready when you're called to come on. He would give me a rocket sometimes and he would say: 'I'm not expecting you to sing and dance and be over the moon, but you need to at least try to make an effort. Otherwise, other players, when they get left out, they will copy that.' He has helped me to be a better captain with advice like that. It hadn't occurred to me that other players might look at me with my long face and copy it. It should have done, but it didn't. I don't want to be setting a bad example. I'm a bit better now. I have got better at thinking about the bigger picture – though I'm sure other people will tell you different!

The day of the first leg of the Barcelona tie, I knew I needed to shake off my resentment. Pep Lijnders, Jürgen's assistant, came over, and I had a good chat with him for about half an hour. He knew I was angry, but he was saying the team needed me. Pep is a great sounding board, and he does an important job assisting Jürgen. He had a six-month spell managing NEC Nijmegen in the Netherlands in 2018 but came back to assist Jürgen after we had lost to Real Madrid in Kyiv. He's a football obsessive, totally committed to helping us reach our goals, and the lads have trust in him. It's the same with the rest of the coaching staff, from Pete Krawietz to John Achterberg, the goalkeeper coach, and many more besides. They aren't afraid to tell us the things we need to hear, and Pep pointed out we had Barcelona, then Newcastle away, Barcelona at home, Wolves at home, all in the space of a fortnight. The problem was, I wanted to play all of them. The conversation helped me a little bit. I thought I just needed to concentrate on the match. Naby Keïta got injured after twenty-four minutes and I came on. Two minutes later, Suárez scored to put them one up. Quite an impact I'd made.

We played well in the game. We'd been playing well before I came on. We played well after I came on. But they had players who could seize on the smallest things. Luis snaffled up that first goal, but then we had the better of the game for a while.

Then they took the game away from us in the last fifteen minutes, just when I thought we had them where we wanted them. Messi was the first to react to a ball that rebounded off the crossbar. He chested it down, as cool as you like, and slid it into the empty net. Then they were awarded a foul on the edge of our area eight minutes from the end and Messi curled in a free kick that was special even by his standards. Looking back at it, it was one of the best free kicks I have ever seen. The whip, the precision, the speed of the ball. Alisson is unreal, the best goalkeeper I have played with, and I'd back him to save most things that come his way. Messi, from thirty yards, put the ball in the one area of the goal he couldn't protect. It was unbelievable.

You can appreciate someone's genius, but for fuck's sake! How was this happening again? It was a big ask to overhaul that deficit. After the game, I went into the dressing room and it was a strange vibe. We had lost 3–0, but I was in the ice bath with Gini and Virg and we were saying, 'What the hell just happened, because we battered them?' Somewhere in the back of my mind, I started thinking – if we got an early goal at Anfield and played in the same way, maybe it wasn't over. Maybe . . .

It wasn't doom and gloom, but in the Premier League we were still pushing against a closed door. We had won our last eight games on the spin, but City had been relentless. We hadn't lost in the league since 3 January and we had just secured another nerve-jangling last-gasp 3–2 victory, at Newcastle, with a winner from Divock Origi. But now we only had one game left and we were running out of chances for City to crack.

Our best chance, we thought, was their home game against Leicester City, the night before we played our second leg against Barcelona. Leicester were a good team and they kept City at bay for seventy minutes. Then Vincent Kompany, the City captain, who hadn't scored all season, strode forward and let fly from twenty-five yards with his right foot. It was an absolute screamer of a shot that flew into the top corner. Are you fucking joking me here? I sat there in disbelief as the ball went in. To make it worse, Hamza Choudhury put Kelechi Iheanacho through late on. It was a glorious chance and he side-footed it wide. If Leicester had drawn that game, we would only have had to beat Wolves in our last match of the season, at Anfield, to win the league. But City hung on for the win and that meant everything was depending on a miracle.

Jürgen always holds a meeting before we leave the Hope Street Hotel, where we used to stay before home games. What he said the afternoon of the Barcelona game will always stay with me. He looked around the room before he started to speak.

'If it was any other group of players in the world 3–0 down to Barcelona after the first leg,' he said, 'I'd say we've got no chance. I'd say play for pride. I'd say play for dignity. I'd say go out with your heads held high. But this is not any other group of players. And, because it's you, we have a chance.'

The way that he delivered that, the pride it instilled in us, made us all feel ten feet tall. I went out of that room at the hotel thinking, 'Come on then, let's have it! We can do this, miracles happen!'

There were still some feelings from the trip to the Nou Camp six days earlier. We knew they didn't like our intensity and we had played a lot better than the result suggested. Anfield . . . An early goal . . . You never know. And Barcelona had blown a three-goal lead against Roma in the Champions League the season before. Against that, Mo had been concussed at Newcastle and Bobby was injured. So we were expected to overhaul a three-goal deficit against one of the best teams in the world without two of our best three attackers. Those were more reasons for people to say we had no chance.

I was starting this time. Gini wasn't. So it was his turn to be fuming. Divock started up front with Xherdan Shaqiri in for Mo. A much-changed team didn't matter to the fans, who knew what was expected of them in a

Champions League semi-final. They knew we needed them like never before. We got to the stadium and came out for the warm-up, and I could sense it was going to be a special night. Barcelona at Anfield. A proper European night in Liverpool with the crowd right up for it.

And off we went. It was madness. The whole night was like a kind of beautiful madness right from the start. We got a corner early on, and I looked round and I could see Messi running after Robbo. Messi was pointing at him angrily. I thought, 'What's Robbo done now?' I saw afterwards on television replays that Robbo had ruffled Messi's hair as Messi sat on the ground appealing for a foul. We have so much respect for Messi, a guy who is the best player in the world, but when you're on the pitch, it is eleven versus eleven and I don't really care who you are. You're at Anfield and you're playing against Liverpool, so I liked that from Robbo.

That was our attitude. We weren't bothered about reputations and we didn't care who they were. When a team comes to Anfield, they should know we are fighting for our lives; we are not going to give you an inch and we are going to make things as uncomfortable as we possibly can for you. It's a fine line we were treading, because you have to respect a player like Messi and a team like Barcelona, but as soon as you cross the white line, it's war. What Robbo did encapsulated everything about that night. It went back to what my dad had once said to me about how, when you get on the pitch, we are all equal. Messi is a wonderful player and nobody admires him more than I do. But that night a place in the Champions League final was at stake. So he was treated as a normal opponent. Nothing else would have made sense.

Anfield was electric. The atmosphere was so good I knew we were going to score. It only took us seven minutes to get the first. Joël Matip pumped a long ball forward and, when Jordi Alba tried to head it back to a team-mate, Sadio intercepted it and helped it on to me. I burst into the box. The adrenaline was pumping through me more than ever before. I turned inside Gerard Piqué, who tried to make a tackle but the ball ricocheted between us and I broke past him. I was suddenly ten yards out with a chance to shoot with my left foot. All that time practicing with my weaker foot was about to pay off. I should have practised harder. I hit it too close to Marc-André ter Stegen, but at least I hit it so firmly that he couldn't hold on to it. All he could do was push it out with his right hand, and it went straight into the path of Divock and he slid it into the empty net. It was bedlam, and you felt the stadium was ready to take off.

I didn't stop. I ran into the goal and caught the ball as it came back out, and sprinted to the centre circle with it and put it down on the spot. I didn't want them to have any respite. I didn't want them to have a single second to be able to catch their breath and regroup. None. I wanted the pressure on them to be relentless.

From that moment, it was game on. We knew we had to take chances and we knew that they were going to create chances. Messi was still a brilliant, brilliant player and he made a couple of opportunities in the first half that Alisson saved really well. Messi had a shot of his own that

Ally tipped over the bar. It wasn't all pressure from us, by any means. Our hopes of staying in the tie were still on a knife-edge. I had been struggling a little bit because I had got a stud right on my kneecap from Clément Lenglet towards the end of the first half. It was agony at first, and then it went dead and I couldn't move it. I couldn't run. I was struggling, but I knew it was a stud and an impact and nothing worse.

We went in at half-time and I could barely walk, so I got on a spinning bike and started pedalling to keep my legs moving. I swallowed painkillers and had an injection in my backside for some more pain relief. At the start of the second half, I thought it was going to be touch and go, but the adrenaline took me through it. Robbo had picked up an injury in the first half too, so Millie moved to left back at the start of the second half and Gini came off the bench. He was like a raging bull. He had a point to prove after being left out and it only took him eight minutes to make an impact.

Trent won the ball back from Jordi Alba on the right touchline and swung a low cross into the box. Gini ran on to it and got to it first. He smashed his shot close to Ter Stegen, but he hit it so hard and true that the goalkeeper couldn't keep it out. Now it was 2–0 and the dream was starting to get real. Two minutes later, we were level on aggregate. It was Gini again. Shaq crossed the ball in from the left and Gini rose highest and headed it in at the near post. Ter Stegen barely moved. It was mayhem. I was one of the first to get to Gini in front of the Kop, and I was just screaming at him. I can't remember what I was saying, and he probably couldn't hear anyway.

I'd dreamt that something like this would happen, but I still couldn't quite believe what was actually happening. There was half an hour left for us to get one more – or for Barcelona to ruin the story. I thought we had them. They still made chances, but their body language wasn't good. Barcelona were wilting and the stadium was like a furnace. It was as if the memory of what had happened in Rome was burned into them. It had scarred them. I was thinking, 'We can't lose here, this is too good.' But in the back of my mind I also knew they had Messi, they had Suárez, and I knew that it could all be over in the blink of an eye with players of that ability. One chance and it could be done and it could be game over and we would have done all this for nothing.

And then it was Trent's moment. There were twelve minutes to go and we'd won a corner. Trent was standing over it, but Shaq was marching over to take it so Trent started to walk away. He saw that the Barcelona defenders had switched off and were trying to organize the area, and so he made a snap decision, turned around and took the corner.

Piqué was aware of what was happening because he was watching, but most of the Barcelona players weren't even looking at the ball. I'd never seen Trent take a corner like that before. It was just an instinct, a reflex in the moment. It wasn't something we had practised in training, it was just a stroke of genius from an unbelievable player.

His corner arrowed its way towards Divock, who had turned in time and had a chance to steady himself. I think Trent had shouted to Div just before he took it. I had turned away too. I was trying to sort protection out for somebody else's run, but then I heard the sudden change in the atmosphere and turned again in time to see the ball coming into the area.

It sat up for Div and, even though it was coming at him fast, he guided it towards the top corner. Ter Stegen didn't have time to react and, even though Piqué made a desperate attempt to clear it off the line, it was too high for him to kick away and too low for him to get his head on it. Anfield went wild, to the point that you could physically feel the stands shaking. Even in all the great, great European nights that our stadium had seen, it had never seen anything quite like this. These are the moments you dream about as a footballer, the chance to write your name in history and create memories that will last a lifetime.

I was still worried about Messi. There was still time for him to ruin this for us. One goal was all they needed. Luckily for me, he was more on the right, and I felt we had dealt with him really well as a team. You can't deal with him one v one, but we had surrounded him in twos and threes and hunted him down really well the whole game. In the dying minutes, the ball went back to their centre half and I was sprinting to close him down, and then I sprinted to close someone else down and I knew I could do that all day. I had a keen sense of what was at stake. We were on the verge of one of the greatest comebacks of all time and there was no way we could concede.

I was going to run all night until that whistle went. I was dying for it to go. It was a huge moment for us as a club and a team. When the final whistle did go, I collapsed on to my knees and I couldn't get up. All the emotion came out. We sang 'You'll Never Walk Alone' in front of the Kop, and I left the pitch chanting '*Allez! Allez! Allez!*' to the fans in the main stand, one of their favourite anthems. It was the greatest game I have ever played in, without a shadow of a doubt.

Maybe it was the most important, too.

11. Reaching the Summit

The following Sunday we faced Wolves in the last game of our domestic season. The fans were still on a high from the Barcelona game and we made the journey to the stadium along Anfield Road amid more amazing scenes of fanatical support, but we knew the state of the situation: all we could do was win and hope that City dropped points at Brighton.

Sadio put us ahead after seventeen minutes and, for the next twenty-one minutes, we were top of the table. That summed that season up: we were fifty-two minutes away from becoming champions for the first time in twenty-nine years. There was bedlam in the stadium, an atmosphere like I'd never really experienced before. The best way to describe it was hope and desperation mixed together, knowing that we were so close but, really, it was still so far. The situation was best explained when news started to spread that Brighton had gone ahead, only for it to prove to be a false alarm.

Then there was this huge roar that was bigger even than the one that had greeted Sadio's goal. This time it was real – Glenn Murray had scored at the Amex. For a few minutes, it felt like this was going to be our time, but we also knew not to waste too much emotion. It was another one of those glimpses of hope that we had been given a couple of times in the past in our battles with City.

We were right to be cautious. Brighton had barely stopped celebrating when Sergio Agüero equalized for City. We were still top of the league, but our stay there had lasted only twenty-one minutes when Aymeric Laporte headed home unmarked from a corner seven minutes before half-time. City were ahead, cruising, and eventually won 4–1. We won 2–0, but it didn't matter. We set all kinds of records, but we didn't get the trophy we wanted. Sadio and Mo finished joint top-scorers in the Premier League with Pierre-Emerick Aubameyang on twenty-two goals each. Alisson was the Golden Gloves winner with twenty-one clean sheets. We had only lost one league game all season. And we had finished on ninety-seven points, which was the third-highest total in Premier League history. Only the City of that season, who had just pipped us to the title with ninety-eight points, and the City of the previous season, who had won with a hundred points, had ever amassed more.

It had been one of the greatest title races of all time and it was nice to hear people say so many positive things about us, but as I walked around the pitch at the final whistle, with Elexa and Alba in my arms, there's no point saying anything else other than I was devastated. I love my kids more than anything in the world but, on this occasion, I wish I'd been walking around with a trophy in my hands and they could have been dancing by my side. Fair play to City, because they were incredible, but the margins were so fine. We both kept winning, and nobody blinked. Could we have done any more? I doubt it. All I know is that it made us even more determined not to be second again in the Champions League final.

Spurs had beaten Ajax in the other semi-final in a match that had a storyline almost as dramatic as our victory over Barcelona, with Lucas Moura scoring a hat-trick. Everyone made us favourites straight away, but they had a great manager in Mauricio Pochettino, someone we had huge respect for, and they had beaten City in the quarter-finals. That showed that Premier League form can be turned on its head in the Champions League sometimes.

I hated the idea that everyone thought it was ours to lose. For starters, it was disrespectful, and sometimes I feel people truly don't understand how hard it actually is to win any game. Then I started running things through my mind: imagine losing the final to another English team? It shouldn't make any difference, but the fear of failure would be even greater than if we were playing a team from another country. Spurs were more than capable of upsetting us, and our game against them was to be played at Atlético Madrid's Estadio Metropolitano in the Spanish capital.

There was a three-week gap between the Wolves game and the final. We were given five days off straight away to go on holiday, but all I could think about was Spurs. Every single day. When I woke up, it was Spurs. When I went to bed, it was Spurs. During the day, trying to relax, it was Spurs. It was all I was thinking about.

The year before, we had lost the final. We had just missed out on the league. Now, there was a lot of speculation it was happening again. The fear of failure was almost unbearable. It haunted me. It was almost overwhelming. We just couldn't lose this time. I wanted us to show everyone how far we had come, and the motivation for it was off the scale.

I had played five finals as a Liverpool player. I'd lost four and won one. And in the one that I'd won, I had been substituted early. I couldn't lose another. I just couldn't. I felt like everything was on the line in this match. Everything. It would have been a huge blow to us all psychologically. That thought kept going round my head. We cannot lose, simple as that. It was constantly on my mind. It was getting to the point where it was getting a bit unhealthy. I couldn't go on like that for another couple of weeks. I was thinking about all the 'what ifs'. Particularly, 'What if we lose?'

I was applying a lot of pressure to myself. After I had taken a few days of holiday, we had a week in Marbella at a training camp and then five days at the training ground in Liverpool. I was trying to use the league defeat to urge myself on, but I was waking up with a knot in my stomach every morning about the Spurs match. I couldn't stand it any longer. I texted Steve Peters and asked if I could give him a call. He called me back and I told him I was struggling with thoughts about the final. I knew I was thinking about the wrong things. I was becoming consumed by the fear of losing. So we went back to the first sessions we'd had a few years previously and talked about what was important.

'What's the worst that can happen?' he said. 'Let's get that on the table.'

'The worst that can happen is we don't win the game.'

He said, 'Have you lost a game before?'

'Yeah.'

'Have you lost a Champions League final before?'

'Yeah.'

'And did you recover?'

'Yeah.'

'Were you all right? Were the family all right? Were the kids all right? Are you healthy?'

'Yeah.'

'So now you've got another opportunity to play another Champions League final and that's because you have dealt with it well, you've recovered well, you've done all the right things as a team. So, worst-case scenario, you can deal with it. You have dealt with it before, you can deal with it again. Best-case scenario is you win the game. How do you think you'd feel if you win the game?'

'Well, I'd feel like it was the best thing that's ever fucking happened in the world, in my life,' I said. 'This is everything.'

'Well, think of that feeling, and keep thinking about that feeling, and when you get nervous and excited before the game, that's good. That's what you want, the adrenaline and the emotion and the energy. Use all that within the game and keep thinking about that feeling of winning.'

After I had spoken to him, I felt like a weight had been lifted. From that point, I changed to thinking about the positive of winning. I thought of what it would be like to win that trophy that I had worked my whole life to lift. I was ready from that moment. I was ready to play. It was the best I have felt physically and mentally.

Four days before the final, on the Wednesday morning at Melwood, Millie and I called a players-only meeting and stood up in front of the lads. It wasn't anything too heavy,

I wouldn't even say it was out of the ordinary, but we spoke about what we had been through the previous year against Real Madrid and how we would use that experience to be even better prepared this time around. I knew from talking to Steve it was important to put past experiences to good use.

I couldn't sleep the night before the final in Kyiv, but when we got to the hotel in Madrid everything was a lot calmer and more relaxed. I went to bed a bit earlier, and I was thinking happy thoughts; I went straight to sleep and slept fine. I knew I was more relaxed than in 2018 and I could sense that in the rest of the players too. On the day of the game, I felt there was no way we were losing. It was our time. We were all ready.

And so I made it into the starting line-up for the biggest match of my life when, at one stage that season, it had seemed like I wouldn't. And I started at number 8, on the right side of Fabinho, who played in the middle, with Gini on the other side of him. Everything felt right. It was now or never.

Gini doesn't normally say much, really, before a match, but this time he broke with tradition. He waited until we were about to leave the changing room before kick-off and then he made a short speech about how proud he was to be part of this team. He said this was our moment to go out and show the world how good we were. Gini's a quiet, unassuming guy. For him to stand up like that had a big effect on everyone.

We tore into Spurs right from the kick-off. I won a header in the first exchanges and then the ball dropped to me midway inside the Spurs half. I lifted a ball over the top to Sadio on the left and he checked inside and chipped the ball into the box. It was blocked at close range by Moussa Sissoko, who had his right arm stretched out high to his right. The ball hit his arm and the Slovenian referee Damir Skomina pointed straight to the penalty spot. Twenty-five seconds had gone. Mo took the kick. He went for power rather than placement and the ball went over the dive of Hugo Lloris and almost burst the back of the net.

From that point on, some people would say it wasn't the greatest final of all time, but I couldn't care less what they say. I had no interest in it being the greatest final if we lost it. What that final showed was that we used all our experience in big matches, all our experience under pressure and all our experience in working for each other to manage the game. Maybe we were a bit deeper than normal, but I thought we were always in control of the game and I never felt Spurs created that many chances. Ally made a couple of good saves. I can remember one from a free kick from Christian Eriksen, but Trent and Virgil – who made one unbelievable recovery run to stop Son Heung-min – and Joël and Robbo defended brilliantly; all of us as a team did, really. To win titles and trophies, you need to defend well. Kane had come back from injury, and we kept him quiet. We didn't allow situations where he and Son could hit us on the counter-attack, which is a quality of their game that they have elevated to an art form. Then, three minutes from the end, when we were as comfortable as a team could be with only a one-goal lead, came the moment.

Millie put a corner in that was half cleared. We thought there was a handball and we all appealed, but the attack was kept alive. Joël helped the ball on and eventually it landed at Div's feet, and he fired his left foot shot across Lloris into the far corner. Two–nil. This is it – it's happening. Everywhere I was looking, you could see everyone knew we were nearly there. Virg collapsed to the floor when the ball went in, Robbo and Fab ran faster than they had done all night to get to Div. I wasn't far behind, arms outstretched, screaming at the top of my voice. Still, it wasn't over, but we had one hand on the trophy, so I kept going and going and going. Then the final whistle went and it was probably the best feeling I have ever had in football.

It was like an out-of-body experience. Happiness, relief, the removal of all the worry. Suddenly, the lost finals and trophies we have missed are a footnote, and here I am, the captain of a Champions League winning team. This had been *the* dream, ever since I was a kid and me and my dad were at Old Trafford in 2003 for Juventus versus AC Milan, and there were so many things that had built up to that moment. Everything we had been through as a team, all the setbacks, all the finals, all the disappointments, all the determination to come back stronger – when that final whistle went, each little thing along the way had been worth it. You have reached the pinnacle of the club game, the highest level. No one could take that away from us. We will be remembered.

I felt incredibly emotional. I was gone, unable to keep things under control. I didn't even try to fight it. I was either in tears or on the verge of tears while mayhem reigned around me. And then in the melee on the pitch, I saw Jürgen, who was also in tears. I went up to him and hugged him and he just said, 'We did it!' I had my head buried in his chest and I kept saying, 'Thank you, thank you.'

It was more than a football match for me, that Champions League final. It was more than a victory; it was everything for me as a player and as a person. Finally, finally, I felt that I would be respected as a footballer. Jürgen and I are emotional people, and we had suffered a lot of setbacks together at Liverpool. I don't deserve to be bracketed with him, because he was the driving force behind everything that happened at the club, but we were the two leaders of the club, as manager and captain, and we were both close to being written off as nearly men.

The gaffer understood what I had gone through, in terms of the captaincy. Everything was always traced back to Stevie and questions about how he used to do it. But Jürgen helped me to become my own person. That moment when we won the Champions League, I stepped out of the shadows and I had my own story. Jürgen helped me through the difficult moments, all the turmoil. And this was the defining moment. That was the first time when I felt people had some sort of respect for me as a player and as a captain. Not my team-mates and the manager, but from the outside. That was the moment.

Now I knew we were going to be remembered for something great rather than being heroic failures. No more 'if onlys'. No more 'what ifs'. All that heartache, all that sacrifice and pain. The flight home from Basel. The flight home from Kyiv. Full-time against Wolves. Knowing the

Premier League trophy lift is happening somewhere else. All those setbacks drifted away. They were not a millstone any longer. They were not something to use to criticize us as a team. They were part of our fight to get here and, without those setbacks, what we achieved in Madrid that night would not have had the same meaning. It's our moment now. All those setbacks make it even more special when you actually get over the line. To have setback after setback and keep going, to go on again after losing, makes it even more special.

All this was in my mind as the stage was assembled for the trophy presentation and, because of everything that Jürgen had done for the club, I wanted him to lift the trophy. While we were standing on the pitch, watching the Spurs players collect their medals, I leaned over to Millie and told him he and I were going to lift the trophy together.

'Fuck off,' he said, in a way that only he can. 'You're the captain – you're lifting the trophy.'

I did the same with Jürgen. I got the same reaction. Of course, it was a massive honour for me to lift the trophy, but I also knew instinctively in that moment that winning the trophy was enough for me. The weight of a lifetime of striving for acceptance had fallen away from my shoulders. Winning was enough. That was my dream. That's all I wanted. To get over the line was everything.

In the end, I listened to what Millie and the gaffer said and, if I'm honest, I didn't protest too hard that I was going up on my own! The UEFA president, Aleksander Čeferin, handed me the trophy with the big ears. I heard him say 'congratulations', but my concentration was elsewhere and I turned to walk the few steps with it to the part of the stage where the lads were waiting. I wanted to be able to see my team-mates when I had the trophy. I wanted to be looking at them, not have my back to them. I wanted to be able to see their faces and how happy they were.

So I took the trophy over to them, then I did a little shuffle, turned and lifted it over my head, and I don't think I've ever shouted or roared like that in my life. I let it all out. At some point after that, as we walked around the pitch, celebrating with our fans, I spoke to Des Kelly, BT's interviewer, and tried to sum up what I was feeling. 'It has been difficult over my career,' I told him at one point. 'But I kept going – just like this team kept going.'

I thought I had let it all out, but then I found myself on the other side of the pitch and I saw my dad standing there. If I thought I had let it all out before, now I went completely. To see my dad so soon after winning the Champions League final, something he and I had dreamed of together, and after all he had been through . . .

He was standing with some of the other players' families, and I walked over to him with my arms out wide. That was a moment for me that was meant to be. I don't know how he got there, and I don't know why I was over there. As soon as I saw him and we embraced, I was so emotional. It wasn't just the dreams we had had about me winning the Champions League. It was also because I knew what he had been through over the last few years. He lost his brother, his mother and his sister all in a very short space of time. It nearly destroyed him. My nana had been a big part of my life too. She was there for me when my mam and dad split up and I went to see her whenever I could. Anyway, my dad had been hit by one thing and then another. It seemed like our hug was going to last for ever.

I was emotionally spent by the time we got back to the Eurostars Hotel. You would think that when you win the Champions League, the high would last all night and that you'd be bouncing up and down and laughing and the life and soul of the party, buzzing with the joy of it all. But I was the opposite. I was gone. People were coming up to talk to me and congratulate me, and I wasn't there. It was as if I couldn't take it in. I couldn't believe that we'd done it. I couldn't believe that this quest I had been on, this quest for fulfilment and for respect, was over. What brought everything home to me was seeing my best mate, Ryan. Here we were, twenty-six years on from when we'd first been together in nursery, standing with the greatest trophy of them all. I couldn't tell you how many Champions League games we watched together growing up, so for us to be holding that trophy together was just incredible. Being with him that night meant the world to me.

I know that what I was feeling wasn't particularly unusual. I've heard sportsmen talk about it before. You chase a prize for so long that, sometimes, when you win it, it feels disconcerting. It's amazing, but there's something missing too. One of the things that drove you has gone. The quest that has dominated your life is over. There was something I couldn't process and, in the days after winning a trophy, you feel emotionally drained – hung over, almost – because you want the rush of the celebration but don't know when it will come along again.

I had been chasing the Champions League all my life, and now I was just dealing with disbelief. I was trying to work all that out when somebody came up to me and said, 'Stevie's here.' I looked around the room. We were in a basement area at the hotel and the lights were low and I couldn't see him. Someone pointed to a far corner. Stevie was there with a few of his friends and family, right out of the way. He was delighted, as a Liverpool fan, to be there, but he wasn't there to get in the glory. He had always embodied so much of what I aspired to be, but he was also someone who had been a support to me when I took over the captaincy from him. Even after the first year of having Jürgen as manager, I had sought him out when I was on holiday in Los Angeles and asked him if we could have lunch.

When I was feeling vulnerable, unsure of my place in the team and unsure of whether I was wanted as captain, we sat down for a couple of hours, and he was brilliant. He told me to get my head down, to be ready to take my opportunity and to try to enjoy having a great manager at the club. As I walked over to the corner of the room where he was sitting, I thought about what he'd said about how I'd be judged as skipper on what the team won. I went over and hugged him. I asked him if I could have a picture with him if I brought the trophy over.

'Not tonight, mate,' he said, smiling as broadly as I'd ever seen him smile. 'This is your night, go and enjoy it. This is nothing to do with me.'

12. Surf's Up

The days after beating Tottenham were a blur. We returned to Liverpool for an open-topped bus parade with the trophy the following day, and I wish my words were as good as the pictures I've got in my head for what I saw that day as we made our way around the city. I'd been told all about what had happened in 2005 and the homecoming ovation that Rafa Benítez's squad received, but this was a joke. I kept getting messages from people saying they'd had the best day of their lives. I could only reply to them, 'To be fair, mine's been better!'

There was to be no rest. A couple of days later, I was in Trent Alexander-Arnold's room in Portugal. We were there for the Nations League finals. We'd just had a training session with England, but our heads were still in the Estadio Metropolitano, and Trent had an idea.

'Let's get tattoos!' he said. 'We should get the Champions League trophy tattooed on our calves.'

I haven't got many tattoos. Just ones of my kids, which are on my ribs. Straight away, I said I was up for it, though. 'You'll do it, too, right?' I said. It was he who had suggested it, after all. 'One hundred per cent,' he said.

We were both going to Los Angeles for our summer break, so I thought I'd send Daniel Agger a message. Dan knows everything there is to know about tattoos; he's covered in them and is a qualified tattoo artist. I was sure there would be someone he would be able to fix us up with in LA. I liked the idea we could turn up and know we were getting it done properly by someone who had been recommended.

I told Trent I'd contact Dan and that we could get them done while we were in LA; we could just turn up and know that they'd do a good job. 'Yeah, yeah, yeah,' Trent said. 'Brilliant. Love it.' I wanted to triple-check with him before I organized it. 'You're sure, aren't you?' I asked again. 'You're absolutely sure?'

He said, 'Yeah, yeah, yeah. Absolutely.'

So I texted Dan. He said it wouldn't be a problem; he knew someone not far from LA and that he'd arrange it. A week later, he messaged again. All sorted, he said. He gave us the date, the time, the location, who we needed to see. Everything. Brilliant.

It was a place called the Klockwork Tattoo Club in Covina, California, about twenty miles east of downtown LA. I'd worked out the route for us and everything. The night before, Trent and I had gone out to get food. We were both staying in Beverly Hills. I was in a hotel; he was in a villa somewhere. At the end of the evening, I arranged to pick him up the next morning and we'd head out to Covina.

'I'll pick you up at eleven,' I said.

'Yeah,' Trent said. 'Sound.'

So I pulled up outside his villa at 11 a.m. I thought he might be waiting, but it was quiet. I waited for a bit, then he came out. He was looking a bit sheepish.

'Come on,' I said. 'Get in.'

'Erm,' he said quietly. 'I can't come.'

'You what?' My face dropped. 'What do you mean, you can't come?'

'I can't come,' he said again. 'I can't come because my mam says I'm not allowed.'

This is a wind-up, surely, I'm thinking to myself.

'You fucking what?' I said. 'Get in the car, man. We've got to go. Are you serious? Your mam says you can't get a tattoo?'

He *was* serious. It turned out that Trent had mentioned the tattoo to his brother, Tyler, and Tyler had mentioned it to his mam, and his mam had rung Trent up and basically said, 'You're not getting a tattoo. End of.'

I hadn't known any of this while I was standing there like a lemon, waiting outside his villa. I kept telling him that we needed to go, that everything had been sorted out. Next thing, he had appeared, looking very serious, and said his mam wasn't happy. It started to sink in that this really wasn't a wind-up.

I shook my head. I thought about not going at all. But I thought about Dan and the trouble he'd gone to and I didn't want to let him down. So off I went. It was an hour's drive out of LA to get this tattoo on my quad. I waited around for a bit when I got there, but the guy was brilliant. He got the details of the trophy, put the date on and everything.

That night, I'd arranged to meet up with Trent for some food.

'Go on then, can I see it?' he asked when I got there.

'I shouldn't even be speaking to you, should I?' I said. I forgave him, but I still haven't forgotten. He still owes me a tattoo . . .

Tattoos aside, I've got an awful lot of time for Trent in every way. I remember the first time he came to train with us at Melwood. At that time, we were on separate sites, with the Academy down in Kirkby. Immediately, he had a different feel about him personality-wise. He was quite serious, intense, but I liked that about him. He trained hard, he wanted to impress. I could see similar traits from when I was that age. I don't think it's unfair to say he didn't stand out straight away in terms of vision and passing in those sessions at Melwood, but his work ethic was beyond reproach. For Trent, coming over to Melwood must have been like coming into a different world. I'd say it was quite daunting for him too, but he made sure the basics were right first and then he built on that.

It seemed to come out of nowhere when he made his full Premier League debut against Manchester United at Old Trafford in January 2017. Nathaniel Clyne had fallen ill the night before, and during our pre-match walk near the Marriott Hotel, opposite the old Granada Studios site, the gaffer took Trent to one side to break the news to him that he was playing.

He'd played against Tottenham in the League Cup a few months earlier, but he'd known that was coming – Jürgen had told him twenty-four hours before kick-off to give him time to get ready. But this was a big deal. Here it was for him: *bam!* Premier League, Old Trafford, 75,000 in the stadium. The thing is, I didn't really worry about Trent. He seemed to have that composed mentality and steady ambition, even though he had not long turned eighteen.

I was a fan of his, for sure, but our relationship at that time was very formal.

Trent would go everywhere with Ben Woodburn, another talented young lad, and we called the two of them 'The Pups'. They would stand with their arms behind their backs when they were speaking to the senior members of the squad, like they couldn't relax. Things changed for Trent and me when we were in Russia at the World Cup the following year. Trent had been outstanding in 2017–18, so much so that he was one of our better performers against Real Madrid in the Champions League final and he did a great job on Cristiano Ronaldo. But he was a shy lad and it was hard to get anything out of him.

It was all very professional, I'd say. In Russia, though, we bonded. It changed from being just professional to friendship off the field. *Love Island* was a big thing, then – yes, I know it still is now – but he would come to my room, we'd watch it together and have a bit of crack about it. Then a few more lads would come in, and we'd start talking about different things – holidays, personal life. Normal stuff, really. From that point, it just blossomed. We'd go to play table tennis and we'd be on it for hours because we both absolutely hate losing. We are quite competitive, to put it mildly. But I won – obviously!

Trent seemed different then, after he came back from Russia. He felt part of the group. I'm still quite hard on him. I love him to bits, but I want to keep him on his toes. His mum and his dad and his brothers are a great influence on him. He's been brought up well, with that work ethic, and he's very respectful. I could see straight away when I met his mum, Diane, that he'd had good people around him to get to where he has got to. Diane came up to me in one of our first meetings: 'You tell me if he's not doing the right things – I mean it,' she said.

Over the past year, I've had to think about our relationship more carefully. As a young lad, you can offer pointers and you can joke, and maybe I could even patronize him a bit with the benefit of my experience, but when you become more established and successful in your own right, as he has become, I have to think about what I'm saying.

His talent is frightening. He's a potential Galáctico. He's a generational talent, someone who has to achieve everything that he can. He's so calm. He'll make a mistake in a game, and it doesn't bother him. He'll try an ambitious pass and he'll lose the ball. The next time he gets it, he'll try the same thing and lose it again. I'll be glaring at him, as if to say, 'Are you sure about this?' Then he tries it again and it comes off. He does what he thinks is right. He's got that level of confidence to keep doing the right things rather than taking the safe option.

I wish, when I was his age, that I'd had that level of confidence. Even now, I wish I was like that. Trent can run a game from right back. He deals with situations like he is thirty. It's not arrogance; he's just got confidence that others don't have. His development was one of the reasons we flew out of the blocks at the start of the 2019–20 season.

We still had unfinished business with the Premier League trophy. It was the one thing that had eluded us. It was the thing that had caused us more pain and heartbreak than any other trophy we had chased. It would be thirty years at the end of the season since we had won it. It was time to bring that sequence to an end. Winning the Champions League in Madrid was a big moment for us. It was huge for everyone – the players, the manager and the club. That gave us a massive confidence boost. We had proved we could be winners and we were determined to prove it again.

And add to that confidence the fact that we had an extra desire to put things right in the Premier League. When we came into the new season, the Premier League was the one that we wanted. The focus had shifted. The focus was heavily on the domestic title.

We did a pre-season tour of the States in the summer after we won the Champions League. We played at Notre Dame in South Bend and at Fenway Park in Boston, and the big screens at those stadiums were always showing a montage of the win in Madrid and the amazing crowds that had greeted us in Liverpool when we paraded the trophy through the streets the next day.

But there was a feeling among the lads – and from the manager – that we had to draw a line under this somewhere. This wasn't a victory parade any more. We'd had the parade. Jürgen called a team meeting, and he said that when we left America, we were going to draw a line under the Champions League. That was gone now. We had more to do.

We went to Évian-les-Bains in France, on the shores of Lake Geneva, when we got back from the States. We had been there the year before too, and that's where we did the hard pre-season graft, double sessions and intense training. And this year, Jürgen asked Sebastian Steudtner, the world-champion high-wave surfer from Germany, to put on a presentation for us at our hotel.

It might seem unlikely, but it was a critical moment in our season before it had even begun. We had come up short against Manchester City in the league before even when we thought we had given absolutely everything and could have given no more, but Sebastian's demonstration was all about showing us that people can find new limits all the time. Essentially, it was about dealing with mental pressure. It was about mind over matter and how to remain calm in the most difficult moments when you are trying to find new ways to overcome things that have stopped you before.

Sebastian started off by showing us a montage of himself in action, focusing on incidents when he'd come off his board and gone under water. He was talking about dealing with pressure and having to be ready for any moment. He said he could go months without riding a big wave but then suddenly he would get a call telling him he needed to be at a certain beach the next day because the big one was coming and he had to be ready.

When he's on his board, it's life or death. If he makes the wrong decision, it's game over. So it's all about being clear in your mind and not fearing what the consequences might be. It's doing what he's practised and learned. After the introductory part of his talk, he took us away to the swimming pool in three groups of ten. His first challenge was for us to get our heads under water and see how long we could last before we had to come up for air. Plenty of us were emerging spluttering and coughing after twenty or thirty seconds.

He told us to work on a technique. He asked us to hold on to the side of the pool and lie face down in the water and then to concentrate on our bodies, to think about our toes, our legs, our arms – anything other than our breathing. Then he told us to go under again. Part of the point of it was that when you reach that moment of stress and you're desperate to gasp for air and you think you can't last any longer, find a happy place, change your focus to something else and remain relaxed. Don't fight the feeling. Think about relaxing your fingers, arms, shoulders, legs, toes. I went under again and focused on what he had said. I thought about being at home with the kids and relaxing with them and, rather than rushing up for air, I came up slowly and they told me I had been down there for more than two minutes.

Adam Lallana's time under water was something crazy, like three or four minutes. Everybody had improved their numbers. The whole idea was that when you feel you're at the end, when you feel you have reached your limit, you are actually only at about fifty per cent of your capacity. It was all about positive psychology, how the body can keep going when the mind is trying to tell you there is nothing left. Maybe it was a coincidence, but it was a feature of that season that we won some crucial games with a series of late goals. Millie got the winner for us at home to Leicester with a penalty in the fifth minute of added time on 5 October; we got a draw at Manchester United on 20 October when Ads scored an equalizer in the eighty-fifth minute; we got past Spurs with a seventy-fifth minute winner from Mo at Anfield on 27 October; Sadio grabbed a winner at Villa Park on 2 November in the fourth minute of added time after Robbo had got a late equalizer; and Bobby got the decisive goal at Crystal Palace in the eighty-fifth minute on 23 November.

Towards the end of that sequence, we had swept Manchester City aside 3–1 at Anfield. I'd had a bit of flu in the build-up to the game and hardly trained, but I managed to play for over an hour and I set up the goal for Sadio that confirmed that win. When we beat Palace, it took us nine points clear of City. We felt we were unstoppable.

With that comes the confidence that, no matter what stage the game is at, you've always got a chance. Our attitude was that we never give up and we always go right until the very end. It was something the manager addressed early on at Liverpool. He could see that if we conceded a goal, the mood would change a little bit. He talked about changing doubters to believers, and that's exactly what happened, in the crowd and in the dressing room. We kept going and going and going until the whistle blew and it was over.

The main idea that Sebastian had wanted to get across was that you might be tired, you might suffer adversity, but keep going; change your focus, think about what you're

When Virgil Van Dijk has got your back, like in this match at West Brom in April 2018, it's never a bad thing. I knew his signing would help us make the next steps.

Feeling the pain in the Champions League semi-final against Barcelona in May 2019, but nothing was going to hold me back that night.

What a feeling when Mohamed Salah scored our first goal from the penalty spot against Tottenham in the 2019 Champions League final.

Tears with my dad after our victory over Tottenham in Madrid had been confirmed.

A hug with Jürgen Klopp that was my way of saying 'thank you' to the gaffer.

erpool fans sing how we have 'conquered all of Europe', and this was our crowning moment in
drid's Wanda Metropolitano stadium in June 2019.

ing the trophy with my best mate, Ryan Royal, he after-party. We've known each other since were three and he's like my brother.

A permanent reminder to that victory over Tottenham!

We will never stop the fight against racism and all other forms of discrimination.

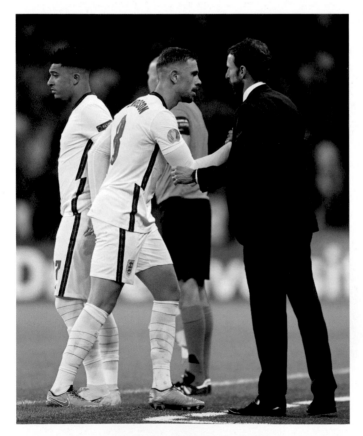

Making my way off in the fina[l] of Euro 2020 before the pen[alty] shoot-out.

y ultimate ambition when I joined Liverpool in June 2011 was to win the Premier League one day, and
achieved that aim in 2020. It was an unbelievable journey, and you can see in my face the contentment
scaling that summit. It was a surreal night, being in Anfield without any fans due to the pandemic, but
ting the trophy on the Kop felt symbolic for everyone.

is is me, Adam Lallana, James Milner, Andy Robertson and Trent Alexander-Arnold the night we got
trophy in July 2020.

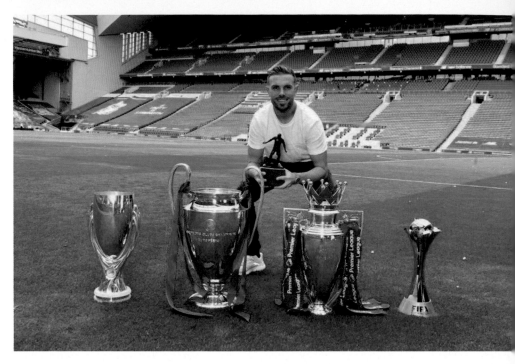

At Anfield with the European Super Cup, the Champions League, the Premier League and the Club World Cup.

Receiving my MBE from the Duke of Cambridge at Buckingham Palace in July 2022.

...ttling with Chelsea
...ender Marcos Alonso
...*) in the Carabao Cup
...al, February 2022, and
...*ow*) in the FA Cup Final,
...y 2022. These were two
...es of unbelievable
...ensity, but we got our
...ards and I was over the
...on to be able to lead our
...m up the steps at
...mbley on both occasions
...get the trophies. It was
...y the second time in
...erpool's history they had
...n both domestic cups in
...same season.

The bus tours around Liverpool, parading trophies, were two of the greatest days of my life, experienc
I will never forget. This picture was taken in 2022 after a remarkable season had just ended. Calvin Har
(*centre*, white shirt) supplied the soundtrack to an unbelievable party.

I am surrounded by winners at Liverpool and I'm surrounded by winners at home. Everything is right i
the world when I am with Rebecca, Elexa, Alba and Myles.

doing, and whatever you think your limit is, double it or triple it. That's where you should be aiming. If you feel tired, tell yourself you're not tired. That's the attitude we adopted the whole season.

Just before Christmas, when we already had that healthy lead at the top of the table, we travelled to Qatar for the Club World Cup and beat the Brazilian side Flamengo in the final. It was another proud moment – I was humbled to be the first Liverpool captain to lift that trophy. I was getting a taste for it too, as we had also won the European Super Cup in August, beating Chelsea on penalties. I knew which trophy I wanted more than anything, though. City had lost to Manchester United just before we flew to Doha, and they lost again on 27 December, to Wolves. We hit the ground running when we got back and stuck four past Leicester on Boxing Day. By 2 January 2020, when we beat Sheffield United at home, we were fourteen points clear of City, with a game in hand.

Our lead grew and grew. We just kept winning. Internally, the narrative was always 'Next game, next game, next game,' and we didn't look beyond that. The lads would always wind me up because I was the king of caution. In front of the cameras, I would always stick to the line that the next game is the biggest game and it's not over until it's over. It's boring, I know, and it doesn't give the headlines people want, but that's not my way. I didn't just say that on camera either. I said that in the dressing room too. I never really looked at the league table. Robbo would wind me up the worst. He'd ask me whether we were going to go to Las Vegas to celebrate when we won the title, then he'd ask me where I'd organized for the title party. I'd have to walk out of the room. We had been so close before, and I just wouldn't tempt fate.

I also knew what City could do. I'd seen them put together incredible runs before, and it would have come as no surprise if they could do it again. You had to basically prepare for City winning every game until the end of the season, so I told Robbo if we won every game until a certain point, then fine, I'd accept we were going to win it. But then we did win every game and still I couldn't bring myself to acknowledge it.

People started talking about whether we would go the whole season unbeaten too. We'd got to the New Year without losing, and I would be lying if I said it wasn't a goal. When we got to February, we started thinking that would be pretty special. Only two teams – Preston North End in 1888–9 and Arsenal in 2003–4 – had ever done a whole season without losing a game. Jürgen used to get asked about it at most press conferences, and I know he saw it as an irritation. Maybe he didn't quite see it as an irrelevance, but he wanted us to keep our eyes on the prize, which was the title. Nothing else mattered.

We beat Manchester United 2–0 at Anfield on 19 January to move into a sixteen-point lead at the top of the table, and for the first time our fans sang, 'We're gonna win the league!' Carra even started singing it in the Sky commentary box too. When we got to late February and we had a twenty-two-point lead with eleven games to play, even I had to accept that if we didn't win it from here, something would have had to have gone dreadfully wrong.

When we went to Vicarage Road on Saturday, 29 February we knew that a win there would establish a new English top-flight record of nineteen victories in a row. Watford hadn't won for their last five matches and were on the edge of the relegation zone, but they outplayed us that day. We couldn't deal with Ismaïla Sarr and Troy Deeney, and they won comfortably, 3–0.

Maybe we were starting to slow down a little bit. We had lost to Atlético Madrid in the first leg of our Champions League second-round match in the Estadio Metropolitano and we had squeezed past West Ham 3–2. But the title was in sight now. Media outlets were calling us 'champions-elect'.

I had just started to become aware of Covid-19 by then. I'm quite insular during the season, like a lot of players. I don't pay too much attention to anything apart from football. I bury myself in it. Covid wasn't something that I was giving a lot of time to. I was aware that there was an issue in China, but it seemed remote. We'd had scares like this before, with things like bird flu, but the effect on us had always been marginal. I assumed this would be the same.

I'd read about it on the BBC website, but I heard Millie, who is probably the most engaged of all of us in current affairs, saying this was different, this was serious, but I still did my best to bury my head in the sand. But on the day we lost to Watford, five Serie A matches, including Juventus's home game with Inter Milan, were postponed due to the coronavirus outbreak in Italy. It was getting real.

The Premier League banned pre-match handshakes; matches in Spain and France were played behind closed doors; PSG's Champions League game against Borussia Dortmund was played behind closed doors. There were suggestions that the Cheltenham Festival should be cancelled, but it went ahead. There were also suggestions that the second leg of our Champions League tie with Atlético should also be behind closed doors, but it went ahead as normal, including a large contingent of travelling fans from Spain. That influx of fans was later linked to a Covid outbreak on Merseyside.

Things were closing in and there was more and more concern about Covid and its effects. Suddenly, it felt like a matter of time until we stopped playing. We tried to focus on the Atlético game, but Covid was looming over us. It wasn't an excuse for us losing the tie after extra time, though, because it was the same for both of us.

We still played well and should have won the game. I wasn't aware of how tense the manager was, but he did say to the media later that that game was the only time in his career where his head wasn't properly in it. When he'd walked down the tunnel out on to the pitch beforehand some fans had leaned over to try to high-five him, but he'd waved them away. When Diego Simeone, the Atlético manager, went to shake his hand before the match, Jürgen bumped elbows with him instead.

The day after the Atlético game was a day off. I saw on the news that Mikel Arteta, the Arsenal manager, had tested positive for Covid and that Arsenal's game against Brighton, scheduled for the weekend, had been postponed. The second leg of City's Champions League tie against Real Madrid was also postponed, after the Madrid players were forced into quarantine. The next day, 13 March, the inevitable happened: the Football Association, the Premier League, the EFL and the Barclays FA Women's Super League and FA Women's Championship collectively agreed to postpone the professional game in England until 3 April at the earliest.

We had come in for training that day, and we didn't know what was going on. I was bewildered by it all. When we arrived, it was fairly apparent we were turning up for training for the last time in a while. Jürgen got everyone in the canteen and he said the league was going to stop, we weren't allowed to come into training and that he didn't know when we'd be back. He told us to go home and said we would stay in touch via WhatsApp groups.

He sat on the side of the snooker table and made a short speech to everybody. He talked more about community than football. He told us there was something more important going on here. He said we had to take care of each other. He reminded us that some people in the squad and on the staff would be by themselves. It woke me up to the seriousness of what was going on. It was a very powerful message. I know it was naïve, but part of me was still thinking this couldn't happen in our society, but the manager cut through that. He said we had to become a community and we had to look out for each other. He was very worried.

Driving away from Melwood that day, it all felt very unnerving and surreal, but I still thought it would last a couple of weeks and then we would be back in. How wrong I was.

13. #PlayersTogether

I trained at home to begin with. Then my family went to the Lake District for a few days, so I went with them. I did a bit of road running around Lake Windermere and then it was announced by the Prime Minister that there would be a lockdown so we went home and stayed in the house. I was okay. I was with my kids. We've got a decent garden. But what about the lads who were on their own in a flat in Liverpool? What were they doing? How were they getting food? How were they getting by?

Most days, we would do a Zoom group session, just trying to talk and joke and have some interaction, being there for each other, trying to keep each other's spirits up, thinking about what Jürgen had said about looking after each other. I did a bit of yoga and we organized some group sessions that we all filmed on our phones so Jürgen could see we weren't slacking.

I thought about football. I thought about the league. I felt guilty about worrying about whether football would resume and whether we'd be allowed to come back and win the title. I couldn't help it, but I felt shallow and selfish for worrying about that when people were dying and the news was full of images of nurses in PPE, working themselves to exhaustion, trying to save people's lives.

But even when we were talking about life and death, even when I was worrying about my dad, because I knew he would be in a vulnerable category, thoughts crept in about the league. I was also aware some people in football were trying to use the situation for their own benefit and get the league annulled. Some were agitating for the leagues to be cut short and decided on a points-per-game basis.

Their stance usually had more to do with self-interest – particularly whether a certain method of ending the season would save them from relegation or guarantee them promotion – than it did with the interests of public health, but that's normal in football. It's a business, and these people were trying to protect their own business interests, though it didn't look great.

Was there a point when I thought the league might be taken away from us? Yes. I'd like to say I wasn't thinking about it because there were more important things in the world, but that would be a lie. And I was aware that some people were making the argument that the Premier League season should be declared null and void and we should just start again next season.

My own opinion was that we didn't know how long the lockdown and this crisis were going to last, so we should wait until it was safe to start playing again and then resume from where we left off. It was easy for me to say that, I know. It was a simplistic solution that didn't take into account complex issues like television contracts and rebates to broadcasters.

The thing is, we had put everything into a season that was three-quarters done, and it was my view that you couldn't just cancel it. You have to finish it off. That might be in August, September, October, November. Whenever it was, we'd just restart. What was the rush? The priority was making sure that everybody was healthy, everybody was fine, and then, at the right time, we'd take off from where we'd left off. This wasn't about me, or Liverpool, or football. It was about people's health.

What I didn't want to do was to get into a public slanging match about what was to be done. I felt that would be utterly inappropriate and totally insensitive. I was coming under pressure from some people outside the club to speak out against the idea of null and void, but I didn't want to do that. I spoke to Jürgen about it, and he was very much of the same mind. It was just too ugly to do that. It didn't sit right.

I wasn't going to start moaning about wanting to start playing again. How would that look to people who were dealing with the loss of their loved ones, or were worried about their jobs, or were clinically vulnerable and desperately worried about their health? Of course I wanted to start playing football again, but not so much that I wanted to ignore what was right and wrong.

I didn't see my mam and dad for a long time after lockdown began. My dad got Covid quite early, and he texted me to say he was struggling to get up the stairs because he couldn't catch his breath. I was conscious, obviously, that he'd had cancer and that his system might be compromised. I was aware that this could go wrong quickly.

My cousin, Stephanie, is an NHS nurse, and I was hearing stories about nurses holding iPads for loved ones so that they could say goodbye to patients because no visitors were allowed into the hospitals. There were reports about all the people on ventilators. When my dad came down with it and was starting to struggle, I spoke to the club doctor and we got an oxygen monitor sent up to his house.

The doctor told me that if the reading was below a certain level they should call the ambulance, because it sounded like he was close to being in trouble. I got my dad to do it and told him to tell me what the reading was and to send me a photo of it, because I didn't trust him not to play it down. The reading was just in the safe zone. Not far into the safe zone, but it was in it.

It took him a month or so to get over it properly, but he was all right in the end. I worried about the kids a bit, but then you heard it didn't really affect kids. I was in the same boat as everyone. There was so much uncertainty and so much that was unknown.

Very much on the lower end of the scale of worry, I had to get Bec to cut my hair at one point. I had my barber on FaceTime, trying to tell her what to do. I had ordered some trimmers for her to use, because my hair had got to the stage where it had got ridiculously long. It was a bit of a massacre, that haircut. At least it was obvious I hadn't broken the rules by getting a professional in to do it! People took one look at mine and said, 'Yeah, that was definitely his missus.'

I appreciate I was in a fortunate position, but there were elements of the lockdown that I loved. I hardly see my kids during a football season, and I felt that lockdown brought me closer to them. I was doing online lessons with them at school, Elexa and Alba were doing guitar lessons on Zoom, and I was doing them with them.

And I was rested, too, even if we had just welcomed a new addition into our house. Myles, my son, was born on 6 February 2020, and the beauty of lockdown was the ability to see him every day — that wasn't the case when the girls arrived, so to have this opportunity to be with him, undisturbed, was amazing. The bond we formed must have been strong because he's now my little shadow, following me everywhere I go.

There was quite a lot of dialogue between players at different clubs, particularly through Captains Calls that were held on Zoom at least once a week. Early on in the lockdown, when we had all seen pictures of nurses working to breaking point in hospitals, overwhelmed by the numbers of coronavirus patients, we began to formulate plans for collective donations.

We didn't quite have time to finalize them, though, before some politicians decided that in the midst of this national crisis, it would be a good idea to turn footballers into scapegoats. 'I think everybody needs to play their part in this national effort, and that means Premier League footballers too,' Health Minister Matt Hancock said. 'The first thing that Premier League footballers can do is make a contribution, take a pay cut.'

It was a strange intervention. In fact, I found it bizarre. I can only assume Hancock was under pressure and felt the need to deflect. And well-paid footballers were an easy target. 'He felt the players should be doing more,' Tyrone Mings said soon after that. 'Maybe some players felt the government should be doing more. It wasn't a time to be concerned about who was doing the most or being seen to be doing the most.'

As I said, the discussions about the players doing something had started before Hancock got involved. I had spoken to a few different players who wanted to try to help but didn't really know how. You're sitting at home and seeing that we haven't got enough PPE and the NHS staff are overwhelmed. We're sitting in a privileged position – nice house, nice garden – but on the television, it's carnage. What can we do to help?

I had got a sense of that desire to help on the Captains Calls anyway. There was a consensus that a lot of people looked up to footballers and that people love football in this country, so let's try to earn that a bit more at a time when so many people are facing hardship and pain. I rang all of the captains individually to get an idea of what they thought. Every single one of them was on board immediately. What can we do? How can we get together? By doing something together, it made it more powerful. Regardless of what team you play for and the rivalries in which you're involved, this was bigger than all of that. This was helping the people that need it the most.

So I organized a separate Zoom meeting for all the captains and I had a list of things I wanted to speak about. Other people threw ideas around too. Everybody agreed it would be more powerful doing everything together rather than in our individual teams. We decided that the people who needed help the most and who we could make an effective contribution towards helping were the

NHS staff. I had family members who were working for the NHS, and some of the other lads did as well. Stephanie works at a hospital in the north-east, and she told me they were overwhelmed. Some of the detail was like horror-movie stuff. She was working on the wards, and she's a very bubbly and positive person and will always try to keep her spirits high, but it was tough to listen to what she had to say.

We came across NHS Charities Together, a charity whose slogan is 'Making the NHS go further'. Among its aims are ensuring that staff have somewhere to rest during busy shifts, providing dedicated counselling support for those who are struggling with their mental health and funding training for staff so that they can support each other better. I spoke to Ellie Orton, the NHS Charities Together chief executive, and we talked about channelling money towards staff, volunteers, gift packages, paying for occasional hotel stays for staff who couldn't go home because they were working such long hours, and funding the provision of more PPE. I went back to the other club captains with the information and they were all in favour of any money we raised going to the people who needed it most.

I knew that however much we gave, it would never be enough. The lads could give tens of millions and I knew it could be spun that it should be tens of millions more. We all decided that whatever we raised between the players and whoever else got involved would be kept private. It wasn't about putting figures out there and saying 'Look what we've done.' It was about raising as much as possible and giving that support to the staff emotionally, giving them a boost by feeling they had our support.

I went to my Liverpool team-mates and told them the proposal we had discussed. I told them it wasn't compulsory. And, by the way, there were lads donating to foodbanks and putting money elsewhere that no one will ever know about. They were doing things off their own back. We didn't ask them to give a specific amount. It could be £200 or £200,000. It was up to them.

Setting it up was a lot harder than I thought. I was having meetings constantly. Bec was asking, 'What are you doing? I've got three kids here – I've just had a baby by the way!' I was upstairs on the phone all day. I knew I needed to sort it out, and it took over my life for a while. I was trying to organize everything. Other players at the club were helping. Millie was brilliant in the background.

If we were all going to donate money, how was that going to work practically? If we set up a fundraising page, it would be public and everyone could see it, and part of the idea was that it should be confidential. I didn't want it to be public. I spoke to a bank and asked them to set up a private account; the money would then go from the account to NHS Charities Together. We had to have a few different players as guarantors. We set all that up. We gave the details out to the captains, and they went to their players and gave them the account number and we went from there.

Some teams said it was up to the individual players. A lot of players agreed to donate a percentage of their wages so that it was deducted at source. The lads at Liverpool were amazing with that. I didn't want to know, really, about other teams and how they were organizing it. It wasn't a competition. It was just about chipping in and seeing what we could raise.

We raised a lot of money. How much was never made public and I don't think it's right for me to make the figure public, but we're talking millions and millions of pounds. And I've visited hospitals that have benefited from the money footballers donated and I've seen the great work the charity has done with it in terms of the staff's mental health and well-being.

On 8 April we released a statement that made the initiative public. It read:

Over the course of the last week, we, as a group of Premier League players, have held numerous talks together with the vision of creating a contribution fund that can be used to distribute money to where it's needed most in this COVID-19 crisis; helping those fighting for us on the NHS frontline as well as other key areas of need. This is a critical time for our country and for our NHS, and we are determined to help in any way that we can.

'We can confirm that after extensive conversations between a huge number of players from all Premier League clubs we have created our own collective player initiative, #PlayersTogether, and have partnered with NHS Charities Together (NHSCT) in order to assist them in generating and distributing funds quickly and efficiently to where they are needed most.

NHSCT is the national umbrella organization for over 150 registered NHS charities, working closely with the

Charity Commission, the Department of Health and Social Care and NHS England to represent, champion and support the NHS's official charities. NHSCT is the official charity partner of the NHS nationally.

The contributions that this initiative will generate will help NHSCT quickly grant funds to the front line to support in a number of ways, including to help enhance the well-being of NHS staff, volunteers and patients impacted by COVID-19 as well as helping them in their work supporting many other critical areas of need both now and in the longer term.

#PlayersTogether is about we, as players, collaborating together to create a voluntary initiative, separate to any other club and league conversations, to help get much needed funds to those that need it right now. To try and help, along with so many others in the country, make a real difference. Our prayers and thoughts go out to everyone affected by this crisis. By sticking together, we will get through this.

The England and Scotland women's players got involved, and so did players from the lower leagues. I think the statement was the powerful thing for the NHS staff, the idea that we had come together for them. Troy Deeney and Mark Noble were brilliant in helping to formulate the initiative; Kevin De Bruyne, too. They were all great. Every single captain.

Everybody blames each other in politics and it never seems to be about what's best for the country. I wanted what we did as footballers to be a positive for the whole country.

There are lots of rivalries in football, but we all came together. There were players who didn't know each other, maybe there were some who didn't like each other, but we all came together for something that was much bigger.

I feel massively proud of what the players did as a collective. Players get judged. I know a lot of players who do endless stuff behind the scenes, for different charities and organizations and foundations, and no one will ever know. The public perception of players is probably based around the idea that the majority of footballers don't really care and are a bit arrogant. That's not the case in the dressing rooms that I'm in. There are other players from other clubs who I know well, and that is not the case with them either. Most players want to help as many people as possible. You go through our leagues and there will be a lot more players doing good than otherwise.

Yes, I understand people who question the money some leading footballers earn. When you put it into perspective and you have someone who saves lives and someone who plays football, then the money we earn doesn't marry up. I get that. I understand why people say they should be earning a lot more and we should be earning a lot less. That's why a lot of players feel like they want to help: because we know we're in a privileged position.

That's why more and more players have charities and foundations. Most of us come from working-class backgrounds and that brings a conflict of feelings when you suddenly have money. When you're a kid, you don't want to become a footballer to earn millions of pounds. You don't understand money. You play football because you love playing football. Even if we went back to a time when players earned minimum wage, I would still have wanted to be a footballer. Fortunately for me, at the time I became a professional footballer and was able to pursue a job doing what I loved, clubs were paying a lot of money to employ us.

I didn't create that; none of us did. It's the way it is. To get to play at the highest level in English football, to play in the Premier League, is an odds-against ambition. Hundreds of thousands of kids fall by the wayside trying to make it. I almost fell by the wayside. The ones who make it are one in a million. You've got to be extraordinarily lucky to have football as your profession.

If you play in the top tier of English football, the money is high. It's a market. It's supply and demand. When you think about transfer fees, it's mind-blowing, but that's not something I can control. I don't play football for money. I try to teach my kids that this isn't normal, having a nice house and nice holidays. I'm not extravagant, and I try to keep their feet on the ground as much as possible. I want them to have a nice life, but I never, ever take the money for granted.

Being in this position, I can help people who are less fortunate than me. Look at what Marcus Rashford did: he helped people that couldn't afford to eat. We have got money, but if we do good things with it, if we use some of it to help others, then I'd like to think that is a positive for our society, not a negative.

Look, English football's changing. In fact, it's already changed. In a football dressing room, all I'm interested in is 'Are you a good guy? Are you good at football? Are you going to help the team?' Creed, colour, sexual preference – none of that matters to me. You be who you are going to be and you will have my support a hundred per cent, as long as you give everything for the team.

I haven't really been educated on it. I haven't taken lessons about diversity and acceptance. It's just what I believe in, and if I can use my platform and profile to help people who don't have a voice, then why wouldn't I do that? Our dressing room at Liverpool is tolerant and diverse, and if a player came out, it wouldn't matter at all. I am totally convinced of that. And it would be the same in the England dressing room.

We are more enlightened as player groups now, I'd say. Social media can also bring positives. It can educate you, too. I might be wrong, because I can only judge on the dressing rooms I'm in with Liverpool and England, but from where I'm sitting, it doesn't matter about any of those things at all. Religion, sexuality, colour of skin – it's irrelevant.

Yes, it's about 'Can you help us win?' But it's more than that. Are you a decent person? Are you going to fight for me? Because I'm going to fight for you. When the chips are down, are you going to have my back? Because I'm going to have your back, and I don't care about anything else. It's about the core of people. How they are as a person inside. Everything else is irrelevant.

I started playing in an era that was still a bit old school, but things have evolved now and I have adapted the way I think. I'd say I am fairly typical of what footballers are like today, to be honest. I'm uncomfortable with getting credit for, say, sticking up for my black England team-mates who were jeered and abused and targeted in Bulgaria. Everyone else stuck up for them too. We're a team, we're friends, and we know what's right and wrong. It's fairly basic stuff.

There's no point me preaching about these issues either. Who am I to tell people what to do when I am white, privileged and straight? I can offer my support, but I can't really hope to understand the pain of being discriminated against when I haven't experienced that kind of dis-crimination myself. All I can do is do what I think is right.

I've never liked seeing people ostracized or bullied. It's how I was brought up, I think. It's how most of us were brought up, I'm sure. If there are campaigns that promote inclusion, I'm keen to back them. I've worn a Rainbow captain's armband and rainbow laces in my boots on England duty. Again, I don't see that as worthy of praise, really. Why should I get praised?

It's part of a simple message: football is for everyone.

14. #BlackLivesMatter

In the midst of a world of so much turmoil and uncertainty, George Floyd, a forty-six-year-old black man, was murdered in broad daylight on a street corner in the US city of Minneapolis by Derek Chauvin, a forty-four-year-old white police officer, on 25 May 2020. The murder was filmed by a passer-by. We watched it on our televisions.

A wave of outrage washed across the world, and the reaction in sport was no different. Sportsmen and women everywhere used their profiles to call for change and education and to support the idea that black lives matter. Sport was still dislocated by the coronavirus crisis, but when the NBA resumed in the US at the end of July, every person present knelt in support of the Black Lives Matter movement during the national anthem before the New Orleans Pelicans and Utah Jazz played in Orlando.

All the players, coaches and staff members of the Pelicans and Jazz, along with all the officials, wore shirts reading 'Black Lives Matter', and it was also printed on the court. Many locked arms with those next to them, while some players raised fists in the air.

When England played the West Indies at the First Test in Southampton on 8 July, players dropped to one knee in support of the Black Lives Matter campaign and West Indies players wore black gloves on their right hands in an echo of the Black Power protests made famous by US athletes at the 1968 Mexico City Olympics. 'All we want is for black lives to matter now. It's as simple as that,' the former West Indies fast bowler Michael Holding said.

Soon after the murder, Virgil and Gini came to me and said they wanted to make a gesture of some sort too. On the first weekend after Floyd's death, four Bundesliga players, including Jadon Sancho, had made gestures of support. Jadon wore a T-shirt calling for 'Justice for George Floyd'.

I agreed that we ought to do something, and I thought it would be more powerful if we did it as a collective. We were still more than a fortnight away from the resumption of the Premier League, but we were in training again by then and Virgil and Gini came up with the idea of taking the knee at Anfield after our session there the next day, 1 June. All the lads were on board and felt it was the right thing to do to send a statement out there, and hopefully, others would follow. We knelt around the centre circle and the club posted the image on social media, accompanied by the caption 'Unity is Strength #BlackLivesMatter'.

On one of the Zoom calls with the Premier League around that time, we were discussing Project Restart and the initiatives we were taking around the NHS and the logos on our shirts, and Troy Deeney voiced his frustration and anger about the fact that the topic of race had not been mentioned. He and Wes Morgan felt that we should be doing something as a league. He felt the subject was being ignored because people felt awkward about it. I don't think people knew what to do. Troy was a bit angry that

that conversation hadn't happened yet. He wanted us to do something as a league and all the other captains agreed.

That was when we came up with the idea of having Black Lives Matter on the back of our shirts and taking the knee before kick-off. That was led by the players. It was something that we had seen happening before NFL games in the past when the San Francisco 49ers quarterback Colin Kaepernick had taken a knee to protest against police brutality and racism.

It was what we felt was right. Troy and his wife also designed a logo for the sleeve of our shirts to keep that momentum going once the Black Lives Matter words came off the back. We got a bit of criticism around that time because of suggestions that the Black Lives Matter movement had become political and people said we were supporting a political movement. We had stated very clearly it was nothing to do with that. It was not political. We just felt that racism was wrong and we were not going to stand for it in the English game. We wanted to raise awareness, set an example and start conversations that would promote education and openness in the discussion of racism in our game and in society.

We knew that some people would try to take us down and misrepresent the message because a lot of people are still uncomfortable with footballers having an opinion and having the confidence to air it. Some people still look at players having a view about anything other than groin strains and 4–4–2 and say, 'Stick to football.'

I'm sorry, but the time has passed when footballers kept their mouths shut about important issues because they were scared to court controversy. Social media and the reach that it carries has changed a lot of things. You have a platform and a profile, and you have a responsibility, I think. If it's something you're passionate about and you have experienced yourself in life or you want to help people, then why not express an opinion? Why wouldn't you help people? Why wouldn't you use your profile to achieve some progress in something you are really, really passionate about?

If Marcus Rashford had kept his mouth shut and stayed in his lane, would millions of kids have benefited from what he has done? And what he has done is incredible, by the way. He made a huge difference to families across the UK who are struggling, all because of his profile, and he is passionate and he understands being in that situation because he has been there himself and he has been through it. For him to remember where he has come from and to work to bring about real change – I think it would be a sin not to do that.

Look, I don't think I should have an opinion about anything and everything if I'm not properly informed about it. People can look at me and say, 'You're white, you haven't got a clue what it's like to be racially abused.' I get all that. But I have friends who are black and they tell me I can still make a difference by speaking out because I am white.

I saw Danny Rose, Raheem Sterling, Wilfried Zaha and Marvin Sordell racially abused when we were playing for the England Under-21s in Kruševac in Serbia in 2012. I was alongside Danny and Raheem when they were racially abused, again, in Podgorica, Montenegro, in March 2019, and I saw Marcus and Tyrone, in particular, racially abused when we played against Bulgaria in Sofia in October 2019. That kills you. You feel helpless. We're close. We're friends; we've known each other for years and years. It would be wrong not to support them.

I would have walked off the pitch there and then in Bulgaria if one player had wanted to. No problem. We all said that if anybody wanted to walk off, we would stand with them. On that occasion, all the lads felt that if we had walked off, we would be letting the racists win. By staying on and punishing them in a football way, that was better. That was the consensus.

I was really angry in that game, and I had an argument with the Bulgaria manager, Krassimir Balakov. I could hear what was going on. Every time we scored, I was overly aggressive in my celebrations. We just felt as a team that not one player wanted to walk off. We made it clear I didn't mind being the person to lead us off, and Harry was the same.

I'm pleased that we're still taking the knee. Again, I know there has been opposition and, even though I wasn't there, I heard about the tens of thousands of Hungarian kids booing us for doing it in Budapest during a Nations League qualifier earlier this year, in a game that was supposed to be behind closed doors. Some people say it hasn't achieved anything and, if that's the case, that's a reason to keep doing it. But I think it *has* changed things. When we were doing it in the build-up to Euro 2020, some booing went round, first at the Riverside Stadium in Middlesbrough, and even at Wembley. You can hear that while you're on the pitch, and you're thinking, 'This is exactly the reason we are doing this. People are not getting this.' Eventually, those boos became fewer and fewer and the cheers louder and louder.

It was decided after that Zoom call with the Premier League executives that the anti-racism message should be an integral part of Project Restart, but we still had to be aware that different people had different views on whether and when we should start playing football again. I spoke to different captains about their views and what the general consensus was among their team-mates. I wasn't trying to convince them one way or another about going back to training. I wanted to try to understand what the differing views were at other clubs.

We started a regular Captains Call on Zoom, and there were occasions when we talked to experts, like the government's deputy chief medical officer, Professor Jonathan Van-Tam, and the Premier League's medical officer, Mark Gillett, about the conditions that would have to exist in order for the players to think about returning. I tried to be as honest as I could, forgetting about our position in the league, doing what was best for my team-mates but also what was best for players across the league in general. If players didn't feel comfortable going back, then my stance was that I was more than happy to wait until they were. The idea that players should be rushed back against their will was unacceptable.

Professor Van-Tam would come on the Zoom calls and explain the risks. He was under pressure from some of the lads, who were asking questions, and maybe sometimes he could not give definitive answers, but he would answer as honestly as he could and, from that, you have to make your own decision. I was relaying this back to the lads, and there was so much to process and pass on I felt like I was becoming a health-care administrator.

Some of the worries about going back were clearly absolutely legitimate. There was a period where there was evidence that ethnic minorities were disproportionately vulnerable to Covid compared to the rest of the population, and Professor Van-Tam gave a really strong answer about that. I was trying to feed this back to the players.

The dialogue was useful, but I did feel that whatever the players said, ultimately, was irrelevant. We could have been on those Zoom calls and we could have said we didn't want to go back and they would have ignored that because the Premier League is in charge. It doesn't matter what the players say. It matters what the owners say. 'We are commodities in the game and we accept that,' Tyrone said, and he was right.

If the players had said they didn't want to go back, the owners would have said we were going back anyway. The more we understood about the virus, about how it was transmitted and how the risk of spreading it could be reduced, the more players wanted to go back. I wanted to go back because I was listening to the advice I was being given by people whose learning and expertise I trusted.

The initial plan was to restart training in twos and threes, keep socially distanced, so the risk was reduced, keep your family at home, come in in your car and kit, turn up, park, walk on to the pitch, do a bit of a session, get straight back in your car, drive home and have a shower there.

Most of the Liverpool lads were satisfied with what they were being told. Most of them seemed to be happy with the new protocols. I said anyone could ring me privately if they were concerned about coming back, but no one got in touch. We were all happy to listen to the experts and base our decision on their advice. When we restarted training, everyone came back in. We were still at Melwood then, and the weather was beautiful, which helped with the fact that everything was outdoors. We had to drive to the academy to get our Covid tests first. Then we had time slots for training.

There was a marquee outside at Melwood at one point, and you could go into it in a small group and perhaps do a few stretches in there. You could have a massage, but for a maximum of ten minutes, and the masseurs were dressed head to toe in PPE. I think we all understood it was necessary, but it was still a bit disconcerting.

The plans for Project Restart accelerated when it was announced that the Bundesliga would resume, behind closed doors, on 16 May. And on the twenty-eighth, the Premier League agreed to a new provisional restart date for the 2019–20 season of Wednesday, 17 June, provided that all safety requirements were in place.

I want to give credit to all the medics who put that plan together. It would have been easier not to go back, but we preserved the sporting integrity of the league through an extraordinary feat of organization and logistics. We can argue about motive all we want, but as players, it came down to one thing: we were going back.

15. The Formby Hall Barbecue

I was desperate to start playing again, but the world had changed since any of us had last kicked a ball competitively. I don't want to be glib about it, but I had changed, too. I'm fond of saying that football is everything to me, but when football stopped, I had to look at the world around me as well. And I couldn't just go back to football as if nothing had happened when a lot of people were still mourning for loved ones they had lost in the pandemic and trying to come to terms with the restrictions that were still being imposed on them.

Yes, I wanted to play again. But I was also acutely aware of how lucky we were, as players, that we were being allowed to go back to our jobs and do the thing we loved when that luxury wasn't available for most of the population. I told myself the return of football would allow supporters stuck at home a form of escape and that it would be a distraction from the hardships they had suffered.

That's what sport is for many of us, isn't it? A distraction, an escape. A release from the pressures of the real world. I thought football could fulfil that role more than ever at that point, after so much turmoil and isolation. It was the first time since the Second World War that English football had been stopped like this and, even if the matches were going to be behind closed doors, at least families could watch together at home. We had followed all the protocols, all the advice from Professor Van-Tam, and done all the testing, so we were as reassured as we possibly could be that we were not putting either ourselves or anyone else at risk. We knew nothing could be a hundred per cent safe but, by then, we were just eager to get going again.

There were more selfish reasons for me to embrace the restart too. I've already mentioned the guilt I felt about wanting football to begin again so that Liverpool could win the title for the first time in thirty years. There were times during the lockdown when football had felt insignificant set against the suffering so many families were going through, but now that we were on the verge of playing again, it was tantalizing to be so close to something the club had craved for so long. We needed a maximum of six points to win the league.

It was more than a hundred days since Leicester had beaten Aston Villa at the King Power Stadium in the last match before the shutdown on 13 March, and the first match back looked different as well as feeling different. The players of Aston Villa and Sheffield United took the knee before their match at Villa Park on Wednesday, 17 June and, as we had agreed, the words 'Black Lives Matter' replaced their names on the back of their shirts.

The second game of the restart was Manchester City's home game against Arsenal, and we knew that if Arsenal could win at the Etihad, we could win the league when we played our first game back against Everton at Goodison Park that Sunday. No such luck. City played brilliantly and won 3–0. We were still twenty-two points ahead, but we wouldn't be able to finish things off in the Merseyside Derby.

There had already been ten Premier League games since the restart when we played at Everton that Sunday evening, so we had a bit of an idea of what to expect. An empty stadium was the main thing. The only atmosphere was generated by the players themselves and by the support staff and substitutes in the stands. It felt a little eerie.

The night before the game, we stayed at the Formby Hall Hotel just north of Liverpool and travelled to Goodison in three different buses. We sat at tables for two instead of tables for five or six. And when we got to Goodison, instead of going to the normal away changing room underneath the Main Stand, we went to a Portakabin behind the Bullens Road end.

To be honest, the Portakabin was an improvement on the usual changing facilities we get at Goodison, so there were no complaints there. It was much bigger and a lot nicer, so we were happy with that. The dressing room was all spaced out and our shirts, with 'Black Lives Matter' on the back and the NHS logo on the front, were hung on our pegs. We took the knee there in front of the cameras for the first time. It was a bit surreal because there were no fans. It felt a bit like playing for the reserves or a practice match at the training ground. I'd played a proper match behind closed doors once before, when England played Croatia at the Stadion HNK in the port city of Rijeka in 2018.

Croatia were being punished because a swastika had been imprinted on to the pitch before the country's Euro 2016 qualifier against Italy. That was the first time England had played a match without fans since 1872. Now, we were going to have to get used to it happening a lot more regularly. In that game in Rijeka, I was very conscious that I was the loud one on the team. Sam Wallace wrote in the *Daily Telegraph* that one of the things he had learned from the match was that 'Jordan Henderson plays football by talking his way through a game.' It was a fair observation, and I was conscious now that we were going to be playing in empty stadiums for the foreseeable future that I might have to rein my language in a little bit.

Someone said my language can be a bit 'raw', and I suppose that's a nice way of putting it. But there are up sides, too. When it's quieter, you can use your voice to greater effect. People can hear you. When it's a full stadium, I am screaming to try and make myself heard. Ten yards away, someone can't hear you if the atmosphere is really good. Or they can pretend they can't hear you.

But when there are no fans, it's a lot easier to get people's attention – and create an atmosphere on the pitch. If there's a tackle or we win the ball back, then you make sure that's acknowledged vocally – *and* it has an adverse effect psychologically with the other team as well. There was very little I could cling on to as a positive with the absence of our supporters, but I was determined to try and get any advantage we could and adapt to the circumstances.

I was certainly more conscious of how I spoke to the referee or to other players. I know I can get carried away, but we had prepared for what we were going to face by training at Anfield, specifically to get used to playing in an empty stadium. We played a practice match at Anfield too, against Blackpool. We wanted to replicate a match day, and they even played 'You'll Never Walk Alone' over the loud-speaker system before kick-off. We wanted to reproduce what it was like to play in a sterile stadium, but all it did was underline to us how important the fans are. Not that we needed reminding, but it underlined it. We missed it particularly at Anfield because our fans make the stadium a fortress, but having fans at an away game – fans that are often particularly vocal – is so important too.

Football's a totally different sport without fans. Every-thing is different. When you are playing in front of a crowd of fifty thousand people, you've got so many things to factor in: the effect when you make a mistake, how the reaction from the crowd affects you mentally, how it affects the team mentally. When you're subjecting a team to con-stant pressure, it's difficult for them to break out of it if the crowd is roaring you on.

Say you win the ball back high up and it goes out for a throw-in – it doesn't affect the other team that much with-out a crowd. With a crowd, at Anfield, it's a different world. When the atmosphere gets up, we increase the tempo and you can see panic in the defenders, who don't want to get on the ball. That changes the whole dynamic. Without fans, there is nothing. So we tried to create an atmosphere on the pitch ourselves by using our voices, screaming when someone made a tackle.

It was weird, but at least we had a reason to be energized by it, because we were trying to win the title. The Everton game was very sterile. Some people need a crowd to be able to perform. Some people perform better when there's no crowd. Some players would have liked the idea of going to play without a crowd, as if they were a kid and they were playing football for fun. Some people are liberated by an empty stadium.

There was definitely a theory during that spell of matches that strikers felt more prepared to shoot and be ambitious than they would have in a full stadium when they would be anticipating the groans they would get if they blazed the ball high over the bar or their fancy trick didn't come off. There may have been some truth in that.

I perform better when there's a crowd. However, I can get motivated without one. If I look at my performances in that period without fans, I can still see my motivation and my hunger. You try to forget everything in that moment and focus on the game. You just want to win. That's what it comes down to for me, ultimately. Just win. Things change. Crowd, no crowd; home stadium, away stadium – the goal is always to perform and win, and I have always wanted to win.

I didn't like hearing myself in those circumstances, though. We played Atalanta away the following season, when there were still no crowds, and Liverpool's social media team made a montage of me screaming throughout the game. I was trying to encourage my team-mates, at least. I seemed to say 'Love it' quite a lot. I think the social media people thought it was a compliment to me, but I hated it and I told them to get it off. I didn't want to see it – or hear it – but it did show how much I wanted to win.

Everton was like nothing I had ever experienced in English football. It's usually so hostile and loud and there's always a capacity crowd, and now there was no one there and you could hear everything. I like the hostility of Goodison when it's full. Our players love that. You don't realize how much you love it and how much it motivates you until it's not there. It was something we all had to adapt to.

We drew 0–0. It was the strangest Merseyside derby I've ever played in or ever will play in. The quietness of the environment just seemed to dominate everything. It had to happen, just to get it out of the way. It turned into an occasion that both teams had to overcome and, once it was over, there was a feeling we would relax into the next game a bit more. That was at Anfield, against Crystal Palace.

It was emotional being at Anfield that evening. Before lockdown, Palace at home was being circled as the game in which we could become champions, and you could imagine that the atmosphere would have been off the scale. So the sound of 'You'll Never Walk Alone' being played in the empty stadium and the thought of all the fans who would love to have been there hearing it in those seconds before kick-off made it very moving, and it inspired us. We were top drawer in that match.

The counter-press was very good and sharp and hungry, and we were all over Palace. Trent scored a brilliant free kick, one of those he whips over the wall so the goalkeeper has no chance; Mo got the second when he ran on to a great through ball from Fabinho. Fab bagged the third with a screamer, and then we scored a lovely fourth when Mo played a brilliant first-time pass to Sadio, who slotted it past Wayne Hennessey, their goalkeeper.

There was no crowd noise in the stadium, even if they added it artificially on the television, and it made the game seem completely different at times. I hit a volley through a crowd of players in the box and it cannoned off the post. It made a kind of metallic thud that you'd never be aware of normally when Anfield is bouncing. Its echo told me it hadn't gone in, but it didn't matter in the end. The win and the performance told us we were right on the brink of the title.

I came into the dressing room after the match and it was different level. People started banging lockers and it was getting louder and louder and louder. People were getting emotional. We were trying to create our own atmosphere and our own celebrations. There was a release after that Palace game, because it was such a good performance and we were so nearly there. There was this energy and relief. I'm the worst at celebrating, but this noise was like thunder.

There was no emotion from me. Not really. Not yet. I'm all for celebrating when we've won something, after a Cup Final or a Champions League, but we hadn't won anything yet. We were close, really close. But we weren't over the line. As far as I was concerned, I'd leave the celebrating and the emotion until no one could catch us. In this match, we hadn't won anything, so I wasn't dancing in the dressing room. We had another game coming – Manchester City away in eight days – and we'd celebrate when we'd won the title. So you're asking the wrong person if you want me to remember a dressing room where we haven't won any-thing. When it's done, I'll celebrate. But that Palace game, it wasn't done.

And I had more guilt creeping in. I wanted the fans to be there, and I felt cheated on their behalf, but I felt cheated myself too. The experience of winning this prize that the club had been chasing for so long wasn't going to be the same without them. I had to keep reminding myself how lucky we were just to be playing at all.

You've got people dying, people stuck in the house for months on end, and I'm disappointed because the fans aren't there and the atmosphere isn't better? Come on. You feel bad for thinking that. But Liverpool fans are obsessed with football and they had waited thirty years to win a league title, and for them not to be able to be there to share it with the players was hard. It was hard for the players and the fans because it means so much.

We went home that night, back to our families, as we weren't allowed to see anyone else outside our bubbles. The following morning, 25 June, we had to go back into Melwood to do a recovery session. A few of us had been calling each other on the way in, wondering if there was any possible way we could be together that night. Manchester City were playing Chelsea at Stamford Bridge and they needed to win to keep the title race alive. Most of the lads assumed they wouldn't drop points, but Jürgen was different. He told us, when we had all gathered at Melwood, that he had a feeling about the night and said we were all to go to Formby Hall.

A lot of the Formby Hall hotel staff had made considerable sacrifices for us, because they were part of our bubble and so they couldn't go home to their families. We couldn't bring our partners or our kids, but Jürgen said the entirety of our first-team bubble, including the kit men, the medical staff, the masseurs, and the players and coaches all had to be at Formby Hall that night.

The rules meant we couldn't have organized anything like going round to my house or another player's house in the same way that Jamie Vardy had hosted a party the night Leicester won the league in 2016. That would have been breaking the law, but we could all go to Formby Hall together. Everyone who was on Liverpool's Red Zone list could be there, legally and responsibly, as a work event.

Our staff had to do the cooking because there were no other guests allowed at the hotel, so we had a barbecue outside and put television screens up on the patio and had some food while we watched the Chelsea–City match. City dominated things early on, so the atmosphere was a bit subdued, but then, ten minutes before half-time, there was a mix-up between Benjamin Mendy and İlkay Gündogăn on the halfway line and Christian Pulisic took the ball on and slotted it past Ederson to put Chelsea ahead. The atmosphere at the barbecue wasn't subdued any more, and even Kevin De Bruyne equalizing with a stunning free kick couldn't dampen our spirits.

There was shouting and yelling everywhere as the game went on, people punching the air when Raheem Sterling's shot bounced back off the post and then holding their heads in their hands when Kyle Walker made an amazing clearance to block Pulisic's shot on the line. Then, thirteen minutes from the end, there was bedlam. There was a scramble in the City goalmouth and, in the melee, Fernandinho batted the ball off the line with his hand. The referee didn't see it initially, but VAR did, and Fernandinho was sent off. It was a penalty for Chelsea. It went quiet on that patio. Willian took it. Willian scored. Mayhem. It was carnage.

Then there was the wait for the final whistle. And when it blew, well, I did celebrate then. City were twenty-three points behind us with only seven games left to play. They couldn't catch us. It was over. Liverpool were the league champions for the first time in thirty years. Finally, I could admit to myself that we had done it and that no one was going to take it away. We were all hugging each other, high-fives, singing songs – it all went off. It was special because we were all together. Everything we had been through, missing out when we got ninety-seven points, all the worries over the pandemic, coming back together, wondering whether we would be allowed back to finish it – it all melted away for a little while.

I was very emotional. I'm normally emotional on the pitch, but this was different. Seeing how much it meant to them in that moment got to me. I was celebrating with people, and they were crying and hugging me. I realized how much it meant to everyone, some of them lifelong Liverpool fans, to be a part of winning the league. It was a special night. I spoke to my mam and dad on the phone and I was in floods of tears. My dad couldn't speak properly. I phoned him and I saw he had answered, but I was saying hello and there was nothing on the other end of the line. I was looking at my signal and thinking, 'Have I lost the connection?' but then I realized he was there and he just couldn't speak. Eventually, he got some words out and said how proud he was of me and the team. That got me, the fact that he was so moved. That really got me.

I got off the phone, put my sunglasses on to try and hide my red eyes, got myself back together, then went upstairs to do some interviews. Only our Red Zone personnel were allowed at Formby Hall so there were no broadcasters with us. We did stuff on the laptops for Sky News. I did some of the interview with Sky, and then I had to walk away from it. The emotion of it got too much for me. Jürgen had been the same. Sky had cameras in different places, one at Kenny's home, and that did for Jürgen when he saw him. Jamie Redknapp was in a studio in London, and I started welling up when he spoke to me; Jamie Carragher was at his house and lightened the mood when he started spraying champagne, telling me 'to get absolutely rotten' – I started laughing then and quickly made my exit, as the lads were running up and down the corridors singing 'Campiones!'

Usually, straight away, when you win a big trophy, you want to see your family. This time, I knew the family couldn't be there, and because I knew that wasn't even a possibility, I enjoyed celebrating with the players and the staff in a tight-knit group. When your families are there, all the players get lost with their own families. It's just the way it is. But this was just the players and the staff, people who had been on this journey together and lived every moment of it, all its highs and its lows, its setbacks and now its triumphs.

I'd always had this dream of winning the Champions League, and that night in Madrid had given me a kind of peace, but I also knew that winning the title in England was incredibly important to the club, perhaps even more important than winning the Champions League. The club has this amazing, emotional history with the Champions League, and I was all in with that, but the failure to win the Premier League for so long had left the club and the supporters desperate to get the trophy back. Liverpool used to own the title and we all knew deep down that, until we won it again, there would be something missing from the achievements of this team. We knew that the fans would never be satisfied until we had won the league again, until we could ram the taunts of United fans, about how long it had been since our last title, back down their throats.

Now we could do that. Now we were the club in the ascendancy and we had done it our own way and written our own place in the club's history. Jürgen has always been respectful of the legends who went before, but he was determined we should create our own story for the club, to give a new generation of fans their own memories. We deserved to stand with the giants who had gone before. It didn't mean we were their equal, by any means, but it did mean that we had done at least a part of what they had done by being able to be called the best team in the country and bringing the supporters the kind of happiness that the great teams of the past had brought them.

I will never forget the celebrations that night (nobody present will ever forget Jürgen's moves on the dance floor!) but the emotion of it all ensured the next few days were a blur. Maybe it's easy to forget but we were strictly limited about what we could do, so there were no big parties with friends or nights out in Liverpool. I found it difficult to sleep over that weekend, as things began to sink in, and I'm sure it was the same for the other lads. It meant all the tension had gone out of the meeting with Manchester City now. We still wanted to win it, obviously, but knowing we had been celebrating after clinching the title, I suspect not too many people would have had us down as favourites to beat Pep and his team. They would have been right.

City gave us a guard of honour as we came out on to the pitch, but they didn't look too happy to do it. They were 3–0 up by half-time and added a fourth when Ox scored an own goal. Some of the frustrations they may have had about conceding their title to us, they got out of their system that evening at the Etihad. It was a reminder of what a fine side they were.

After that, it was business as usual. We beat Villa at home and then, on 8 July, we played Brighton at the Amex. The game was going well until the seventy-eighth minute. We were 2–0 up within eight minutes and I had got the second of them with a curling shot from the edge of the box, but then, twelve minutes from the end, when we were leading 3–1, I challenged Yves Bissouma for the ball.

It was an innocuous challenge. The worst ones often are. There was no blame attached. It was just an awkward tackle and I landed badly and felt something in my knee. I heard a noise and I felt sore immediately. I tried to play on because I didn't want to believe it was as bad as I feared it might be. I thought it was my cruciate. I hobbled around for a minute, and then I had to come off. I sat in the changing room afterwards. I put a towel over my head and started crying. It was less than two weeks since we had won the title. I had had two weeks of uncomplicated happiness, but now that was over. All sorts of bad thoughts were going through my head. This could be serious. I could be out for the rest of this season and most of next season too. I heard what Jürgen had told the media when he saw me coming off the pitch.

'We all felt very concerned,' he said. 'It was an awful moment when he went down. We knew immediately. In Germany, you would say he is an animal. Hendo fights with everything. If he has pain, he will never tell you. He can really deal well with pain so in this moment it was a complete mood killer.'

Straight away, I started sending messages. Chris Morgan, our old head physio, who was working at Arsenal at the time, received one, because he is someone I trust implicitly. He has been there by my side through a lot of difficult times. He's always on the end of the phone, no matter what time of day, and has always got my welfare in mind. He'll put long hours in for you and you know he's got your back. I asked what he thought about the diagnosis. I knew he wouldn't want to tell me, but I also knew he could diagnose off the mechanism, by looking at the clip of how it happened. He could judge an injury sometimes by looking at the tackle and the way a player has fallen. He wouldn't want to say that. He might say to the manager what he thought it might be, but not the player.

I knew he wasn't going to tell me, but I was still saying to him, 'Come on, what are you thinking, because it doesn't feel great to me.' So I had the Game Ready, an ice compression to keep the swelling down, wrapped around my knee, and I left the Amex on crutches. I was fearing the worst. I was partly going off other people's reactions. And I looked at the incident back on screen. It looked awkward in terms of weight transference and, when it's awkward, it's never good. When I'm injured, I'm never the most optimistic. When I feel something, I know it's bad. I can deal with a bit of pain. That's fine. But when I've heard something pop and seen something, then I am fearing the worst.

Chris, who was about to rejoin us, will always give you positives. He'll tell you what you haven't done. He's good at reassuring players. There's no point worrying about stuff until you get the scan results back. When mine came back, they weren't great, but they could have been a lot worse. My big fear was that I had torn my anterior cruciate ligament, and that hadn't happened.

It was a medial ligament issue, but it wasn't going to need surgery. It would repair itself with rehab. I had thought I might be looking at seven or eight months out of the game, but actually it was going to be seven or eight weeks. The gaffer texted me: 'Brilliant, best-case scenario,' he wrote. I have been told subsequently that when Jürgen came out at Melwood and told everyone it was only going to be eight weeks, there was a big cheer.

I was relieved. But I was also upset. I'm not good with injuries. I hate being out of the game. After a few days, the relief wore off and the frustration set in. I started thinking about missing the rest of the season. Then I started thinking about things like the fact that I was supposed to be lifting the Premier League trophy after our last home game, with Chelsea, in less than two weeks and that I wasn't going to be able to be in my kit. The gaffer kept asking me when I was getting rid of the crutches because I needed to be ready for the ceremony.

There had never been a trophy lift in an empty stadium before. The Premier League asked us where we wanted to do it, and one of our ideas, given the country was in lockdown, was to do it in the dressing room. The Premier League said that wasn't feasible because there was a presentation party, it had to be formal, there had to be cameras, and it couldn't be enclosed. It wouldn't work.

'What about doing it in the Kop?' I suggested.

The Kop is the heart of the club. Lifting the trophy there was as close as we could possibly get to lifting it with the fans. So they dressed the Kop with banners and a tribute to those who had been lost at Hillsborough, and they built a platform in the middle of that stand for the presentation. It felt like the most fitting place possible to lift our nineteenth top-flight league title.

We tried to make it unique. The local authority allowed the players' families in for the trophy lift, but not for the game. They declared it two separate events. There were five hundred people allowed in for the game and then, after the match – which we won 5–3, by the way – was over, the families were allowed in the lounges in the Main Stand. I was off crutches and in a knee brace by then. The physio said they could tape my knee up and it would act as a temporary brace, just for the ten or fifteen minutes when I was at the ceremony. I made one more attempt to pass the duties on to Millie. He's helped me a lot since he came to the club. Millie doesn't get the credit he deserves for being a top player because he's another one that has maximized his career. He's the most professional player I've played with. Everything is done properly. He is so important to a successful team and everything that goes on in the background that people don't see. But he is a world-class footballer, more than anything. You can talk about all this stuff about him working hard, about him being a leader but what never actually gets recognized is that he is one of the world's best players. There aren't any other James Milners out there, I'll tell you that now.

'You're lifting it,' he said. 'Even if I've got to put you on my shoulders to do it, you're lifting it.'

The good news was, come the day of the game, my knee felt fine. Saying that, it still felt odd getting dressed in my kit when I hadn't played in the match we'd just won. I felt a little bit like an impostor. Again, I understand that there is a pattern here: someone who's keen to be a leader but who is uncomfortable in the spotlight. It wasn't that I felt like a fraud. I earned my share of what we had achieved, so there were no worries about that. But that was the point. I'd earned a share. I hadn't earned this prominence. I had the same old feelings: this wasn't down to me. If I was in an individual sport – tennis or golf – then that would be fine, but football is all about the team. Only teams win trophies, never individuals. This was everyone. Everyone had made the same sacrifice. I was the captain of a team that had achieved something. This team goes down in history, not me. I know people are just being nice, but it doesn't sit right with me.

Jürgen doesn't really get the captaincy thing. Or he certainly didn't when he first arrived in England. For him, the German culture is that it's the longest-serving player. He didn't get the obsession with the captaincy that the English have, but I think he came to appreciate that it's just a cultural difference. Liverpool have a tradition of great captains. It is a special privilege at this club. I did want the captaincy. But I wanted it in order to lead and to help.

It was glory enough for me to win these trophies, to be part of the team, to earn respect by winning the greatest competitions in club football. I didn't need anything more. Millie is as much of a leader as me, so why shouldn't he lift the trophy? He has done as much as I have in terms of the culture, leading by example, demanding everything from others.

Virgil has done the same, so has Robbo. We have got so many leaders, which is what you need in a successful team. That's where I find it difficult. If I hadn't met Jürgen Klopp when I met him, I wouldn't have become the player or the person or the captain that I became. He has helped me grow and do that. Surely he should be lifting the trophy? In my head, all this is down to him and to my team-mates. It's not down to me.

Yes, I have got to follow instructions and do what I do best and perform. But I can't do that without everybody else. The same thing applies to the #PlayersTogether initiative. None of that happened without all the other captains. So it came as a complete surprise at the end of the season when I was named Footballer of the Year by the Football Writers' Association. I was shocked and humbled. This was a massive honour, particularly when you see some of the legends who had won the award before.

And so I made it up the stairs to the special platform they had built in the Kop for the presentation. I forgot about my damaged knee when I saw Kenny standing there waiting for me in a red mask with the club crest on it. He hugged me when I saw him and told me he was proud of me, and that meant so much because, without him, I wouldn't even have been here. I was then handed a medal by Richard Masters, the Premier League's chief executive, which I draped around my neck, as was the custom in those days. I then took the trophy off the plinth, gave it a kiss, and then I walked on to the podium where the rest of the lads were waiting.

Bobby in a cool pair of sunglasses, Virgil with his hands raised to the sky in thanks, Robbo doing the shuffle, Sadio, Curtis Jones and Naby filming it on their phones; Mo with a flag draped around his neck, Div with his hair dyed silver, Ally bouncing up and down, Millie laughing, Jürgen hanging back with his black baseball cap turned back to front.

And it felt incredibly moving to be standing there together on the Kop. It was as if we could feel the spirit of the fans there, the ones who are still with us and the ones who are not. Everyone who has stood on the Kop down the years, everyone who has stood on its terraces or sat in its seats, everyone who has heard 'You'll Never Walk

Alone' being sung, everyone who has seen that wall of scarves held aloft on a Saturday afternoon or a Wednesday evening – every one of them shared that moment with us when I lifted that trophy into the air and we all roared out our cries of triumph. I joined Liverpool from Sunderland with the dream I would one day become a title winner. Fantasy had now become reality.

16. Strength in Adversity

We tried to sign a centre half to complement Virgil, Joe and Joël before the start of the 2020–21 season, but we couldn't get the transfer over the line. At the time, I wasn't too concerned. For some time, the club's strategy had been not to sign any player but to sign the right player, and even though occasionally this approach required a bit of patience, no one could possibly claim the strategy hadn't served us well. This was just one of those occasions and, anyway, my mind was more occupied with who we did sign. I'd played against Thiago Alcântara when I was a lot younger and I knew that he was a dream of a midfielder.

Thiago had just won the Champions League with Bayern Munich, but my most vivid memory of him was when England played Spain in the Under-21 European Championships in Herning, Denmark, in the summer of 2011. I was feeling quite pleased with myself because I had just signed for Liverpool, but then I came up against Thiago. That was a good Spain team. The midfield had Juan Mata, Javi Martínez, Bojan Krkić and Ander Herrera. David de Gea was in goal, but Thiago stood out above all of them. He was on another level. He was so good on the ball I couldn't get anywhere near him. His awareness and his touch were outstanding. I had never played against anyone like him before. I had nightmares for years after that game. We drew 1–1, and let's just say that result was better for us.

It brought me right back down to earth. It was one of those sobering experiences that made me realize I still had a long way to go. After that, I had always watched him and followed him and loved the way he played and now, suddenly, he was coming to Liverpool. That was a real thrill. He was something else, a player who would give us a different gear.

We made a decent start to the season. The first game, against Marcelo Bielsa's Leeds at Anfield, was a thriller that we won 4–3 with a late goal from Mo, who scored a hat-trick. It was a brilliant match, end to end, and I was impressed with Leeds. They played some terrific stuff. We beat Chelsea away and Arsenal at home. New season, just the same as last season. Except then we went to Aston Villa and lost 7–2.

It is hard to explain that result except to say it wouldn't have happened if we had been playing in front of supporters and not behind closed doors. We had also suffered the late blow of losing Alisson to injury on the eve of the game. When you lose such a key player and such an important presence at the back at a point when your preparations are already done, it is only ever going to be unsettling.

Sometimes, playing without supporters encouraged freak results. As I said before, strikers tried things they wouldn't normally try, and the team that's losing don't have their fans in the stadium to lift them. I'm not making excuses. I'm just seeking explanations. On the same day we lost at Villa, Manchester United lost 6–1 at home to Spurs. Some of those results were madness.

Losing 7–2 at Villa was nowhere near as big a setback when you compared it to the events that occurred in our next game, against Everton at Goodison, though. We took the lead inside three minutes when Robbo found space on the left and crossed for Sadio, who lifted his shot into the roof of the net from just outside the six-yard box. Again, no fans were present, but the joy of a derby goal can only ever be massive. We had started well and were looking to build on our advantage.

Three minutes later, though, catastrophe struck. Fabinho lofted a clever diagonal ball behind the Everton defence and Virgil ran to it. As he tried to play it, Jordan Pickford came flying out of his goal and launched himself at Virgil. He took Virgil out at the knee with his left foot and then cleaned the rest of him out with his trailing foot. It was a terrible challenge. It should have been a straight red card, but Jordan wasn't even booked. At the time, I didn't quite realize what had happened and how bad the tackle was. I could see that Virgil was in a lot of pain and then that he had to go off. I was thinking, 'Please, no, surely not.' The game finished 2–2 and, to add one last twist, I had what would have been a late winner ruled out by VAR for a very, very marginal offside against Sadio. To make matters even worse, we had also lost Thiago to injury, following a terrible challenge by Richarlison, for which he was rightly sent off.

If I couldn't get my head around the result at Villa Park, I found this result an irrelevance. We got back to the dressing room and Virgil was there. He was very quiet. In fact, the whole dressing room was quiet after the game, and it was nothing to do with the draw. You look back at the clip of the tackle and your hands go over your face. Why did VAR not see it? It was a horrible, horrible feeling in the dressing room. I could tell Virgil knew something was really wrong. Jordan contacted me shortly after and said he didn't mean it but I wasn't the one who needed the apology. It also wasn't the right time to speak to Virgil. He knew as he was sitting there that he was going to be out for a long time. Experience told him that.

On a practical level, we also knew how big he was for the team and what a massive blow his absence was going to be. The day after the derby, our worst fears were confirmed when scans revealed Virgil had damaged his anterior cruciate ligament and would need surgery. We knew when we heard that news that he would probably miss the rest of the season. It wasn't only the fact that Virgil was injured that made it so hard to take. It was also how the injury happened, and I think Virgil would have struggled to comprehend the same – how it happened and why the player who had injured him was not punished for what he did. As players, you know injury is part of the game, but it was a lot more difficult for him to accept because of that.

So now we were left with two recognized centre halves. Dejan Lovren had moved to Zenit St Petersburg in the summer and we were reliant on Joe and Joel. We knew that, in an emergency, Fabinho could fill in at centre half and that he was a more than decent replacement, but we were keen not to lose him from our midfield options. Less than a month later, though, we were hit with another serious blow. Joe Gomez and I were on the training pitches at St George's Park during the international break, preparing for an England game against the Republic of Ireland.

The day before, Joe and I had been doing recovery runs around the pitch after we'd played Man City the previous Sunday. He had played virtually every minute of Liverpool's seven games in twenty-two days since the October international break, and we'd been talking about different things, but particularly how well he had been playing and what good shape he was in physically. In Virgil's absence, he had really stepped up, and it felt as though this was his time to shine. I have always known he has the ability to be one of the best centre halves in the world. He just needed a decent run in the Liverpool side to start proving it.

The next day, we were training and he stepped in with the ball and tried to play me a pass fifteen or twenty yards between the lines. As he played it, I heard a noise, and then I heard him scream and he fell to the floor. There was no one near him. I didn't know what had happened, but it was clear he was in absolute agony. It was one of the most distressing things I've seen in football.

He was screaming that it was his knee, and the physios put an oxygen mask on him and were giving him gas and air. I stayed with him for a while and then moved away to let the medics have some space to do their job. I had my hands on my head. I was in shock, but more than anything, I was devastated for my mate. Joe is one of the nicest lads you could wish to meet and I was in disbelief that he could have had another setback.

They carried him inside on a stretcher. Gareth Southgate knew how upset we all were so it wasn't long before the session was done. I went in to see Joe. He was distressed, and I was too. He spoke to his wife, Tamara, on the phone, and then we put him in the back of an ambulance. And that was his season over.

When the club fixtures resumed, we were left with Joël Matip as our one remaining centre half and Fabinho as a stand-in. The thing was that Joël was struggling with various injuries too, and had been in and out of the team. Around the turn of the year, he got a groin injury that kept him out for three weeks, and there were games when I had been drafted in as a makeshift centre half. In fact, there were games when I was the starting centre half and players were drafted in to play alongside me. We were that stretched.

Jürgen had spoken to me about playing centre half. It was a real internal battle for me. Selfishly, I was thinking about myself and what I was having to give up, the role I was comfortable in and played in when we won the league. Part of me wanted to keep playing there because that was where I was best. But there was a bigger part of me that knew I needed to play in defence for the team. If the gaffer said I needed to play at centre half, then I needed to play at centre half. But the obvious dilemma we were facing was that we would lose me and Fabinho from midfield so we would just be shifting the problem.

I'd only played centre half once before, when we played the Club World Cup in Doha the previous season and

Virgil came down with a virus before the semi-final against Monterey. It was one game. It was fine. I did okay, we won 2–1 and we got to the final. But I said to Robbo beforehand, 'Don't be thinking you can go bombing forward like you normally do. You are in here with me and nothing gets down this side.'

That was one game and, of course, I was happy to do it. The idea of playing there regularly, however, scrambled my head, but the gaffer knows what he's doing and, in the dire straits we found ourselves in, his priority was to get as many senior players as possible on the pitch. We were going through a tough moment and we had lost big, big players, so I understood the need to go with established players, even if we were out of position.

By the end of January, we had officially lost all three of our starting centre halves for the entire season. Joël was the last to succumb. We played at Spurs at the end of a bad run of results and Joël injured both ankles before half-time. I don't know if he actually injured both ankles at the same moment or whether he'd come into the game carrying an injury to one and then hurt the other as well. But he left the ground in two surgical boots.

There was a level of farce attached to it now. I felt a bit guilty about it, because when he hurt himself, he was saying to the physio, 'I'm all right, I'm all right.' The physio was saying, 'You're not all right,' but we were so short of players already and I was yelling at the physio to let him play on if he was saying he was okay. When I saw him leaving the ground in two surgical boots, I realized I'd probably called that wrong . . .

I was playing centre half pretty much every week from Christmas. I did okay in some games, and I was trying my best, but we were missing so many good players. I didn't find the aerial stuff too difficult, but I did have a lot more respect for centre halves after that, which I'm sure would make Virgil laugh. What I did find difficult was that we play with a high line, so it's knowing when to drop, when to stay, when to play offside if there are runs coming. If an opponent has time on the ball and someone makes a run, it's hard to know whether to drop or go with the run. That was hard to gauge because there was a lot of space in behind sometimes, and it wasn't as if I had a load of previous experiences in my memory bank to use as appropriate.

Positional sense when there were crosses coming into the box tested me, too. Playing out with the ball was fine, easy, and that was what the gaffer was concentrating on. I felt comfortable with that. So it had its moments but, in the key moments, it was difficult. Through it all, we actually did well until midway through the season. We went top in December and won 7–0 against Crystal Palace at Selhurst Park the week before Christmas. We were top at New Year too, but then we went on a run of five games without a win, we were further weakened by Covid absences we could ill afford and things started to go suddenly downhill. In February and March, there was a spell where we lost six league games out of seven, including home defeats to Brighton, Man City, Chelsea and Fulham – a run that dropped us to eighth place. In total, we lost six straight matches at Anfield, which was just unbelievable. Now, instead of fighting to defend our league title, we knew we were facing a bitter struggle just to qualify for the Champions League.

By then, my club season was over too. On 20 February, in the first half of a Merseyside derby defeat to Everton, I ripped my adductor muscle off the bone and had to have surgery to repair it. I had an outside hope that I might be fit for the Euros that summer, but I didn't play another league game. In a way, though, my domestic season wasn't over. It turned out that even in this horrible year, there was more trouble around the corner. On Sunday, 18 April, the day before we were due to play Leeds at Elland Road, news broke that we were one of twelve founder clubs from England, Italy and Spain that had agreed to take part in a new European Super League.

It was being reported that six Premier League clubs – Liverpool, Arsenal, Chelsea, Manchester City, Manchester United and Tottenham – had signed up to a new Super League, along with Juventus, AC Milan, Inter Milan, Barcelona, Real Madrid and Atlético Madrid, which would see the establishment of a 'closed league', without the threat of relegation for the twelve founding members. Those twelve members, which included Liverpool, were quickly branded 'the dirty dozen'.

I couldn't believe that we would sign up to something like this. I was disappointed that our club's name was being associated with it, and I was disappointed that, by implication, I was being associated with it. Neither the manager, nor I, nor any of the Liverpool players, were told anything about the Super League ahead of time.

At the time, this hurt. Emotions and tensions were running high, especially for those of us who were caught up in it. With the benefit of hindsight and a cooler head, I've come to the conclusion that maybe our owners deserve a little bit of credit for that part of it. The fact that they hadn't told us meant we couldn't be blamed for it or implicated in it, at least by those who were willing to look into the situation properly. There was no sales pitch to players or agents, no attempt to sweeten the pill and no bid to use whatever popularity we had to try to influence supporters. Nevertheless, it still felt at the time as if they had put us in a desperately difficult position. There was, quite rightly, a massive outcry about the plans, and English fans showed again that they're the best in the world by mobilizing against the Super League and leading the opposition to it.

The opposition was pretty much across the board. From a personal perspective, I couldn't believe that our club was putting its name to a plan that would kill the Champions League less than two years after that competition had given us and our supporters one of the best nights of our lives in the Estadio Metropolitano. The trophy that I had lifted in Madrid didn't just mean something – it meant everything.

At Anfield, not far from the statue of Bill Shankly, fans had tied a banner on the railings that read 'Shame on You. RIP LFC 1892–2021'. It quickly became evident that there was going to be a popular uprising and, still being a football supporter myself, it meant I understood, respected and identified with what our fans were saying. How could I not? I know competitions change, and sometimes changes in football can ultimately be successful after initially being incredibly unpopular, but this felt like it was all too huge, too sudden and too ill thought out. Again, Liverpool's history informed my thinking. The European Cup had done so much to forge our entire identity, and while I'm not daft enough to think it will always remain the same competition run by the same people in the same way, I was absolutely certain that trying to kill it off in this way was not right.

What I disliked most of all about it was the fact that it would essentially be a closed league. Fifteen of the twenty teams playing in it each season would be immune from relegation. The whole essence of football, to me, is sporting integrity. It's about rewarding excellence, whether you're a big club or a small club. It's about clubs like Leicester being able to win our league or make the top four and then play in the Champions League.

I couldn't get my head around why we had signed up to it. I have spoken to our owners, to Mike Gordon and John W. Henry and Tom Werner, on many occasions, and they are bright, knowledgeable, smart people who have done an awful lot of good things for the club, and I couldn't marry up this plan with what I knew about them. I racked my brain trying to understand their approach, and what I would say is that, as owners, they have proved themselves to be innovative and brave enough to make the kind of decisions that others would shy away from because they are either too difficult or too unpopular. On most occasions, this has served them well, and we should remember that, but this time it was their undoing.

The day after the news broke we played Leeds at Elland Road and, as one of the founder members, we quickly became the focus of opposition to the ESL. Our coach was booed and there were shouts of 'Scum!' when we arrived at the stadium. Liverpool fans held up a banner as the players got off the bus. 'Love for the Working-Class Game Ruined by Greed and Corruption. Thanks for the Memories. RIP LFC.'

I was injured, and I wasn't allowed to travel to Yorkshire because of Covid restrictions, but when the lads got into the dressing room Leeds had put T-shirts underneath every peg that had the words 'Earn It' written on the front next to the Champions League logo. The Leeds players wore those shirts in the warm-up. I was angry about what was happening to our players and the way they were being targeted. It was as if it was the players who had come up with the idea and we were all behind it. We know we've got to earn it. Our whole attitude is about earning it. That's what drives us, earning it, so don't level this stuff at us. This wasn't Liverpool. This had been dreamed up by owners across Europe. The anger directed towards the twelve clubs was growing. Gary Neville and others were suggesting that the clubs who had signed up to the Super League plan should be docked points. Jürgen was asked about the proposals and it was put to him that a couple of years earlier he had voiced his opposition to the idea of a European Super League.

He said he hadn't changed his mind. He was still against it. 'I understand the fans' frustration,' he said. 'I'm in a different position. I don't have all the information, I don't know why the twelve clubs did this. The Champions League is the aim, I want to coach there, I like the competitive element, I like that West Ham can play maybe next season.'

We drew the match 1–1, but no one was too interested in the game. Someone pointed out that there wasn't too much point in us trying to qualify for the Champions League if we weren't going to be playing in the Champions League. Millie was captain that night, so he fronted up when television asked for an interviewee after the match. They asked him about the Super League, obviously.

'I can only say my personal opinion,' Millie said. 'I don't like it and, hopefully, it doesn't happen.'

The anger inside me grew about the way our players had been turned into targets. Things were getting deeply unpleasant for club staff too. They were being abused on their way into Anfield. At that point, I hadn't heard anything from the people at FSG so I phoned Mike Gordon and left a message asking if I could have a few minutes of his time. He rang me back, and the first thing he did was apologize for putting the players in this position. He also said that I and the rest of the players were free to say what we wanted about the Super League. We did not have to parrot a party line. There would be no repercussions for us if we spoke out against it.

To my mind, this was crucial. Mike has always hammered home the point that speaking your mind isn't just encouraged at Liverpool, it is obligatory, but it's one thing saying something like that and another thing entirely living up to it when the issue is as controversial as this one was.

It's for this reason and many others besides that I've always had a lot of respect for Mike, and this has never changed. He said he knew there were flaws in the proposals and that they had been released prematurely. He pointed out some of the issues FSG had with UEFA and with scheduling and he said they believed that if the plans had been presented properly, in time they could have benefited not just Liverpool but the English pyramid too.

Some of what he said made sense. It's not as if the way everything is run at the moment is perfect. I've been outspoken about some of the issues myself. The number of games we're asked to play, the way supporters are treated – these should be at the top of any reform agenda and football has a responsibility to hold itself to the highest possible standard on all fronts. We should always be looking to make the game better and to seek improvements wherever they can be found. We should also encourage ideas and new thinking because, without that, sports can stagnate and become stale. Innovation should be cherished. But with the Super League, there were three things in particular that I couldn't get past. The first was the way it had been launched out of the blue. The second was the lack of any kind of consultation beforehand. And the third – and most important to me – was the failure to enshrine sporting integrity as an absolute principle. Nothing was going to change my mind about that, and nothing ever will.

You shouldn't have an automatic right to play in any league. I know it works differently in the US, and that the NFL, the NBA, the NHL and Major League Baseball are essentially closed leagues. That's absolutely fine for those leagues, and they have been very, very successful, but that has never been part of our culture here and I hope it never will be.

I just couldn't comprehend the idea that a club would be given a place in this competition and then that club would never lose it. As a sportsperson, I couldn't get my head round that. We can discuss and debate UEFA's failings as a governing body, and the rights and wrongs of the Premier League voting system, and how money is distributed, but as an athlete I found the closed-league aspect of what was being proposed impossible to accept.

We hadn't had a home game at that point, but fans had left those banners I mentioned outside the stadium to convey their disgust about what was happening. A lot of our players were against the plans and were coming under pressure from supporters to take a public stance. We had a players' meeting and decided, as a group, to post a statement.

I said I would post it on my Twitter first so that, if there were going to be repercussions, they'd fall on me. The agreement was that I would post it and then the other players were free to repost it or not – whatever they wished. The feeling was that even though some of us might be in discussions with the owners about contracts or whatever, this was more important. We were against the proposals on sporting merit, and we were going to say so. The whole team rallied against it and I posted the statement up at nine o'clock on the Tuesday night. 'We don't like it and we don't want it to happen,' our statement read. 'This is our collective position. Our commitment to this football club and its supporters is absolute and unconditional. You'll Never Walk Alone.'

That evening, there had already been protests outside Stamford Bridge ahead of Chelsea's match with Brighton, and there were dramatic scenes when Petr Čech, who had an executive role at the club, went into the crowd to try to quell the unrest. There had already been reports that City were going to pull out of the project. It then became apparent that Chelsea had lost their nerve, too. The plan was falling apart. Two hours after we released our statement, FSG confirmed that they were pulling Liverpool out of the ESL too.

By the end of Tuesday night, every single one of the six English clubs involved in the European Super League plan had withdrawn and apologized to their supporters. The popular uprising by the supporters had shown again the power and the importance of the fans. The game belongs to them, and they had made their voices heard.

On Wednesday morning, John W. Henry released a video message attempting to draw a line under the whole affair and apologizing to Jürgen, to Billy Hogan, the chief executive, to the players and to the fans. 'I want to apologize to all the fans and supporters of Liverpool Football Club for the disruption I caused over the past forty-eight hours,' he said.

It goes without saying, but should be said, that the project put forward was never going to stand without the support of the fans. No one ever thought differently in England.

Over these forty-eight hours you were very clear that it would not stand. We heard you. I heard you.

And I want to apologise to Jürgen, to Billy, to the players and to everyone who works so hard at LFC to make our fans proud. They have absolutely no responsibility for this disruption. They were the most disrupted, and unfairly so. This is what hurts most. They love your club and work to make you proud every single day.

I know the entire LFC team has the expertise, leadership and passion necessary to rebuild trust and help us move forward. More than a decade ago, when we signed up for the challenges associated with football, we dreamed of what you dreamed of. And we've worked hard to improve your club. Our work isn't done. And I hope you'll understand that even when we make mistakes, we're trying to work in your club's best interests. In this endeavour I've let you down.

Again, I'm sorry, and I alone am responsible for the unnecessary negativity brought forward over the past couple of days. It's something I won't forget. And it shows the power the fans have today and will rightly continue to have. If there's one thing this horrible pandemic has clearly shown, it's how crucial fans are to our sport and to every sport. It's shown in every empty stadium. It's been an incredibly tough year for all of us; virtually no one unaffected. It's important that the Liverpool football family remains intact, vital and committed to what we've seen from you globally, with local gestures of kindness and support. I can promise you I will do whatever I can to further that. Thanks for listening.

This intervention was crucial, and it was also welcome. John W. Henry was one of the few who fronted up over the entire saga, and I think that is to be respected. Other clubs did not have the benefit of this kind of leadership, and it helped us that our owners had publicly drawn a line in the sand and accepted responsibility for what had happened. It wasn't quite the end of the matter, though. Ten days later, our match against United at Old Trafford had to be postponed because thousands of fans protesting against the Glazers and the Super League plans had massed outside the stadium and hundreds had then broken in and occupied the ground. It was another illustration of how trust can break down between owners and supporters in the top tier of English football. The only consolation for me is that I knew FSG were already working to repair the damage that had occurred. Like everyone else, myself as much as anyone, they can and do make mistakes, but history has proved that they also learn from them. By doing this they have restored Liverpool's reputation as one of world football's greatest and most powerful clubs, so as much as the Super League idea hurt me, and as much as I knew it to be wrong, at no point did I question that our owners were acting in what they believed to be the best interests of Liverpool FC. I just knew they had got it badly wrong.

When we finally played the rearranged game, on 13 May, we were in sixth place in the Premier League table and seven points adrift of Chelsea, who were fourth. We had two games in hand on them, though, and four games left altogether. We knew that, to salvage a Champions League spot from a desperately difficult season, we would need to win all four of those games. We won 4–2 at Old Trafford, but then three days later we went to the Hawthorns to play West Brom and it felt as if that dream of making the top four had disappeared. Hal Robson-Kanu had put them ahead early on, and even though Mo equalized after half an hour, the scores were still level going into injury time. A draw wasn't going to be enough.

We got a corner in the fifth minute of added-on time. Alisson came up for it. The idea that we had had a terrible season because the football hadn't gone particularly well felt shallow compared to what we knew he had been through. He was from a very close family in Brazil and a few months earlier his father had died in a swimming tragedy. I knew how deeply he had been affected by it and I was full of admiration for him for the way he had been able to perform on the pitch in the months that followed. Alli's the best goalkeeper in the world, but he's an even better lad, and we were all devastated for him. Covid travel rules meant he hadn't even been able to attend his father's funeral.

Trent swung the corner in and Alli got to it first. It was a brilliant glancing header, a header that any centre forward would have been proud of, and it flew into the back of the net. It was the last touch of the game, and when Alli emerged from the players who were mobbing in, he pointed his fingers to the sky and stared upwards. It was the first time a goalkeeper had scored a competitive goal for Liverpool in our entire history, dating back to 1892. It also moved us just a point and a place behind Chelsea in fourth, and three points worse off than third-placed Leicester with two games to go.

'You can't explain a lot of things in my life,' Alli said afterwards. 'The only reason is God, and he put his hand on my head today and I'm feeling very blessed. I'm too emotional, this last month, for everything that has happened with me and my family, but football is my life. I've played ever since I can remember with my father. I hope he was here to see it. I'm sure he is celebrating with God at his side.'

Jürgen's mother had also died a few months earlier and he, too, had been unable to attend the funeral, and the emotion of what had happened to Ally was very important to him too. 'We are really close,' he said, 'and I know exactly what it means to him. It's outstanding, really touching. It's only football, but it means the world to us.'

When we beat Burnley at Turf Moor in the penultimate match of the season, it meant we were in the fourth Champions League spot, level on points with fifth-placed Leicester City and with a goal difference four better than theirs, with our last game at home to Crystal Palace still ahead of us. We won the game 2–0 and finished third. There were ten thousand fans there for the first time since the pandemic, and they made it sound like there were a hundred thousand. When they sang 'You'll Never Walk Alone' at Anfield, after everything that happened, after the tragedies that had enveloped so many of the people we loved, it was incredibly moving.

Gini made his final appearance for us and got the incredible send-off he deserved. Nat Phillips and Rhys Williams, who had done such an amazing job at centre back in the second half of the season in such difficult circumstances, boys who had grown into men and helped the club when it needed them most, got the clean sheet their contributions had deserved. At the end of the storm, there was a golden sky.

It was a season where every nightmare seemed to have been folded into one campaign but, somehow, we had come through the chaos and the pain with something beautiful at the end of it. 'From nowhere to the Champions League in five weeks is a massive achievement,' Jürgen said. 'Fighting through this and finishing here in third is the best lesson you could learn in life.'

17. Penalties

It wasn't a good evening. I was on the bench for England's last Euro 2020 warm-up match, against Romania at the Riverside Stadium in Middlesbrough, and I was listening to jeers ring around the stadium when the lads took the knee before the start of the game. It had been the same earlier that week when we played Austria. What the hell's that about? A few days before a major tournament, and we get that reaction? I was disgusted by it.

We played okay in the game. It was a friendly, so the pace was fairly sedate. I came on at half-time for Kalvin Phillips, and this was important. Gareth Southgate wanted to give me forty-five minutes, and it was his last chance to gauge whether I was going to be fit enough to play a real part in the tournament. Gareth had been great with me, to be fair, and I was desperate to prove to him that I was in good shape.

It was good to be back, but I was conscious of the fact that I was patched up and there was no secret about that. I had been injured during the Merseyside derby at the end of February and needed to have surgery on my groin. The issue ended my season and it was going to be touch and go whether I made the Euros. Nobody wanted to miss this tournament, given that most of our games were going to be at Wembley, with the potential of playing the final of a major championship on home soil. I had been in contact with Gareth during my rehab to let him know how I was getting on. I've got a good relationship with him and I was grateful that he was going to give me every chance to prove my fitness.

In the end, though, it came down to this: there were internal stitches wrapped around the tendon to help it heal properly inside. Sometimes you can leave them in and they won't cause an issue. On other occasions, the body can react to them because you've got foreign matter inside you and the body naturally tries to push it out of the wound. I found it amazing that my body knew this and was trying to push the stitches out.

When that happens, there's always fluid and puss coming out, so the wound won't heal. I knew it wouldn't heal until I got them out, but I couldn't get them out until after the tournament if I wanted to play. So I made the decision to put up with it and made sure I looked after the wound until the time came when I could have a procedure to get them taken out.

Then again, this was a bit different. I needed help and I was having painkillers and anti-inflammatories to get through it all. I was meant to have some involvement in the game against Austria, but I'd felt a bit of discomfort in my groin before the match, so we left it alone. A few days later, I was more confident about the problem and when I got on, it felt good to be back. Things were going okay; we got a penalty in the sixty-eighth minute when Jack Grealish got fouled and Marcus Rashford took it. He buried it low to the goalkeeper's left to give us the lead; Marcus had done his job and, soon after, Gareth took him off.

A couple of minutes after his substitution, we got another penalty. Dominic Calvert-Lewin had been fouled. He might have been expecting to take the penalty, but I told him I was having it. That's not like me and, looking back, I know I wasn't thinking straight. I felt I needed to make an impact in the game to make sure I was in the squad, but it was stupid. There was also another thing. I'd won fifty-eight caps, but I'd never scored, and I wanted to change that before the tournament started. So I took the penalty. I hit hard and true to the keeper's right, but he guessed correctly and pushed it out. There was a rebound, but we scuffed it.

We won the game 1–0. I gave an interview after the match and I tried to make light of the penalty miss but, inside, I was fuming. What the fuck had I been doing? It didn't cost us and it was a friendly, you could argue, but that wasn't the point. I felt I had let people down and, for the first time I can ever remember, I had let my own agenda get in the way of the team. I still can't believe I did it and I hate the fact I did it.

I saw Roy Keane later on the television, giving some analysis, and he spoke as honestly as he always does. I know Roy knows me inside out.

'Jordan's not fit,' he said. 'I don't think he should be involved. He can't be right. People say they want him around the place. For what? Does he do card tricks? Does he have a sing-song? Does he do quizzes in the evenings? Surely he doesn't want to be around, being some sort of cheerleader?'

Still, I made the squad. We were allowed three extra players because of Covid, so Gareth could afford to get some people in that wouldn't necessarily have made it, and maybe that's what got me in. I told myself that even if I didn't start to begin with, after the first couple of games I would have trained more and hopefully had some minutes to then start later in the tournament.

My desperation to be involved, aside from the fact that we were going to be based in England for a tournament that was being played right across Europe, was down to my belief that we could go all the way. I knew enough about tournament football to know we would need everybody to play a part if we wanted to win it. I wanted to make sure everybody was ready to go when they were called upon – even if they were not involved to begin with.

Our first game of the tournament was Croatia at Wembley. I was on the bench and didn't expect anything else. Kalvin and Declan Rice started the game as the two holding midfielders in front of the back four, and they were both superb; Kalv got rave reviews and Raheem got the winner in a 1–0 victory. It was a good way to start, a solid performance in difficult conditions, as it was roasting hot. There was a good crowd inside the stadium too. It felt a bit as if life was getting back to normal.

I was on the bench again for Scotland, and I could still feel some discomfort in my groin. It was the day after my birthday, and Gareth had ensured that the occasion was marked by getting everyone to sing to, as he put it, 'the old man of the squad'. I didn't play and we drew 0–0. The last group game was against the Czech Republic. Mason

Mount wasn't involved because of a Covid issue that meant he and Ben Chilwell had to isolate. Raheem put us ahead early on and then, at half-time, Gareth told me I was coming on for Declan. I felt relieved, I felt comfortable and we saw the game out. Bukayo Saka was brilliant. We were into the second round – against Germany. We knew what was coming.

Whenever you play Germany, there are questions about history and how our record against them in the games that matter isn't good. But things were feeling positive around the camp – really positive. You could feel the team was gelling, and the atmosphere was changing in the country, too. Nobody booed when we took the knee against Germany. This was going to be the biggest crowd any of us had played in front of for fifteen months and the place felt electric right from the start. I had never seen Wembley like this, absolutely bouncing, and I had goosebumps, taking it all in. Raheem got his third goal of the tournament fifteen minutes from the end, and then Harry Kane finished things off four minutes from time with a header from a Jack Grealish cross. I was about to come on and, as Harry connected with the ball and we saw it going in, I couldn't control my emotions. I grabbed hold of Gareth, wrapped him in a bear hug and almost lifted him off his feet.

I came on in the eighty-eighth minute for Declan, who had been outstanding again. He was on a yellow card, so it made sense. There were no alarms, and we didn't concede. The elation at the end was unbelievable. We now had Ukraine in the quarters, our first and only game away from Wembley.

We flew to Rome on a Friday. I was feeling better every day, and I was on the bench. Dec and Kalv started in front of the back four and Gareth brought Jadon Sancho in for a start. There was a sense we were building towards something. We were in a different class in the Stadio Olimpico and never had a moment's worry. This quarter-final performance was even better than the one against Russia in Samara three years earlier.

Harry Kane put us ahead early when Raheem played him in with a clever pass and Harry slotted it in; Harry Maguire headed us two up early in the second half; Harry Kane headed a third after fifty minutes. I came on for Declan after fifty-seven minutes. Six minutes later, we got a corner on the right. Mason swung it over and I ran on to it. I was unmarked, six yards out. I headed it to my left and made good contact. The keeper had no chance. I had scored for England. It all came out. Peter Crouch had been to St George's Park to do some filming and had asked me how I would celebrate if I scored. I'm not one for routines and I told him I would probably just start screaming. Now everyone could see what would happen. John Stones tried to grab me, but I was away; the frustration was all coming out. I punched the air, over and over. This was the kind of contribution I wanted to make, and it felt so good. It had been tough watching from the sidelines. Even though I wasn't a hundred per cent, I still wanted to play. Watching us progress was an unbelievable feeling, but I just wish I had had a bigger role, especially as we entered the latter stages.

Now we were going back to Wembley, for the semi-final against Denmark. They were on a roll, playing some great football, but they were riding a tide of emotion too, after Christian Eriksen had collapsed in their first game of the tournament, against Finland in Copenhagen. The Denmark team, and their outstanding doctors, helped save his life. They'd formed a protective circle around him while he was being treated on the pitch. We knew they were heroes, each and every one of them.

'Denmark lost but life won,' one headline in a Danish newspaper read. How could neutrals not want them to win? They scored first against us with a brilliant free kick after thirty minutes from Mikkel Damsgaard, but we equalized before half-time when Simon Kjær inadvertently turned Bukayo's cross past Kasper Schmeichel.

It went to extra time. Five minutes in, Gareth put me on, and I could sense the Danes were tiring. I felt I was making a real difference this time. They were tired and I was full of running. Just before half-time of extra time, Raheem twisted and turned his way into the Denmark box and was brought down. Harry Kane took the penalty, Schmeichel saved it, but Harry rammed home the rebound. It's 2–1. We are not letting this slip now. We're in the final of a major tournament for the first time since 1966.

Putting my feelings into words now, the best way to describe the moments after the final whistle would be overwhelming pride. When the initial roar subsided, we all raced to the corner of the stadium, where our families were. I looked for my girls, Elexa and Alba, straight away, as they had made the trip down to watch the game. Myles, who was only sixteen months old at the time, had stayed at home. No matter what happens in football, they always make me feel better, and everything I do now is for my kids.

They were with Rebecca, my wife, who has sacrificed so much in order for me to be in the best possible shape at all times. She moved down to Liverpool with me at a young age and has always been there to support me. I couldn't have asked for a better mam for my children, and I can always do my job knowing that the kids are safe, loved and all good. I don't take that peace of mind for granted, as I know how difficult it can be for her sometimes, especially when I am away. Don't get me wrong – we are in a very fortunate position that she can always be there for the kids, but it can still be a challenge.

Sitting next to the girls, quite close to the front, were my mam and my sister. My mam was the one who was tough on me, who made sure I was eating the right things. She wouldn't let me stay out late with my friends and always told me to practise the things I wasn't so good at. She played basketball and tennis to a decent level, and I can remember, when I was little, I'd go to watch her play netball and basketball. I'd say I get my energy, enthusiasm and competitiveness from her, as when she played netball and basketball all of those qualities would stand out. I saw her and my sister, Jodi, celebrating as we walked across, and it made me realize the joy we were bringing to our families, friends and, basically, the whole country. To lift the trophy would be unreal.

I knew we had the ability to get to this stage, I knew we had the talent to win, and I thought that was going to happen when we got off to a dream start with Luke Shaw's second-minute goal. We were on fire, and if there is one thing to look back on with regret, it's that we didn't make our dominance pay with a second goal. We just couldn't convert our opportunities. In the second half, we started to protect our lead. We dropped deeper and deeper and then, midway through the half, Italy equalized with a Leonardo Bonucci header from a corner. That was tough to take, because we had been so good at set pieces.

A few minutes later I came on for Declan to try and steady things in the aftermath of the equalizer. It was a dangerous moment, but we regrouped and consolidated. We got to extra time, but we couldn't really hurt them. There was a minute to go, and my number came up on the board. I was going off for Marcus. I knew it was coming, and I understood. Marcus is one of our best penalty takers and we needed him on the pitch.

I watched the penalties play out. I admired the guts of the lads who took them and felt for the ones who missed. I knew how it felt, with the horror and the dread and the guilt. I know the pain and I can still remember every moment of that night in Moscow in 2018.

I watched the dream slip away. I said what words I could and sent a few texts to the people who had the courage to take those penalties. Then I heard about the racial abuse Marcus, Bukayo and Jadon were getting.

They were the heroes when things were going well, but now that we'd lost a game the cowards and the trolls had come running out of the woodwork to pour out their ugliness and their bile? I don't understand it. I never will. What I do know is we will keep fighting against racism.

18. Marathon Men

No one gave us a chance of winning the title at the start of the 2021–22 season. I liked how everyone else was talking about Chelsea, Manchester City and even Manchester United. It meant, for the first time in ages, we could go under the radar a little bit.

I knew we'd be challenging. I didn't need to shout about it.

I understood the reasons for writing us off. We'd endured the season from hell the year before, a load of our best players had been injured and we'd just about scraped into the top four. Chelsea had won the Champions League, and they had paid a lot of money for Romelu Lukaku in the summer. A lot of people were tipping them.

I was glad I'd been through all the physical struggles of trying to get ready for the Euros. It was a fantastic experience to be involved in that run to the final and it helped me with a bit of resilience in the build-up to the new club season. I'd had a lot of time out injured – now I was raring to go.

I didn't have a break after the Euros, and I didn't want one either. I brought a physio out to Majorca, where my family were staying, straight away and carried on training so that when we got to pre-season I was fit. The club's first day of pre-season was the day of the Euro 2020 final, so I joined up a couple of weeks later.

The physio was Matt Konopinski. I worked closely with Matt when he was at Liverpool, and he's really helped me whenever I have been through tough times with injury. His attention to detail is amazing and he will leave no stone unturned to find the cause of a problem. I trust him, and that's why I invited him and his family out to Majorca, so he could be there to help me train but also to give me treatment on my groin. We did sessions in the morning so he could spend the rest of the day with his family.

On the first day, we had the surgeon on FaceTime telling Matt how to take the stitches out properly for my groin. As I explained, I didn't have time to get the internal stitches removed before the Euros, so straight after the game with Italy I went in and had the procedure to get them removed. When the wound healed, Matt just had to remove the external stitches. From there, we had a really good ten days to get me in a good place before going back to pre-season.

I trained with the Under-23s for the first few days and then met up with the lads when they came back from the camp in Austria. The manager said I wouldn't be involved for the first two or three games of the season because I hadn't trained with the team. I didn't play against Norwich, but there were a few injuries to the first team so I started our first home game, a 2–0 victory over Burnley.

Gradually, we began to find a rhythm, and Mo, in particular, was on fire. We drew 2–2 with City at Anfield at the start of October and he scored an unbelievable goal when it seemed like he had dribbled past half of their team. A few weeks later, we went to Old Trafford and had one of those days that seem to have come from the pages of a story: Manchester United 0; Liverpool 5.

Regardless of how United are doing – and they weren't in a great moment at that time – it is always difficult for us to go there and get a result because of the history and the rivalry involved in the match. It is always a special day when you beat United – and this, for our supporters, was special. I was pleased with the performance, and with the way I played too. I got a bit of praise for a pass I played through for Mo for the fifth goal. It took out a few United defenders and Mo ran on to it and finished it beautifully. When you've played together for a long period of time, you have this understanding between one another. You have a feeling about what people are going to do before they know they are going to do it.

I know where Mo's going to run. It's always about the run, more than the pass. If the run's right, the pass is made easier. That becomes easier in a team like ours, where so many of us have been together for so long and have worked together in training and in matches for so long. It becomes second nature to know what your team-mates are going to do and how they think.

Mo and I get on well. In football terms, we are next to each other on the right-hand side. Mo, Trent and I are a unit on that side when I play as an 8. We have a good understanding of what each of us is good at and of our strengths and weaknesses and how we can cover each other's runs and complement each other. Mo and I have a good relationship off the field as well, not necessarily going out socially, but we think the same way about the game. He likes to have a laugh, he's very respectful, but he's an obsessive about the game and that's where we're kindred spirits. He's always first in the gym and he lives for football.

He's an immaculate professional, all about the detail, and I can relate to that. Mo is constantly thinking about how to improve recovery to make sure he is ready for the next game; I've learned a lot from him about recovery, and it's helped me to extend my playing time throughout the season. When I saw Mo and Sadio the day after a game, they'd be ready to go again, whereas I'd be feeling a bit tired. Yes, we have different roles and different positions and maybe a lot of their work is about speed as opposed to endurance, but they still taught me new things about recovery.

After a game, Mo goes in the swimming pool straight away. I went into the ice bath, but that didn't work well enough. Different things work for different individuals. After a night game, I can't sleep. That applies to any game, but especially a night game. It's adrenaline, thinking about what happened, what was good, what was bad, what I ought to have done or ought not to have done. So I thought that instead of tossing and turning, trying to get to sleep, or watching Netflix, I should use that time to start my recovery. Mo told me to go in the pool. So, if we were at home, I'd have a massage after the match and then go into the pool at Anfield. For away games, I'd get back and then go to the training ground and use the pool there at 2 a.m. or 3 a.m. I've done that the last year or two, and it has really helped.

Talking about being fit, I have to mention one of the most crucial members of our squad, a man who has done so much for me. Paul Small has been at Liverpool for more than twenty years. He's a masseur and soft-tissue therapist and he must have spent thousands of hours giving me treatment. Most importantly, he has always been there to support me when I've needed it.

I've been lucky enough to work with the best in the business behind the scenes throughout my career, and Smally is absolutely one of them; it's important to look after staff and recognize all the work they do throughout a season, and I try my best to make sure that is the case. When I took the captaincy, I wanted to make sure I was there for the players.

But I'm also there for the staff and I'll always make sure they are looked after. People such as Smally make sure we are always at our best, and the role they play for us is incredible. All the travelling, all the hours away from home must be hard for them, but they never show it. They are a special group of people.

We lost at West Ham in early November and at Leicester at the end of December, but then we didn't lose another league game for the rest of the season. And soon the race for the title had settled into a pattern we were used to from previous seasons – us and City, neck and neck for the title. Before that pattern had been established, though, there was a point in the middle of January where City opened up a fourteen-point lead over us. We had a couple of games in hand, but people were talking about the title as if it was already over, and Jürgen spoke to us about it.

He held a meeting before our home game with Brentford on 16 January. He said he knew there was a big gap to City but that there were still a lot of games to play, we had games in hand and we had nothing to lose. Everyone had written us off, and so the pressure was gone. Then he asked us to break it down mathematically. They were fourteen points ahead, but if we won our two games in hand, it was eight points, and then if we beat them in April at the Etihad, it would be five points. And so on. He was saying that the gap wasn't what it seemed and that it could change very quickly over the course of the next few weeks of the season. He told us to visualize that they had lost points. In his own way, he wanted to get a message across to the fans as well and, after that Brentford match, which we had won 3–0, he raced up to the Kop to give three fist pumps – something he only tends to do after big occasions – to get everyone going. It worked.

We drew that game with City at the Etihad on 10 April, but by then we were right behind them, only a point adrift. Some people said that was the game where the title slipped away from us, because it was far from being our best performance of the season, but Jürgen often says that, even when you play City, there are only three points on offer, the same as when you play Burnley or Brighton. Maybe it helps psychologically, but it's the same amount of points as any other game. You can't look back on a season and point to one game or another that you think might have cost you the title. Football's not like that. Some games, you lose when you should have won. We give it absolutely everything in every game, and that's all we can do.

The game at City, our second 2–2 draw against them that season, was probably our poorest performance in that run-in. We did not show ourselves in that game. Partly, that was because of City's quality. We came from behind twice in the match, so you couldn't question our mentality. But we didn't dominate the game. We weren't quite as brave as we needed to be on that day. They are such a good team when they have got the ball. They can wear you down because they keep it so well. They don't force it, so you can be running for long periods without the ball. Andy Robertson said we are the hardest opponents for teams to play physically and City are the hardest to play mentally, and I'd agree with that.

When teams play against us, they know they're going to face the counter-press and aggressive pressure and that it's going to feel as if we've got two or three men everywhere. With City, it's more of a mental battle where you have to stay in your shape, keep your concentration, chase and not switch off for a second. The gaffer was disappointed that we didn't do the things we are normally really good at and played into their hands a little bit. They had a lot of chances and we didn't play well, so a draw wasn't a bad result. When we beat them later in the FA Cup semi-final at Wembley, it was more like us.

We only lost two games in the league all season. The only game we lost in any competition from the turn of the year was Inter Milan at home in the second leg of the Champions League last sixteen, until the Champions League final, but even that didn't have a negative impact because we had a 2–0 lead from the first leg. The domestic cups provided us with some more unbelievable memories, and the two games against Chelsea at Wembley, in the Carabao Cup and FA Cup finals, were incredible occasions. Some people never get the chance to walk up the steps to get a trophy on the national side, and here I was, leading Liverpool up twice in the space of three months to receive the prizes. The FA Cup, especially, meant everything to us because it meant we had won every competition we had contested in the last five years. You always want more in football, that's the nature of it and why you always try to improve, but we can't ever lose sight of the fact that this has been a golden period for the club. It's been an honour to be a part of it.

We kept trying, we kept pushing, we kept doing our best to put pressure on City and see if they would crack. We kept chasing them and hoping that sooner or later they would drop points and we would be in a position to take advantage. The thing is, City don't really drop points. They don't lose many games. The level they have got to and the level we have got to are products of the standard both teams have set. We both know we can't lose. We can't afford to lose, or else the other team will take advantage of it and then you have to wait for a long time to make the points back. We kept the pressure up as relentlessly as we could. We'd been here before. We didn't want to contemplate another final-day heartbreak when we chased them right to the finish line and saw them sprint over it just ahead of us, but City are not a team that give you a lot of encouragement.

I did a post-match interview with Carra late in the season where he asked me if I watched City's games, and a lot of people misinterpreted my answer. I said that normally I avoided watching them.

'The way they play, it's never nice to watch, so I put the kids' channels on,' I said. Some suggested I'd been having a dig at City and hinting they didn't play attractive football, but it wasn't that all. I have nothing but respect for City and the way they play. They're an astonishing team with fabulous players and an unbelievable manager. What I said was meant as a tribute to them. I don't like watching them because I always assume they're going to win. So why watch your rivals winning again and again and again? I'd rather get a break and take my mind off how good they are by watching something with my children.

We dropped points when we drew 1–1 with Spurs at home on 7 May, but there is no shame in that. Spurs beat City at the Etihad last season too. They were one of the best counter-attacking teams last year under Antonio Conte, and that style works for them. Harry Kane drops deep, feeding Son, who is a world-class player in his own right. They defend deep and stay in the game, and Conte is a top manager with a winning mentality who demands everything from his players. They were coming from behind in the race for fourth place, so it wasn't as if they had nothing to play for when they got to Anfield. They had everything to play for, and Son scored one of their classic counter-attacking goals to put them ahead. Luis Díaz equalized fifteen minutes from the end, and we threw everything at them, but we couldn't get the winner. I thought we deserved to win, but it could have been worse – much worse.

There were only three games left after that and we knew it was going to be difficult, but we still had a little bit of hope. That point took us to the top of the table on goal difference, but City had a game in hand, which they won. We needed a City slip-up and, if there was a slip-up, we were there. We made sure they had to keep looking over their shoulders, and I heard Pep say more than once that he knew if City lost, it would cost them the title. It was that tight.

We were chasing them most of the season, but they always knew we were there. When they dropped points and we were right there, psychologically, that could have been damaging for them because their lead had dwindled, but they're a mentally strong side too. They regrouped when they needed to. I respect them massively. I hope I've made that obvious already. Pep Guardiola has been unbelievable wherever he has been and is a tactical genius. My favourite in that team is Kevin De Bruyne, and it's a high bar when you're picking a favourite in that side. I can relate to the position and I love how he plays in that 8 role. He is more attacking than me, and I love the quality he has, how he can change a game, the goals he scores, his assists, his work rate. He is one of the best in the world. He is the stand-out one for me. And, I'll say it once again, it's a high bar.

And so it went to the last day again. There was something inevitable about that. We played Wolves at Anfield, and City played Aston Villa, who were managed by Steven Gerrard, at the Etihad. If they won, they were champions again. I didn't text Stevie before the game –

why would I do that? I didn't send a message to Philippe Coutinho, who had signed for Villa earlier in the season, either. Stevie knew the importance of the game to us. He didn't need me to text him. They wanted to win the game for themselves, not for Liverpool. They've got enough pride to want to win, irrespective of the effect it has on anyone else.

We'd had a similar scenario in 2018–19, where we had one eye on City's game at Brighton and we'd allowed ourselves to become distracted by cheers in the crowd at Anfield, and by rumours. That only led to a loss of focus and disappointment. I thought we might deal with it better this time, but I knew it was still going to be difficult if the crowd was cheering other scores. This time wasn't a repeat, but it wasn't far off. We didn't play to the level we're capable of against Wolves. They scored early, but at half-time we were level and City were 1–0 down. Trent said the only score he knew at half-time was that City were losing and he wasn't really bothered because he knew how City could transform a match.

We knew they could score two or three in quick succession. They've done it before. I kept telling myself just to win the game. The noise when Villa scored to go 2–0 up, you couldn't help but hear it. I think there were louder cheers when the news came through that Villa had scored than when we scored. Then the Wolves fans started cheering, so I presumed City had scored. I wasn't really sure. It all felt a bit confused. When Mo scored to put us 2–1 up six minutes from time, he celebrated the goal as if we had won the league. He thought it was still 2–2 at City, but City had scored three goals in five minutes late in the game and were on the verge of the title.

I wasn't celebrating the Mo goal as if we'd won the title. I'm too wary for that. Too pessimistic. Too long in the tooth. The reaction from the Anfield crowd told me that they were not celebrating to an ecstatic level that said we'd won the league. When our match finished, I asked Pep Lijnders the score at City and he told me it was 3–2 for City.

I tried to be relaxed about it. I wondered how it had got to that point, what the sequence of scoring was, whether perhaps Villa had got a late consolation goal to get back within one of City. When I got back to the changing room and saw how the scores had gone and that Villa had been so close and that they were 2–0 up with fifteen minutes to play, it made it worse. It made it harder.

I can't imagine what it was like for the Liverpool fans watching the games at home. It must have been torture. I just know that our dressing room at Anfield was a devastated one. It was the dressing room of a team that has lost a final. A squad of twenty and the best part of twelve staff were in there. There were forty people in a tight space and you could hear a pin drop. And Jürgen stood at the front and made a speech. He talked about how we had won the League Cup and the FA Cup. He talked about how we had become the first team in English football to contest every possible game we could have contested in a season.

I won't lie – it felt like it was the end of the world. We had made this huge effort for a whole season, we had poured our hearts and souls into it, and we had lost the league by a single point on the last day. But Jürgen always sees the bigger picture. He said he was proud that we had already done what no other team in English football had ever done by contesting all four trophies to the bitter end. He said he was proud of our resilience and our dedication and of everything we had already achieved. And he reminded us that in less than a week's time we had a date with Real Madrid and the Champions League final in Paris.

19. Love in a Hopeless Place

We were stuck in Paris traffic. I realized that much. But I didn't pay too much attention. Robbo, Trent, Millie and I usually play a quiz game called Tenable on the way into games, just to keep us relaxed. It's competitive, obviously. It's an app that Robbo has on his phone, and it's hosted by Warwick Davis. A sample question might be: Name the ten English racecourses ending in 'am' or 'er'. Or: Name ten books with a bird in the title.

Robbo is such a great lad. He's the joker in our squad, brilliant for morale in the dressing room. He loves playing Tenable, but there are times when he does passable impersonations of Stuart Little, the quiet mouse. If a topic comes up that he struggles on, the man who can't stop speaking suddenly doesn't have much to say!

Quiz topics aside, there are parts of Robbo's journey that are not too dissimilar to my own pathway. He found life at Liverpool a challenge at first when he came in 2017 and wasn't in the team initially. I can remember him being quite reserved then, but as time went on he blossomed and is now one of the leaders in the dressing room. He's someone you would always want on your side.

Tenable does it for us. It makes the time pass and gives us something to laugh at and argue about. So I didn't pay too much attention to what was going on around us. I didn't notice we were in a kind of gridlock on the Paris ring road. I didn't see the fans running alongside the bus or notice that it was getting a bit late, and it certainly didn't cross my mind that our fans would later be in danger.

When you're about to play in a game like the Champions League final, you try to stay in your bubble. When we got to the Stade de France that evening, about an hour and twenty minutes before the kick-off at 9 p.m. local time, I hadn't seen the massive queues of our fans who were being either herded through narrow pressure points near the stadium or forced to wait in huge numbers outside the turnstiles.

I was aware that we were a bit late and the Real Madrid players were already in the stadium, walking around the pitch, but I didn't think too much of it. I stayed in the bubble. I kept my head on the game. Not much gets through into that cocoon. We went through our usual routines, and then I got changed and went out on to the pitch for the warm-up.

It was our third Champions League final in five years, and we were up against a team that has made an art form out of winning the biggest trophy in club football. It's a cliché, but when it comes to this competition, they possessed the biggest quality of all: they knew how to win. And if we had had a miracle journey to the final in 2019, when we overturned that 3–0 first-leg deficit against Barcelona in the second leg of our semi-final at Anfield, Madrid had done some miraculous things this time around. They had conjured astonishing comebacks and last-gasp goals against PSG, Chelsea and Manchester City on the way to the final.

Our route had been more straightforward. We had beaten Inter, Benfica and Villarreal in the knockout phases and, even if it hadn't been easy, we hadn't needed to go to extra time. There had been nothing like the drama of the Barcelona game.

There was a lot of talk of revenge ahead of the final because of the circumstances of our defeat to Real in Kyiv in 2018, when Sergio Ramos had executed a kind of judo throw on Mo Salah after half an hour of the game. Mo had to be substituted soon after with a damaged shoulder. It was a hard blow for us to take. There were no complaints about the sublime Gareth Bale overhead kick that put Madrid 2–1 up later in the game, and we lost the match 3–1.

But I wasn't really harbouring a grudge. Maybe it was different for Mo, but there was no sense of wanting payback for me. They had a different team now. Cristiano Ronaldo had left and, more pertinently, Ramos had left, too. I didn't need to wind myself up any more to play in a Champions League final. It's the pinnacle of the club game. I had all the motivation I needed.

People have asked me if I noticed when we went out for the warm-up that the Liverpool end of the stadium was emptier than it should have been. The honest answer is no. I was concentrating on what lay ahead. Nobody mentioned to us at that stage that there were any problems outside.

I was more preoccupied with what was going on with Thiago and Naby Keïta. There had been a serious doubt about Thiago's fitness in the build-up to the game, and when we went out for the warm-up, Naby trained with the first team group and Thiago warmed up by himself some distance away. It looked as if he was having a fitness test.

At one point, Thiago went over to Naby and put his arm round him, and it looked as if he was saying to Naby that he hadn't made it and that he was wishing him good luck for the game. But I misread that. When we got back into the changing room, I think Thiago had had a painkilling injection of some sort and he was stripped and ready to go.

Once we were back inside, we were told that kick-off had been delayed by fifteen minutes. That was the first hint any of us had that something was wrong. We were told about the delay, but there was no concern at that point. I just thought there was a problem getting the spectators in. Maybe there had been a transport problem. I think I had seen there had been strikes planned for the Métro. Maybe it was something to do with that.

I wasn't on my phone, or checking messages or hearing radio reports. I was trying to keep my head in the game. I don't think any of the other players had access to any communications either. My mam, my dad, my wife and my girls were all at the stadium. Nobody told us there was an issue. People were vague with us: they're just waiting to get people into the stadium, we were told.

It didn't register at that moment that there might be a problem. When we ran out at the Estadio Metropolitano for the final against Spurs in Madrid in 2019, the atmosphere hit us. This time, it felt quieter, but my focus was on warming up. It wasn't like I ran out and saw the away end sparse and wondered what was going on.

I'd been getting my shin pads on when they said there was going to be a delay. We asked what had happened. 'We haven't got the fans in yet,' we were told; there were problems with some of the gates. They didn't want to worry us, I suppose. They just said there were delays. So then the kick-off was put back to 9.15 p.m., and then to 9.30 p.m.

Some of the lads had a bit of a stretch, listened to music. There was a warm-up area, so I went in there, had a bit of a stretch, came back in, got my boots back on. Then we went out for a second warm-up. I asked if we were doing the whole thing again. 'No, just get moving, pass the ball, get going again.' It was at that point I looked at our end and noticed the crowd. It wasn't as full as it should have been.

I didn't read the message that had flashed up on the big screens at both ends of the ground. I was told later that it said, 'Due to the late arrival of fans, the match has been delayed. Further information will follow in fifteen minutes maximum.'

I realize now that that was the beginning of an attempted cover-up by the French authorities. The police and the government thought they could blame Liverpool fans for their own incompetence. They thought it would be easy to turn them into scapegoats and fall back on the old narrative that it was all the fault of our supporters.

Liverpool fans had been here before, of course. They were blamed for the Hillsborough tragedy in 1989 by a dishonest police force, an eager government and an obedient media. It has taken a heroic fight for justice, led by the families of the victims, that has lasted for more than thirty years, for all the lies to be exposed. It didn't take as long this time. There are plenty of reasons to be wary of social media, but it was part of the reason why the French police didn't get away with blaming Liverpool fans this time. And if the media had been part of the problem in the aftermath of Hillsborough, they were crucial in Paris for exposing the lies of the French establishment.

The first lie was that the match had been delayed because of the late arrival of fans. I know from speaking to journalists and supporters in the days after the match that some supporters were turned away for arriving at the Stade de France too early. The problems weren't caused by supporters arriving late. They were caused entirely by incompetent and dangerous policing that funnelled Liverpool fans, in particular, through impossibly narrow pressure points that led to a mass build-up of supporters.

That was reported immediately by journalists outside the stadium who were trying to get in too. 'Chaos at the Stade de France on a big bottleneck on the ramp by gate U,' Sam Wallace of the *Telegraph* wrote on Twitter about an hour and a half before the game. 'Security guards overwhelmed and lots of fans shoved together. Very unpleasant experience.'

Rob Draper, who works for the *Mail on Sunday*, was forensic in his reporting of what was happening and was so worried by what he saw an hour or so before kick-off that he pleaded with a French policeman to intervene with his superior before the situation spiralled out of control. 'Sad to relate it's chaos outside,' Draper wrote. 'Police funnelling fans into dangerously narrow routes – because their vans are parked blocking the pavement.'

Kelly Cates, the Sky Sports presenter, and the daughter of Kenny Dalglish, was also caught up in the chaos. 'No way in, no way of knowing which way to go,' she wrote on Twitter. 'Stay safe if you're heading in. It has the potential to be very dangerous.' Gary Lineker also wrote about the chaotic situation around the ground.

It still sends a shiver down my spine now when I think how close we came to another tragedy that May evening in Paris. I think of myself sitting in that dressing room with the other Liverpool players, oblivious to what the fans were being subjected to outside, oblivious to the fact they were being tear-gassed and attacked, and it sends a shudder through me to think of what could have been.

Far from blaming Liverpool fans for the scenes outside the stadium, where thousands of fans were kept crowded together for hours in confined spaces, the French authorities should be down on their knees, thanking them for the restraint and the decency and the regard for their fellow football supporters they showed.

Several people close to the situation have said that they believe it was only because Liverpool fans were so intimately acquainted with the details of what happened at Hillsborough that they behaved with an almost superhuman degree of patience and tolerance. If it hadn't been for their nobility, the French would have had an unfolding tragedy on their hands.

How close we came to a deadly crush or a stampede, we will never know. But I do know that when I learned about what our fans had had to suffer and the way they dealt with it and the care they showed for each other, I have never felt more proud to be a Liverpool player. Through their humanity and their restraint, they saved a lot of innocent lives that day.

The game eventually started thirty-six minutes late. Its story, basically, was that we came up against a goalkeeper in Thibaut Courtois who had one of the nights of his life. In the first half, he made one brilliant save when he pushed a shot from Sadio on to the post, and another when he managed to change direction to push out a close-range effort from Mo.

Madrid took the lead after an hour when they worked the ball well down the right side and Federico Valverde cut in and lashed a ball across the face of the goal. It went beyond Trent and fell to Vinicius Jr at the back post, and he tapped it into the net.

Trent was blamed by some people for the goal, but I didn't feel any of that criticism was legitimate. He was damned for not knowing that Vinicius Jr was behind him for the goal, but there was nothing he could do. It was a cross shot from Valverde and he could very easily have turned it into his own net. What was he going to do? It wasn't as if he could have just controlled it and cleared the danger. It was hit way too hard for that. It was difficult for Trent to do anything other than what he did. Listen, I'm on Trent more than anybody in games, but in that moment, there was nothing he could have done to defend it. He was brilliant all game. I thought he was absolutely outstanding.

Vinicius Jr is a top, top player, by the way. He was on fire leading up to that game, and Trent did very well against him. Unfairly, question marks are put against Trent defensively, but in that final he proved again that he certainly can defend. Time after time, we came close to equalizing. Courtois pushed out a fierce, curling drive from Mo, and then he spread himself to deny him again when he tried to squeeze the ball in at the back post. Courtois saved the best for last. When Mo took a high ball down from Fabinho and beat his man, it looked as though his right-foot shot was spearing into the far corner. Somehow, Courtois managed to get his right arm to it and push it wide. Mo couldn't believe it. Courtois was mobbed by his grateful team-mates, who couldn't believe it either. Yet again, against the odds, and against the run of play, Madrid had found a way to win.

We came back into the dressing room, devastated, but that was when our focus began to change. It was now that we started hearing the first hints of issues outside the stadium. I heard someone say there had been problems. I heard someone else say that some of our fans had been attacked and that was what had caused the delays to kick-off. People were also saying there were now issues getting away from the stadium and there were more attacks on fans.

Straight away I thought about my kids. I looked at my phone for the first time at that point. I had a stream of texts saying it was a disgrace what was happening outside.

I rang Bec, and there was no answer. I started to worry. What's happened? Where are they? I hoped they would be in the players' family area. I rang Jane Griffiths, who is Player Care manager; I knew she was with the families. She answered. I asked her if Bec was there. She said they were all there. I asked about the other families. They were all good. She said there had been a few issues getting in, but there had been no real trouble for them and everyone was safe. That was a little bit of a relief, but then we started hearing more details.

I rang some friends, and they were saying I wouldn't believe how bad it had been outside. Everyone said they couldn't explain it, but that it was the worst they had ever seen at a football game and that our fans had been faultless. I was coming to terms with losing the match, but I was starting to be aware that actually there was something a lot greater to be thankful for.

My family had had very minor problems of their own that had given them a small taste of the problems other fans had had to suffer. When Bec was coming into the stadium with the girls, the stewards and the security were very aggressive. There was my wife, the two girls and her dad. The security guards were saying to her, 'You and your dad come in first and then the two girls come in after.'

My wife said, 'No, my dad will come in and then the two kids and then I will come in last.' Any parent would do that. She said the police were already edgy and hostile. The security guys were saying that if they didn't do as they said, they weren't getting in. So Bec said she wouldn't go in. She said she'd rather go home than go in without the girls.

So then a security guy from the club who was with the players' families came over and said the kids would go in the middle, and he sorted it out. Even a little detail like that suggests that something was wrong, that the attitude was aggressive and unpleasant, and this was with players' families, who had the advantage of having security with them.

The experience of the Liverpool fans helped to avert a tragedy. They didn't push, even though they were tested beyond the limits fans should face. They were amazing. They were subjected to more attacks on the way back to the Métro and the RER. The whole experience was traumatic, but it did at least leave me feeling thankful. We were very lucky that the only thing we lost that night was a trophy.

It took six weeks for the French authorities to absolve the Liverpool supporters of blame. A Senate report, released in mid-July, found the French government was wrong to blame supporters and fake tickets for the crowd chaos that led to supporters being tear-gassed and robbed in Paris. The French inquiry said the fiasco was caused by a litany of administrative errors and failings rather than Liverpool fans.

We got back to Liverpool the next day, and a parade had been organized. I was unsure about it to begin with, because we had just lost the Champions League final and our fans had had a hell of an ordeal before and after the game. But we had won the Carabao Cup and the FA Cup and we'd come within a whisker of the Premier League and the Champions League. It had been a great season.

I feel stupid saying this now, but I didn't think anyone would turn up. A friend of mine was waiting on the parade route, and he'd sent me a picture of fans gathering on the roads, and I wanted to know, genuinely, if it was busy. I felt guilty, too, because Calvin Harris was on our bus, the best DJ in the world and a huge Liverpool fan, providing the music. He must have sensed that some of us were unsure about being there.

The parade started down towards the south of the city and made its way slowly towards the Strand on the waterfront near Pier Head and Albert Dock. The further the bus drove, the more fans appeared at the side of the road. Then more and more and more, until we were surrounded.

It was reported that half a million fans came out to celebrate with us and the Liverpool FC women's team, who had won the FA Women's Championship that day. And that was after we had lost the Champions League final. The loyalty and the commitment of that meant so much to me, and to all the players. It took my breath away. It turned into one of the best days of my life, that day. It was a celebration of a year, and of a team and a season, and of deliverance and of the times of our lives. We felt like we'd let the city down by losing in Paris, and the city responded like this. Someone called the show of affection a 'big Scouse hug', and that was what it felt like.

And when we got down on to the Strand, by the waterfront, the crowds were at their height. The air turned red with the smoke from flares, and I looked out at all the smiling faces. It was then I thought about all the dedication the supporters had shown towards this team through tough times, through the pandemic, through years when questions were being asked of the team and if we could ever deliver trophies.

It was then that Calvin Harris played 'We Found Love (in a Hopeless Place)'. And in that moment, it felt as if he had picked the perfect song. The parade gave me comfort, but the sight of my team-mates, knowing the kind of characters they are and the ability they have, gave me the belief that there will hopefully be more days like this in the future.

Our team is evolving, with Sadio Mané having left and Darwin Núñez coming in from Benfica. His impact in the Community Shield was brilliant, and that 3–1 win over Manchester City was the perfect way to prepare us for the next chapter. This story certainly isn't over.

Career Statistics

Club Appearances (goals in brackets)

	Season	League	FA Cup	League Cup	Europe	Others	Total
Sunderland	2008/09	1		1			2
Coventry (*loan*)	2008/09	10 (1)	3				15 (1)
Sunderland	2009/10	33 (1)	2	3 (1)			38 (2)
	2010/11	37 (3)	1	1			39 (3)
Liverpool	2011/12	37 (2)	5	6			48 (2)
	2012/13	30 (5)	2	2	10 (1)		44 (6)
	2013/14	35 (4)	3	2 (1)			40 (5)
	2014/15	37 (6)	7	4	6 (1)		54 (7)
	2015/16	17 (2)		3	6		26 (2)
	2016/17	24 (1)		3			27 (1)
	2017/18	27 (1)	1	1	12		41 (1)
	2018/19	32 (1)		1	11		44 (1)
	2019/20	30 (4)			7	3	40 (4)
	2020/21	21 (1)	1		6		28 (1)
	2021/22	35 (2)	5	5	12 (1)		57 (3)
	2022/23	2				1	3
Totals		**408 (34)**	**30**	**32 (2)**	**70 (3)**	**4**	**544 (39)**

England Appearances

DEBUT: Became the 1,170th player to be picked for England on 17 November 2010; *v* France at Wembley Stadium. Lost 2–1

CAPS: 69

GOALS: 2 (*v Ukraine, Euro 2020 quarter-final; Rome, 3 July 2021; v Albania, World Cup 2022 qualifier; Wembley, 13 November 2021*)

Major Tournaments

EUROPEAN CHAMPIONSHIPS: 2012, 2016, 2020

WORLD CUP: 2014, 2018

England Under-21s

DEBUT: *v* Uzbekistan, 10 August 2010 at Ashton Gate, Bristol. Won 2–0

CAPS: 27

GOALS: 4

Honours

Club

Premier League: 2019–20

Champions League: 2018–19

League Cup: 2012, 2022

FA Cup: 2022

European Super Cup: 2019

Club World Cup: 2019

FA Community Shield: 2022

Football Writers' Association, Player of the Year: 2020

Only British player to captain a team in three European Cup finals
(2018, 2019, 2023)

England

England Under-21 Player of the Year: 2012

England Player of the Year: 2019

Runner-up: European Championships 2020

Fourth place: World Cup 2018

Other

Member of the British Empire, for services to charity: June 2021

Acknowledgements

Compiling this section has arguably been the most challenging aspect of this project. You will have learned by
now how much I hate the idea of ever letting anyone down
and if I was to personally name every individual who has
helped me on my journey, we would be able to publish
another 350 pages. To achieve anything in life, you need
the right support and, from the very beginning, I have
been blessed to have the best. This book is for you all.

Football is everything to me and the last seven years,
in particular, have provided the opportunity to fulfil every
dream I had as a little boy. None of this would have been
possible without the outstanding characters I have had
alongside me from day one – the brilliant team-mates at
Sunderland, Coventry, Liverpool and England. We are
blessed to have some of the best players in the world,
genuine global stars and icons, but at Liverpool – the best
club in the world – the team comes first. We are a collective and everything we have achieved we have done so
together.

That we have been able to enjoy such success is down
to the fact we have followed the direction that the 'Gaffer'
has pointed us in. I have been lucky with all my club
managers – Roy Keane and Steve Bruce at Sunderland,
Chris Coleman at Coventry, Sir Kenny Dalglish and

Brendan Rodgers at Liverpool – but hit the jackpot when Jürgen Klopp arrived in October 2015. His faith and support has been crucial and when I look at the medals I have collected, I will always think about him.

There are not many higher honours for a player than being captain of Liverpool and what an unbelievable privilege it has been to spend eleven years wearing a Liver Bird on my chest. Thank you to the people who believed I had the qualities to succeed in this shirt, thank you to those who stood by me and offered support when times were difficult and, most of all, thank you to the fans who kept faith in me. Winning for you is unrivalled and a number of the best days of my life involve being on an open-top bus looking out on to a sea of Red. I hope you understand the pride I feel running out to represent you every week and your role in my story is huge.

I am a naturally private person and like to keep my family out of the spotlight, but I wouldn't be in the spotlight without everything they have done – and continue to do – for me. Thanks to my mam and my dad for every piece of right advice and showing me the right way. Jodi, my sister, is a big presence in my life and comes to watch me play whenever she can.

To Rebecca, my wife and the incredible mother to our three beautiful children Elexa, Alba and Myles. You are the ones I do everything for.

When I talk about family, I include Ryan Royal, my best friend since we were three. Ryan, you're basically my brother and you have been by my side every step of the way. Without you, none of this would have been possible.

I know the value of teamwork and I have seen it at its finest in the process of putting this book together. Daniel Bunyard, at Penguin Books, has been first class. His availability to answer questions and provide reassuring words has been an immense help. It has been a whirlwind, seeing how everything has come together, but Dan could not have done anymore to get us to the finish line.

There are others: Sarah Day, the copyeditor; Emma Henderson, Nick Lowndes, Paula Flanagan and Ella Kurki have helped see through the process; Mubarak Elmubarak and Gaby Young have worked on marketing and publicity, respectively; Deirdre O'Connell, Katie Corcoran and Stella Newing, who is producing the audio book, have all been crucial.

I have to thank Matt McCann and Tony Barrett at Liverpool for reading and re-reading pages and giving me invaluable pointers. Chris Morgan was always on hand, too, when it came to providing accuracy on the details of the injuries I have suffered. It was never too much trouble for him. Then again, it never is.

Ollie Holt, the Chief Sports Writer of the *Mail on Sunday*, is someone whose views I have respected for a long time and he could not have worked harder against deadlines that I thought might prove to be impossible. We had some brilliant conversations and I couldn't be happier with how all those hours of talks during the summer were pieced together. Thanks, Ollie, for listening.

I have known Dominic King of the *Daily Mail* since 2011, when he was reporting on England's Under-21s and I was playing for that squad. He's been there right the way through my Liverpool and England career and I have total trust in him. His files and records were an enormous help to us and he can't argue with the tag of being called 'Stat Man Dom' now. He's written about all the big days in my Liverpool career. I hope there will be many more to come.

Picture Permissions

1–7, 15, 22–23, 28, 33. Courtesy of Jordan Henderson

8. © Christopher Lee / Getty Images Sport via Getty Images

9. © Clive Brunskill / Getty Images Sport via Getty Images

10. © John Powell / Liverpool FC via Getty Images

11. © Peter Byrne, PA Images / Alamy Stock Photo

12. © Paul Ellis / AFP via Getty Images

13. © Laurence Griffiths / Getty Images Sport via Getty Images

14. © Michael Regan / FIFA via Getty Images

16. © John Powell / Liverpool FC via Getty Images

17. © Shaun Botterill / Getty Images Sport via Getty Images

18. © Alex Caparros / UEFA via Getty Images

19. © PHC Images, Alamy Stock Photo

20. © Jan Kruger / UEFA via Getty Images

21. © Soccrates Images / Getty Images Sport via Getty Images

24. © Andrew Powell / Liverpool FC via Getty Images

25. © Shaun Botterill / UEFA via Getty Images

26. © Laurence Griffiths, PA Images / Alamy Stock Photo

27. © Pool / Getty Images Sport via Getty Images

29. © Dominic Lipinski, PA Images / Alamy Stock Photo

30. © Andrew Powell / Liverpool FC via Getty Images

31. © Robin Jones / Getty Images Sport via Getty Images

32. © Andrew Powell / Liverpool FC via Getty Images

Index